MARTIN SCORSESE

To my husband, John,
with love and gratitude

MARTIN SCORSESE

*An Analysis of His Feature Films,
with a Filmography of
His Entire Directorial Career*

by MARIE KATHERYN CONNELLY

McFarland & Company, Inc., Publishers
Jefferson, North Carolina, and London

British Library Cataloguing-in-Publication data are available

Library of Congress Cataloguing-in-Publication Data

Connelly, Marie Katheryn.
   Martin Scorsese : an analysis of his feature films, with a
filmography of his entire directorial career / by Marie Katheryn
Connelly.
     p. cm.
   Includes bibliographical references and index.
   ISBN 0-89950-845-6 (lib. bdg. : 50# alk. paper) ∞
   1. Scorsese, Martin — Criticism and interpretation.   I. Title.
PN1998.3.S39C66 1993
791.43′0233′092 — dc20
                                                92-56636
                                                          CIP

Manufactured in the United States of America

McFarland & Company, Inc., Publishers
 Box 611, Jefferson, North Carolina 28640

CONTENTS

Acknowledgments	vii
Introduction	ix
Mean Streets	1
Alice Doesn't Live Here Anymore	17
Taxi Driver	33
New York, New York	49
Raging Bull	69
King of Comedy	87
After Hours	103
The Color of Money	113
The Last Temptation of Christ	125
New York Stories	133
GoodFellas	137
Conclusion	157
Filmography	159
Works Cited	173
Index	175

ACKNOWLEDGMENTS

My deep gratitude goes to my mentor, Louis Giannetti, for his kindness, support, and expert advice in preparing this book. He talked to me on the telephone and met with me many times, and he conscientiously read and edited all of my work. I also wish to thank Professor Giannetti for all he has taught me about film, a study which has greatly enriched my life. Most of all, I wish to thank him for believing in me.

I wish to thank Roger Salomon for his kindness and encouragement and other Case Western Reserve University faculty members, Robert Ornstein, Walter Strauss, and William Siebenschuh, for their insightful suggestions. I am also grateful to the staff at the downtown branch of the Cleveland Public Library for all of their helpful assistance in securing reference materials. I wish to thank my father, Gus Pappas, for his help in obtaining Martin Scorsese's movies. I am deeply grateful to my brother, Michael Pappas, for his thoughtful and generous support of my work. Many thanks also to Cathy Skully and June Morris for their interest and encouragement.

I wish to thank Margie Martin for her interest, expertise, and gracious help in proofreading my manuscript. I am also thankful for the help of Lorin Kinkaid Kolek for typing the filmography and for her cheerful companionship. Many thanks to Cheryl Brooke for her kind and generous help with the index. Finally, I am grateful to the staff at St. Paul's Episcopal Church, Cleveland Heights, Ohio, for their interest, support, and help in providing a computer and workspace.

INTRODUCTION

Martin Scorsese was born on November 17, 1942, in Flushing, Queens. He was the second son of Catherine and Charles Scorsese, children of Sicilian immigrants who first came to the United States in 1910 (Thompson and Christie 1989, 1). His parents were born in Little Italy on Elizabeth Street, in the Lower East Side of Manhattan, and they both worked in the garment district. Scorsese lived in Corona, a suburb of Queens, until he was eight years old. Then financial difficulties motivated the family to move back to Elizabeth Street. Scorsese lived with his grandparents for several months while his parents looked for housing. During this period he became aware that the neighborhood in which he now lived was dangerous. He comments, "This was a terrifying experience because I was old enough to realize that there were some tough guys around. You might be playing in a sandbox and something would fall behind you — not a bag of garbage, as you might expect, but a little baby that had fallen off the roof" (Thompson and Christie 1989, 3).

In a way, Scorsese was preparing for a career as a director all his life. He had asthma when he was growing up, so he couldn't play sports with the other boys. Instead of being an active participant in neighborhood children's activities, he was often an observer of the action from a window of his family's apartment. As a child, Scorsese had wanted to become a painter, so he tried to learn to draw. His parents often took him to the movies, and he tried drawing the images that had been on the screen. Making up stories, he also drew his own comic strips. He even began drawing in aspect ratios comparable to movie screens and using close-ups. Another love was music, especially rock and roll, which he listened to avidly and which he was later to feature in many of his films.

When Scorsese was eight or nine, he decided he wanted to become a priest. He was especially interested in missionary work. When he was fourteen, he enrolled in a junior seminary school, Cathedral College. However, he was expelled after only a year. Scorsese admits, "I didn't really have my mind on my work" (Thompson and Christie 1989, 12).

Scorsese chose to attend college at New York University because cinema studies was a part of its curriculum. He also considered majoring in

English, but later decided on film as a major and English as his minor (Thompson and Christie 1989, 13). His film teacher, Professor Haig Manoogian, was a fine educator and a great inspiration to him. Scorsese was a film student from 1960 to 1965, during the period when many European film makers' movies were being discovered in America. It was the era of the French New Wave, and many Italian art films and eastern European films as well were being shown. Also, Director John Cassavetes had made a film (*Shadows*, 1959) in the manner of the French New Wave film makers, using a lightweight, handheld camera.

As a student, Scorsese made a number of films. His first, *What's a Nice Girl Like You Doing in a Place Like This?* was made in 1963. His second was *It's Not Just You, Murray!* While a student, he became friends with Brian De Palma, Michael Wadleigh, Jim McBride, and Mardik Martin, all of whom later achieved distinction in the American film industry. In 1969 Scorsese went back to New York University to teach film. He also worked as a film editor before he began directing movies full time. One of the movies he helped edit was the rock documentary *Woodstock*, directed by Wadleigh.

Critics have recognized Martin Scorsese as one of the finest contemporary American directors. They have praised several of his films for their outstanding artistic achievements. These include *Mean Streets, Taxi Driver, Raging Bull*, and *GoodFellas*. Scorsese's *Raging Bull* was selected by a group of American critics as the best film of the 1980s.

There is no book-length critical study of Martin Scorsese's work. One book, *Martin Scorsese and Michael Cimino*, by Michael Bliss, combines a study of Scorsese and Cimino; however, that book is already outdated. The last Scorsese film included is *King of Comedy* (1983). Another very helpful source has been a book composed largely of writings by Scorsese, *Scorsese on Scorsese*, along with various notes by the book's editors, Thompson and Christie. Marion Weiss's *Researcher's Guide to Martin Scorsese*, published in 1987, has been enormously helpful in writing my own work. The bulk of her work is an extensive bibliography, which served as a guide to excellent materials to read in preparation of this study.

Scorsese's work falls into the category of art films. Usually, his films are not mainstream, and they are often not liked by the general public. There is much to appreciate, however. Scorsese's work improves with repeated viewings: It is complex, provocative, not easily pigeonholed.

One of the most compelling features of Scorsese's work is the humanity he brings to his films. Typically, he chooses protagonists who are outside the mainstream. They are often hard to like, yet Scorsese has chosen to tell their story. It has been said that when people are their least loveable, they are most in need of love. Scorsese shows us these characters' lives not in a sentimental way, to arouse our sympathy. Rather he shows them in some depth: We see how they often suffer for who they are. He also suggests that perhaps those objectionable traits are often not of their own choosing. Scorsese thus transends their superficial traits to concentrate on their spiritual condition, their inner anguish and humanity.

In addition to portraying outsiders, there are several other qualities typical of a Martin Scorsese film. Most of his works are character studies, and plot is often subordinated to this primary end. Sometimes his narratives are ragged, although his more recent work is more neatly plotted. A second quality is attention to period detail. Scorsese is superb at creating the look and feel of a particular time and place. A third quality is superior acting. A number of his actors have won Academy Awards for work in his films. He works well with actors and has a gift for eliciting fine performances. Minor characters are also especially well cast. A fourth quality is Scorsese's technical expertise. A New York University film school graduate, Scorsese is well informed about the possibilities of his medium, and he has experimented widely in his work. A fifth quality is that a Scorsese film typically features an interesting selection of music. His musical choices for each film are usually a significant artistic feature. A sixth quality is humor. Even in his most serious films, there are funny scenes. A seventh quality is violence, physical and often psychological as well. Finally, a Scorsese film is more often than not a version of a revisionist genre. Sometimes, the revision can be so radical that it is hard to recognize the original genre.

I have confined my study to Scorsese's feature films beginning with *Mean Streets*. Scorsese made two feature films beforehand, *Who's That Knocking at My Door?* (1969) and *Boxcar Bertha* (1972). *Who's That Knocking*, a low-budget, early sketch of *Mean Streets*, is interesting but bears too much the stamp of student work to be considered a major film. *Boxcar Bertha* was important because independent producer Roger Corman gave Scorsese an opportunity to make a second film. However, like most of Corman's productions, it is an exploitation film. I have also left out Scorsese's short student films, his television commercials, and his music films, not considering them major works.

Because Scorsese's films are sometimes hard to understand, and because there is no book-length critical study, I have attempted to write an overview of his work. The first part of each chapter includes a plot summary, a description of major characters, and a thematic interpretation of the film. The second part of the chapter is a stylistic analysis, consisting of an examination of the film's major technical elements, including camera work, script, music, humor, and acting. These stylistic elements vary considerably from film to film.

Mean Streets

You don't make up for your sins in the church. You do it in the streets. You do it at home. — Charlie, in *Mean Streets*, commenting on the sacrament of confession

Mean Streets, Martin Scorsese's first important feature film, is a coming-of-age film. It tells the story of a group of friends growing up in the Little Italy section of New York City during the early 1970s. The thread that weaves together many of the scenes in *Mean Streets* is the responsibility Charlie (Harvey Keitel) feels for his friend Johnny Boy (Robert De Niro). Johnny Boy owes a large debt to Michael (Richard Romanus), a neighborhood loan shark. As the movie progresses, Michael grows increasingly impatient at Johnny Boy's dodging repayment. Charlie's involvement, however, not only steps beyond the bounds of helpfulness, but also threatens his relationship with his Uncle Giovanni (Cesare Danova), who is Charlie's employer. Giovanni disapproves of Johnny.

Rather than being plot directed, however, *Mean Streets* has a loosely woven episodic format which focuses on its main characters, capturing in slice-of-life fashion many privileged moments with humor, warmth, and authenticity. The main characters in *Mean Streets* are Charlie, Johnny Boy, Tony (David Proval), Michael, and Theresa (Amy Robinson). At the beginning of the film, each of them, except Theresa, is introduced while performing some characteristic action. As the movie unfolds, *Mean Streets* looks at the life of these characters, whom we get to know well.

During the opening segment, there is a shot of a junkie shooting up in the bathroom of a bar. Disgusted and annoyed, Tony (David Proval) takes swift and clear action in grabbing the junkie and throwing him out of his bar. Tony then chastises his bouncer for not doing his job. Tony is not the type to wrestle over moral ambiguity. Although Charlie agonizes over what the priests have told him, Tony takes a more philosophical and practical approach: "Why do you let those guys get to you?... It's a business, it's work, it's an organization." Tony advises Charlie to apply some common sense when thinking about the church: "You got to be like me.

1

Using the flame motif to represent the fire of hell, Scorsese shows Charlie's (Harvey Keitel) inner struggle. In an interior monologue, Charlie reflects on the pain and decides that between the physical and spiritual "the worst of the two is the spiritual" (*Mean Streets*, 1973).

You're going to be saved." Sensible, responsible, and content with his life, Tony is a warm and giving person and a good friend to Charlie.

Johnny Boy is introduced next. Rounding a corner, he tosses an explosive into a mailbox, then quickly flees. Furtively but excitedly, he glances back to see the results, a big explosion. With just a few bold strokes, Johnny's character is thus quickly sketched in as someone who lacks good sense and who flirts with danger, not thinking through the consequences of his behavior. Interestingly, Johnny doesn't speak in the scene. Rather, the action — maniacal, impulsive, and dangerous — tells all. Later, Johnny will engage in other risky and senseless actions like shooting a loaded revolver from a rooftop and defiantly baiting and insulting Michael, pushing his luck well past the safety zone.

Michael is introduced sitting in a car under a bridge. He tries to negotiate a deal to sell some hot merchandise. However, Michael soon learns he's been duped. His buyer has no interest in the deal. Instead of German telescopic lenses, Michael finds out that he's been stuck with two shipments of Japanese adapters. Always trying to make a buck, Michael sells everything from bootleg cigarettes to PX toilet paper. His schemes, however, don't always go as planned. Although Michael is not terribly bright, he will not play the fool. The sobering, violent conclusion to *Mean Streets* comes about as Michael, furiously and cold-bloodedly vengeful, evens the score with Johnny Boy for hustling and ridiculing him one too many times. Interestingly, Scorsese cast against type with Romanus as Michael. Instead of the stereotypical one-dimensional character, typically an unattractive middle-aged man, Romanus's portrayal is full and engagingly human. Handsome, young, and gentlemanly, Michael is hardworking, sincere, and even funny at times, though often as the butt of jokes.

Although a main character of the film, Theresa isn't introduced until the sixth reel. This delayed entrance violates conventions and contributes to the lack of smoothness in the movie's narrative. Theresa's late entrance was partly circumstantial; Scorsese kept adding scenes to the first part of the movie. However, the delay of her introduction later became a deliberate choice. Scorsese comments, "This seems to me to be the best way to indicate that this is a society dominated by males. Theresa doesn't even get a vignette at the beginning; she has to be the last to be presented if we want to describe, and describe once and for all, a lifestyle. Too bad about the structure" (Ciment and Henry 1975, 14).

Theresa and Charlie have a tender and loving relationship; however, Theresa also contributes to Charlie's angst in life. Charlie's Uncle Giovanni cautions his nephew not to get involved with Theresa, Johnny Boy's cousin. Because Theresa is an epileptic, Giovanni ignorantly assumes that "she's sick in the head." Charlie's uncle also considers Theresa's wanting her own apartment a crazy idea, typical of Theresa and Johnny Boy's family, to whom Giovanni is regrettably related as godfather to Johnny. Charlie's relationship with Theresa, although comforting, is thus also a source of anxiety because he has to keep it a secret for fear of his uncle's disapproval.

Finally, Charlie's introduction is intercut throughout the opening segment. *Mean Streets* opens with his voiceover and a black screen: "You don't make up for your sins in the church. You do it in the streets. You do it at home. The rest is bullshit and you know it." The next shot is of Charlie waking up, as if from a bad dream. The movie thus introduces *Mean Streets* as, primarily, Charlie's story and his conflict of conscience as an important preoccupation.

During the home-movie sequence which follows these brief character introductions, other important dimensions of Charlie's character are revealed. For example, religion is again emphasized as we see Charlie shaking hands with a priest on the front steps of a church and attending a reception for a child's baptism. In other shots, we see Charlie with various people who are important to him: Michael and other friends, for being a part of the neighborhood is important to Charlie; Theresa, who is Charlie's girlfriend; and Uncle Giovanni, who is Charlie's employer, relation, and mentor. All of these relationships are pivotal to Charlie's character and to the story to be presented in *Mean Streets*.

After the introductions of Tony, Michael, and Johnny Boy, we see Charlie in church praying, having just gone to confession. As he prays, he reflects on the church's means for forgiveness of sin. Charlie feels that saying prayers in church as an act of contrition isn't enough. He aspires to live as a good Christian out in the world. Like St. Francis, whom he admires, Charlie feels people should care about others and try to help them.

Throughout the movie, Charlie feels a conflict of conscience about his responsibility towards others and towards himself. Unfortunately, he steps over the boundaries of helpfulness in trying to look out for his friend Johnny Boy. The last thing Charlie would want to do is hurt people, but he ends up doing just that because his attempts to help Johnny, although well intentioned, are misguided.

Charlie repeatedly bails out Johnny. Scorsese raises questions about how people can realistically be of help to others who will not be helped. To what degree should people get involved in the life of someone who is recklessly irresponsible? How much should they intercede, and when does trying to help encourage the person's irresponsible behavior? If they persist in helping in this manner, do they form a dependent relationship with the person they're trying to help? Each of their motivations has to be questioned. Scorsese seems to suggest that this dependency is really self-serving to the giver and unhealthy to the taker , who often resents the giver's actions. Charlie learns these truths under serious and tragic circumstances at the conclusion of *Mean Streets*.

Mean Streets was widely praised and enthusiastically received by critics. "Even though people liked it," commented Scorsese in an interview with Anthony Macklin, "a lot of them didn't understand it. That was interesting" (Macklin 1975, 24). A number of reasons might account for this lack of understanding. One is that because *Mean Streets* was Scorsese's first film of note, critics lacked the perspective of the works that were to come, an understanding of his *oeuvre*, the concerns, sympathies, interests that were to underlie all of his work, his way of seeing the world.

Another impediment is a more delicate issue. Much of the ill-conceived criticism has as its base stereotypical thinking about ethnicity. Ethnic stereotyping, in this case, works to obfuscate the meaning of this work. Critic Richard Gambino points out that Italians are typically presented as one of two stereotypes, as buffoons or thugs, and that such

Robert De Niro (*left*) and Harvey Keitel. In this memorable scene, Scorsese used improvisation to reveal Johnny Boy's character. Charlie knows Johnny is embellishing like crazy and is leading him on. Although Charlie listens with skepticism, in spite of himself he becomes engrossed in Johnny's story (*Mean Streets*, 1973).

stereotyping has helped perpetuate distortions about Italian-Americans (Gambino 1974, 107).

Even people who consider ethnic slurs ill-mannered are often unknowingly inculcated with common myths about ethnicity. For example, in Linda Brandi Cateura's book, *Growing Up Italian*, the contributors shatter many useless myths. John Ciardi, for example, relates the resentment he felt at being the victim of this kind of insensitivity,

> I published a poem in the *Atlantic Monthly* once about Italy and Mussolini . . . Robert Lowell, the poet, wrote me a note saying it was the best Italian-American poem he had ever seen. And I thought, "Does that son of a bitch think he is more American than I am?". . . Because my

name is Ciardi, he decided to hyphenate the poem. Had it been a Yankee name, he would have thought, "Ah, a scholar who knows about Italy" [quoted in Cateura 1987, 149–50].

Stereotypical thinking about Italians has also been applied to *Mean Streets*. In fact, one of its critical problems is that it has often been grouped with the "godfather pictures." Because the characters in *Mean Streets* are Italian, and they are engaged in illegal activities, the movie's plot becomes reduced to a Mafia story and its characters are categorized as criminals. However, *Mean Streets* is not a gangster story. To label its characters as criminals reduces them to types, which prevents us from thinking of them as human beings, one of Scorsese's main points.

Still another prejudice applied to *Mean Streets* is a middle-class bias against the working class. For the middle-class critic, life in working-class districts is claustrophobic, limited, small, and, by implication, inferior. Actually, working class or not, most people's worlds are small, and it is unfair to be condescending towards a different small world than one's own. Critic David Denby noted this trend in some of the criticism, stating, "Why should we care about these working-class hoods, asked some of the film's colder reviewers. But it's hard to see in this question anything but class bias and squeamishness. The reasons for caring are there in almost every scene" (Denby 1973–74, 48). Interviewer Guy Flatley asked Scorsese if perhaps he'd overemphasized the seamy side of life in Little Italy, "There must be some decent, hardworking people living there." Scorsese replied,

> Sure—the majority of the people in Little Italy are decent, hardworking people. My parents are over 65 and they're *still* decent, hardworking people.... But there is also this milieu of young turks. Some people are shocked that these guys are running around, buying and selling hot stuff, but *I'm* not shocked—I'll buy toothpaste from them for 19 cents instead of 50 cents. Why not? It's not as if they're dealing in heroin. And don't forget, even numbers runners are hardworking guys [Flatley 1973, 17].

That *Mean Streets* is a coming-of-age film is significant to an understanding of it. *Mean Streets* is about Charlie's entrance into the adult world. Interestingly, Charlie is in some ways the least clearly defined character, perhaps because so much is unclear for him. He may go through the motions—dressing the part, enjoying the conviviality of his friends, and observing his uncle as a mentor. At the feeling and conscience level though, Charlie agonizes over issues that the others either feel no need to examine or that are simply practical and clearcut matters for them. The mistake Charlie makes in getting involved with Johnny is especially understandable when we remember that Charlie is young, idealistic, and inexperienced, and therefore far more vulnerable to making such an error in judgment.

Mean Streets is a memoir. In it, Scorsese looks back primarily with affection at the neighborhood in which he grew up. Scorsese is critical of the prejudices, narrow-mindedness, and violence endemic to these characters. However, the neighborhood, for the most part, is affirmed here, not maligned. There is meanness, but there is also friendship, humor, and warmth. In fact, the title *Mean Streets* is a misnomer in many ways. It suggests a movie about street gangs, a *West Side Story,* a movie of violence, anger, and anxiety, something much different than the tenor of the actual film.

Mean Streets is autobiographical in that Scorsese has drawn widely from his upbringing. Yet, it is also autobiographical in the way of all of Scorsese's best works. In *Mean Streets,* Scorsese incorporated feelings, conflicts, ideas current for him. From his gut come the power, sincerity, and honesty that characterize a Scorsese film at its best. On *Mean Streets,* Scorsese comments, "See, it's the idea of success—in fact, when I first wrote it, it was like an allegory for what was happening to me trying to make movies. Mardik [Martin, co-writer of *Mean Streets*] and I were working together, writing scripts about ourselves at that time, trying to get things going. . . . I drew from personal experiences about a guy trying to make it" (quoted in Jacobs 1977, 136).

Because *Mean Streets* was a low-budget film, Scorsese had to work hard to keep costs down yet not compromise the film artistically. For example, the six days allotted for on-location filming in New York were rainy, but there simply wasn't time or money to wait for better weather. The result was the wet, overcast, gray urban look to the film.

The film is also dark at times because better lighting was too expensive. The budget reduced much of the night shooting to medium shots and close-ups to avoid the need for hundreds of lights and a large lighting crew. According to Scorsese,

> Much of it was exterior shooting and it was very simple—wide shots, medium shots, close-ups, different angles. But the main thing was to get the atmosphere of the place, to get the characters in their setting. We did some dolly shots and things in the streets, but we were really limited. We had lights, but we didn't have enough lights, enough generator power, enough people and so on [Bobrow 1974, 28].

Scorsese had to make other artistic choices in order to save money. Because filming totally on location in New York was cost prohibitive, part of *Mean Streets* was shot in Los Angeles. Certain characters, Jimmy (Lenny Scaletta) for example, were only photographed indoors to prevent having to transport the entire cast back and forth from Los Angeles to New York. Yet in other areas, Scorsese was unwilling to compromise. For instance, he spent an extra day in New York to shoot the interiors of hallways because they couldn't find interior hallways in Los Angeles that looked like those in a New York tenement (Bobrow 1974, 28). Similarly, Scorsese shot the beach scene on Staten Island because the look of a Staten Island beach is different from a West Coast beach.

Scorsese also economized by using a home-movie sequence as the initial means of exposition instead of using expensive establishing shots. Shortly after the beginning of the film when Charlie wakes up from his dream, the screen goes black once again, and there is a close shot of a movie projector being turned towards the audience. We then watch home movies, shot in super eight in a deliberately amateurish style. They introduce the major characters and the neighborhood where the story takes place. Structurally, this sequence serves the same purpose as one or more establishing shots would at the beginning of a typical movie except that here we get more of a feeling for the neighborhood and the characters than we would with more conventional opening exposition.

Scorsese uses camera movement expressively. Sometimes the moving camera in *Mean Streets* can be fluid and graceful. For example, often Charlie's experience is revealed to us through moving camera shots. We enter Charlie's world through the slow motion traveling shots Scorsese uses at the beginning of the movie when Charlie is in Tony's bar. Through the moving camera and through stationary shots, we experience what Charlie does during this sequence. When Charlie first enters, the camera slowly trucks down the length of the bar, scanning its patrons to the Rolling Stones lyrics, "Tell me you're comin' back to me." We next see a freeze frame of a nude painting; then the camera quickly zooms to the belly of one of the bar's topless dancers. In slow motion we see Tony warmly greeting Charlie as Tony puts an arm around Charlie and shakes hands with him. The camera next follows Charlie as he dances his way through the bar. Tony approvingly smiles and nods at Charlie.

When Johnny Boy enters accompanied by two women, as a gag he checks his pants at the door. Tony jokes with Johnny, asking him if the shorts he has on are the ones with the hearts on them. We then hear Charlie's thoughts in a voiceover, "All right. Okay. Thanks a lot, Lord. We talk about penance and you send this through the door . . . Well, we play by your rules, don't we?" Observing Johnny's entrance, Charlie watches as Johnny Boy, with his arms around the girls, ushers them down the length of the bar to the tune of the Stones song "Jumpin' Jack Flash." This slow motion shot highlights Charlie's contemplative response to Johnny's silly antics.

In addition to emphasizing Charlie's experience, other slow motion shots evoke a mood, a feeling. For example, at the party for the Vietnam veteran newly returned to the neighborhood, Scorsese's use of slow motion draws us into the experience lyrically, as if we'd had a drink or two and were relaxed. Actions seem slower, and we notice small gestures more. Admitting that he's fond of this technique while acknowledging that its most common use is for fight scenes, Scorsese comments, "I wanted to isolate, analyze very simple gestures: a woman lighting a cigarette, a guy having a drink, another observing the scene" (Ciment and Henry 1975, 17).

Yet another stylish technique is the use of a ragged camera in conveying Charlie's drunken state at the party for the Vietnam veteran. In close-up, we see Charlie, his face wet with beads of sweat, looking very drunk as the room tilts behind him. The song, "Rubber Biscuits" by the Chips, complements the visuals, as the song's lyrics reverberate along with the pulsating beat of the song. Soon the party streamers dangle loosely, horizontally, behind Charlie's head, and we too get a sense of the experience, the room spinning, off balance, undulating, feeling drunk.

Much of *Mean Streets* was photographed with a handheld camera. This technique contributes a great deal to its realistic look and feel. Giving the impression of having captured a slice of life, the camera seems to have been a shrewd and astute observer of the action. The effect is that the camera involves us in the action, often making us feel the anxiety, tension, or violence of the scene. For example, after having been warned that he absolutely must meet Michael, Johnny Boy nervously darts down a street in nearby Greenwich Village. The jagged look of the handheld shots of the scene underscores Johnny Boy's abrupt, uptight movements, and we too experience his anxiety, paranoia, and unfocused anger as he lashes out at a guy who happens to bump into him. Johnny Boy punches him savagely.

The narrative structure of *Mean Streets* is weak. On a first viewing, it is hard to know who is who, how the characters are related to one another, and what the story is about. Part of this lack of coherence was the result of the film's small budget and inadequate production time. According to Scorsese, the choppy narrative was also partly a deliberate artistic decision.

The editing seems jagged in part because of the movie's jump cuts and lack of establishing shots. Scorsese later admitted, "if *Mean Streets* looks frenzied, it's because we *were* frenzied" (quoted in Jacobs 1977, 137). He also stated frankly, "I think *Mean Streets* is a very sloppy film, only because we had to shoot it in 27 days. I'm not giving excuses. That's reality" (Macklin 1975, 24). Being under a tight production schedule, Scorsese may have simply miscalculated how much exposition the audience could follow.

Most American movies are plot-oriented: all of the action, with mounting suspense, builds toward the climax and resolution of the story. By contrast, the pieced-together scenes in *Mean Streets* are some of what the story is about. "That's the way life is down there, it's digression," Scorsese commented, "It's never dealing with the realities of life . . . nothing ever really happens, but when things do happen they happen like they do in the film"

(Delson 1972, 29). The loose format and the ragged editing also contribute to the documentary quality of the film.

Freed from the time demands of plot, the characters could be developed more realistically than in conventional movies. Critic David Denby noted that film makers using this technique are increasingly "able to allow characters their own reality" (Denby 1973–74, 49). Scorsese is well aware of his departure from the norm: "I'm striving for an approach to filmmaking where things are simple and direct. Where I can tell a story and it doesn't have to be the longest, most complex or most traditional story in the world. *The Godfather* is a classic ethnic storytelling film, but I'm going in the opposite direction" (Delson 1972, 28).

In addition to the movies, another love of Martin Scorsese's is music, and a study of the uses of music in *Mean Streets* is revealing. Sometimes a song's lyrics simply provide additional information. For example, the lyrics to "Jumpin' Jack Flash" suggest that Johnny Boy is a flashy character. This song appropriately underscores Johnny Boy's entrance to Tony's bar as he shows off to the two women accompanying him.

The various types of music in *Mean Streets*—Italian operatic, band, folk, and rock and roll—richly evoke setting. Most of the musical pieces were selected before filming. Scorsese comments,

> The piece at the end, for example, ends all of the Italian feasts. The one at the beginning, "Be My Baby," by the Ronettes, is very important, because it evokes the music which plays in the street, when the jukeboxes are outside and the kids dance on the street. . . . I remember rock 'n' roll was always in the background of our cruisings and our fights [Ciment and Henry 1975, 17].

Music is often used as a transitional device. Scorsese frequently cuts on music; a song ends one scene and begins the next. Sometimes the song establishes a relationship between the two scenes. For example, when Charlie stands up Diane, a casual date, the scene ends with a close-up of her as she waits expectantly on the street. Charlie is in a cab, but he tells the driver not to stop . The poignancy of this shot is underscored in a quiet but moving way by the quivering anguish of an Italian folk song that begins a meeting Charlie has with his uncle. Charlie cannot see Diane, a black woman, because it would threaten his relations with his racist uncle, and the music reveals the sadness underlying that fact.

Music works in a more overt way in the graveyard scene. Charlie and Johnny Boy hide out in a church graveyard after fleeing from a rooftop where Johnny had been shooting off a gun and tossing explosives. As they run away, the sound of Latin-beat music dominates the scene, setting the tone of adventure and boyish fun. The music also underlines their footsteps, thereby creating a comical mickeymousing (music which tries to complement the action with a musical equivalent) effect. Later in the scene, however, after Charlie has had an unsettling talk with Johnny, the same music grows louder once again, but this time with a more chaotic and faster beat, suggesting the mounting pressure Charlie is feeling.

Music sometimes functions to intensify the action in a scene. For example, at the Vietnam vet's party where Charlie gets drunk, "Rubber Biscuits" by the Chips is as important as are the visuals in conveying Charlie's drunkenness. The song's reverberating, busy, and relentless beat and its silly lyrics complement the dizzying visuals to recreate the sensation Charlie is feeling. Similarly, the frenzied sound of the guitar which precedes and later accompanies the hit man's shooting Charlie, Theresa, and Johnny Boy foreshadows the terror to follow and intensifies the ensuing violence.

By contrast, music serves a lighthearted function in the poolroom brawl scene. When a fight breaks out over payment of a gambling debt, the action is underscored by a girl-group version of "Please Mr. Postman" by the Marvelettes. Here the bubblegum, pop sound of the music adds a playful and comic tone which diminishes the violence of the scene and distances us from its reality.

When the police arrive and the fight is over, there is silence, and the fun ends. Here silence means sobering up after the high, the excitement of the fight. Silence has the same effect after the murder in Tony's bar. The plug is pulled on the music, and again there is the sobering reality. After the shooting, there is a tense, dramatic quiet, followed by a barking dog, a siren, and cans being kicked over as the bar's patrons flee while Tony repeatedly cautions them, "Don't run!"

Perhaps the most sobering silence, however, occurs after Charlie crashes into the fire hydrant, concluding Michael's hit man's shooting spree. This has resulted in a bloodbath, wounding Charlie, Theresa, and Johnny Boy. Only Charlie had realized how serious the situation had become. Just before the shooting, Johnny Boy had been playing the radio, creating a party atmosphere, and Theresa had been playfully teasing Charlie. As the action in the scene escalates, with shots being fired and the car careens out of control, a frenetic guitar intensifies the horror of what is happening. After the crash, the screams, the screeching guitar, and the squealing brakes are all silent. There is only a stunned silence — reality, the aftermath.

There is a great deal of humor in *Mean Streets*, and much of it derives from its often warm, playful, and colorful language. First of all, there are lots of jokes in the movie. For example, although Charlie takes religion seriously, he doesn't take himself that seriously. He lightheartedly allows others to tease him about his religious obsession, playing along by assuming the role of a priest.

Harvey Keitel (*left*) and Richard Romanus. Trying to be a good Christian, Charlie goes out of his way to help his friend Johnny Boy. In this scene, Charlie entreats Michael to reduce the interest on Johnny's loan, so that the money really could be paid back. Unfortunately, Charlie is naïve. Johnny Boy never intended to repay the loan in the first place, and Charlie's good works end in tragedy (*Mean Streets*, 1973).

There are also lots of one-liners. In the car on the way to collect Jimmy's bet winnings, for instance, Charlie, Tony, and Johnny Boy exchange quips as they stop for a light while a bum cleans their windshield. "He's probably an ex-judge," says Tony, while Johnny, annoyed at the lengthy light, quips, "What is this? A coffee and cake light?" During the boring hour just before closing, Charlie good-naturedly tries to pass the time by offering a card game to Michael as a "game you cannot say no to," to which Michael promptly retorts, "No." During the same scene, Jimmy, having drawn a swastika on a table, tells Charlie that he's drawn a portrait of him. Charlie glances at the swastika and comments, "Not quite, but keep trying!"

Jokey scenes help humanize the image of Michael as the Shylock character and contribute to his likeableness. These scenes often reveal a sincerity in his character which makes him vulnerable to being the butt of a joke. For example, at the Vietnam veteran's party, Michael speaks proudly and affectionately of his new girlfriend, saying, "She's going to be a teacher," as he shows her picture to a friend. Tony, seizing the opportunity to tease Michael, tells him he saw her kissing a "nigger" under the bridge. Michael, horrified, says, "What do you mean?" Tony responds, "You know, his lips on her lips," to which Michael responds, "Ugh."

One of the funniest scenes, rich in character-revealing information, is when Johnny Boy explains to Charlie why he has money to buy drinks for the Village pickups, but not the money to pay Michael. Johnny chronicles a long, rambling story which Charlie listens to with skepticism, but also with sympathy and sometimes amusement. To persuade Charlie that he's telling the truth, Johnny constantly appeals to higher authorities, "I swear to my mother," "I swear to Christ." From the dance of the story, which goes on and on, Johnny comes across as someone who lives on the edge and who is always stretching his luck to the limit. Yet there is also an entertaining quality to his story in both its style and its content. He is a good storyteller, and his story's very outrageousness makes it fun to listen to.

The acting in *Mean Streets* is noteworthy. The level of realism is remarkable as is the depth of characterization that results from Scorsese's sensitivity with actors. Some contributing factors to these performances are the use of improvisation, casting, and Scorsese's working methods with actors.

About a third of the dialogue of *Mean Streets* was improvised. Three or four scenes were actually improvised on camera, but the rest came from rehearsals and were later written into the script. Critic David Denby thinks Scorsese uses improvisation better than anyone in American movies so far. He attributes this success, at least in part, to a quality he sees in Scorsese that Bertolucci also noted as important in directors: "Directing actors means, above all, liking people, liking certain things about people" (quoted in Denby 1973–74, 50). Perhaps it is liking people and trusting them that allows Scorsese to let his actors have more freedom than is often the case. Denby notes,

> Scorsese ... stays back from his people, allowing them to draw strength from the streets, the music, their friends. ... Thus Scorsese's improvisation becomes a fast, explosively funny way of extending the actors' expressiveness. The near-musical texture of obscenity, for instance, would be impossible without improvisation; no one could possibly get down on paper the lunatic obsessiveness of the swearing, with its infinite variety of meanings conveyed through minute variations in rhythm and inflection [Denby 1973–74, 50].

Scorsese likes to work with actors who can handle improvisation, actors who can draw from themselves rather than being locked into the script.

> And you need actors with a good sense of humor, that's a key thing. Personality is important too. That is part of what I mean by having a sense of humor. Very often during the shooting of *Mean Streets* the actors reverted to their own personalities. In cases of difficulty, trying to reach out for something in the character, they could always draw from themselves [Bobrow 1974, 31].

Scorsese and Mardik Martin wrote the first draft of *Mean Streets* in 1966 as a sequel to *Who's That Knocking at My Door?* Scorsese's first feature-length film. They had Harvey Keitel in mind as the older Charlie. "De Niro, who lived on 14 Street, was well acquainted with characters like Johnny Boy, the role he was to play, and Keitel, from Brooklyn, knew the neighborhood from experience as well as his part in the earlier film" (Jacobs 1977, 136).

But perhaps most important is Scorsese's subjective instinct. He chose Amy Robinson primarily because of her appearance; she had exactly the kind of look he wanted. Scorsese commented, "There are certain things about certain faces. I think Keitel's is kind of important in holding the whole picture together — it's a strong kind of face. Other people could have played the part, but they wouldn't have given me the same feeling that his face did" (Bobrow 1974, 31).

Scorsese has been able to elicit strong performances because of his rapport with actors. Although both De Niro and Keitel have worked with Lee Strasberg, Scorsese surprisingly admits he knows nothing about method acting,

> I've never set foot in an acting course. I have to like my actors, we have to go out together, we have to become close to one another. I need for them to trust me. I expect a lot from rehearsals. For *Mean Streets*, we had rehearsed ten days, strengthening together the network of relationships among the four main characters and Theresa, giving them the impression that they could invent whatever they wanted. When they were relaxed enough, they felt free to introduce their own jokes in their parts [Ciment and Henry 1975, 18].

In this atmosphere of freedom to improvise, two comic scenes came about. The scene with Harvey Keitel and Robert De Niro in the back room was created from improvisations that were written into the script. However, during the actual filming, Keitel couldn't remeber some of the text, so he had to improvise, and De Niro played along. Also, although the fight for the poolroom scene had been written out, the dialogue was incomplete. George Memmoli (Joey) supplied a funny idea for the scene which worked well with the rest of the plans. The fight is motivated when Joey says, "We're not payin' because this guy's a mook." Jimmy responds defensively with, "But I didn't say nothing!" Then, a moment later, not entirely sure if he's been insulted or not, he asks, "What's a mook?" Tony and Charlie shrug their shoulders in response, "I don't know. What's a mook?" Concluding that being called a mook must be an offense, Jimmy finally responds indignantly, "You can't call me a mook!" Then Joey responds with, "Oh yeah?" followed by the punch that starts the whole bar fighting.

The performances in *Mean Streets* were widely praised. Critic Jon Landau stated, "The often improvised, largely comic, always overlapping dialogue provides a perfect aural equivalent, while the acting virtually leaps off the screen" (Landau 1973, 80). Critics noted De Niro's bravura style, making the most of his flashy role, and praised the character he realized so fully, especially his physical movement and vitality. They were also impressed with Harvey Keitel's performance, more subtle than De Niro's, capturing the torment, humor, and kindness of Charlie's character.

After *Mean Streets*, Scorsese was sent many scripts dealing with similar subject matter. A number of critics too had prematurely typecast Scorsese, expecting him to continue to make more movies like *Mean Streets*. Instead, his pattern has been to make each subsequent movie in a different genre. His second feature-length film, *Alice Doesn't Live Here Anymore* (1974) stands in stark contrast to *Mean Streets* for a number of reasons. This new project had a bigger budget; it was produced by a major studio, Warner Brothers; it was scripted by someone other than Scorsese; it is a woman's story primarily; and it was a far more commercially successful film than *Mean Streets*. For Scorsese, the challenge was more than working in a different genre. He felt the real experimenting was done in the areas of character and exploration of feelings (Howard 1975, 26).

Alice Doesn't
Live Here Anymore

*I was always so . . . so scared of Donald. I was always trying to
please him. I was so afraid not to please him. . . . And now I'm
without him . . . I always thought he was taking care of me, you
know? . . . But he didn't. I just felt like he did just because he was
there. I don't know how to live without a man. That's what it is.*
—Alice, talking to her friend Flo

Alice Doesn't Live Here Anymore, a woman's picture, recounts the
story of Alice Hyatt (Ellen Burstyn), a housewife who lives in Soccorro,
New Mexico. She is married to a truck driver and has an eleven-year-old
son. Although Alice accepts her humdrum life, she also feels emptiness and
hurt because she and her husband are sadly mismatched. They do not communicate, and emotionally there is no connection, leaving Alice's husband,
Donald (Billy Green Bush), mystified and Alice feeling lonely and sad.

When Alice's husband dies in a traffic crash, she feels both guilty and
bereft at her loss. Left penniless at her husband's death, she decides to move
back to Monterey, California, where she grew up. She plans to resume a
singing career which she had begun briefly before her marriage. Having little cash to finance the trip, however, Alice and her son, Tommy (Alfred
Lutter), have to stop along the way so she can earn money to continue their
journey. First she finds a singing job and gets involved with a charming but
violent man. At her next stop, she has no luck finding a singing job and
becomes a waitress instead. She is luckier in love though because she
meets a handsome and kind rancher to whom she is attracted.

Perhaps what is most significant about Alice's story is its ordinariness.
Alice and Tommy are bright and witty, and their lines are well written.
However, Alice is not extraordinary in the usual way of female leads: She
doesn't have upper-middle-class comforts. Also, she is not alcoholic or
neurotic, nor does she have some domestic melodramatic situation thrust
upon her. She is not glamorous, nor does she possess special advantages
like having unusual talent or self-confidence. *Alice* is the story of a more

Left to right: **Billy Green Bush, Alfred Lutter, Ellen Burstyn.** *Alice* **is a film of its time in that it presents the landscape of a section of America at a particular moment. It reflects the look of the Southwest, its dusty streets, stucco houses, wide skies, and roadway motels and truckstops. It also observes the lifestyle of lower-middle-class suburbia and the relationships among its inhabitants (***Alice Doesn't Live Here Anymore,*** 1974).**

average woman than we usually find in a woman's picture. Scorsese comments on his intentions in making this film: "This film attracted me . . . because it was a challenge to make a picture about a woman as realistically and honestly as possible, yet a picture that would be fun as well" (Rosen 1975, 42).

Alice, as French critic Henri Behar noted, is about the experiences of women in general, and it is about relationships. Several important relationships are explored: between Alice and her son, Tommy; Alice and men — her husband, Ben, and David (Kris Kristofferson); and Alice and her friendships with other women — Bea and Flo.

Alice yearns for closeness and affection in her marriage to Donald. She craves conversation and emotional connectedness with her husband, but he doesn't seem to be aware that there is a problem. She tries to attract his attention by preparing special foods and by engaging him in everyday conversation, but nothing works. Each attempt is futile, revealing only emptiness and making her feel all the more lonely.

After Alice's husband dies, it is her loneliness and need to be held that draws her into the relationship with Ben against her better judgment.

Although he later turns out to be a dangerously violent man, Ben initially charms Alice. With a boyish grin, he approaches her and tries flattery to interest her. Alice invites him to sit down with her when, in spite of her bad mood, Ben makes her laugh. However, he wins real sympathy from Alice when he tells her he works in a factory, where he fills bullets with gun powder, "Guess there's not much to say about that." Reluctantly, Alice, seeking both companionship and a physical relationship, gets involved with Ben. Later, when he bursts into her motel suite looking for his wife in an explosion of rage, Alice is both stunned and frightened at his behavior. What is represented is the fear women have of a man's anger and capacity for physical violence.

David is a marked improvement in men for Alice. Kind, gentle, and sexy, he is an attractive potential match for her. He has been called the perfect man for the post-liberated woman of the mid-seventies — masculine, yet nonthreatening, secure in himself and therefore able to be supportive to a woman. Nevertheless, he is still a man, and there is inequality in the relationship between Alice and him.

David sometimes assumes the role of teacher and person of sounder judgment. For example, he points out to Alice that going to Monterey and resuming a singing career don't necessarily go hand in hand. At least in part, Alice finds it hard to assert herself at the end of the movie because her relationship with David is not adult to adult.

In addition to the men in Alice's life, the film also explores friendships between women. One of the most genuine performances in the film is that of Lelia Goldoni, who plays Bea. Bea is introduced in the opening scenes of the film as Alice's neighbor and friend. They share a common experience as women in similar circumstances. They both may not be totally happy, but they accept their lives. Their relationship is memorable because it is such a genuine portrayal of friendship between women. Sketched in just a few scenes, the scenes are effective and truthful in showing the love, joy, and depth that bind women in friendship. The scene in which Bea says goodbye to Alice is particularly moving because of the heartfelt emotion that is conveyed. Though Goldoni's scenes are few, they are noteworthy and contribute to what the film has to say about relationships.

In contrast to the commonality of Alice and Bea's relationship, Alice and Flo's friendship is one of opposites. Alice is at first offended by Flo's bawdiness but later comes to appreciate her colorful style. Again, Alice's humor and openness allow her to get to know someone she hadn't planned on getting to know. The turning point comes when Flo, feeling particularly frazzled, lets out a frustrated curse that silences the diner. Alice finds herself laughing so hard that tears come to her eyes. Flo apologizes, thinking she's truly offended Alice. When she realizes Alice's response is actually delight, they embrace, joined by wimpy Vera, who is drawn to the loving

Alice (Ellen Burstyn) is pictured here with Ben (Harvey Keitel), a man she met at the club where she sings. In this privileged moment, Scorsese shows sympathetically, Alice's vulnerability. Lonely and alone, she surrenders to Ben's charm. Full of physical and emotional needs, she gives in to him, abandoning her better judgment.

display of affection. Despite her unpolished exterior, Flo becomes a loyal friend to Alice, appreciative, sympathetic, and tough-minded towards her when she feels that response is in Alice's best interest.

The character of Alice's son, Tommy, is one of the elements that mark *Alice* as a Scorsese film. Often the boy is uncomfortable to watch. Probably many find him objectionable as a character. He is an outsider and an original. His unusual cynicism and smart-ass comments distinguish him because he is only eleven years old and because those qualities are present to such a marked extent. Yet Tommy is also Alice's son. She takes his remarks in stride, often playing along, but she is rarely offended by them.

In contrast to the heroines of other women's pictures, Alice stands apart because of her level of realism. She hasn't the wealth and stature of Norma Shearer in the thirties' *The Women*; she isn't successful in business and a selfless mother like Joan Crawford in the forties' weepie *Mildred Pierce*; and she isn't virginal, self-assured, and in an enviable position in life like Doris Day in a fifties' romantic comedy like *Send Me No Flowers*.

In contrast to these stylized heroines, Alice has a full range of behavior and feelings. In addition to being funny, appealing, and endearing, Alice curses, acts out her frustrations, and vents her rage, later regretting her behavior. In contrast to the glamorous clothing of previous heroines, Alice, sporting a simple hairdo and a figure that's a bit round, wears clothes that are ordinary—housedresses and plain slacks and tops.

Finally, in contrast to the emotional safety of previous heroines, living lives well within the prescribed norms of movie convention, norms which society recognizes and supports, the loneliness and emptiness of Alice's marriage is far less documented territory. Such experiences are not usually discussed openly; such loneliness is seldom validated. Even Alice's journey to start life over is new, at least the way it is shown here. Alice encounters chauvinism as it actually exists in the world. Women in the films of previous decades usually didn't encounter such obstacles, though they surely existed.

When *Alice Doesn't Live Here Anymore* debuted, critics accused Scorsese of selling out to Hollywood, of commercializing his work for greater box-office success. Also, having liked his realistic portrayal of the macho world of Little Italy, they were disappointed with the softer subject matter of this new film. Of the scripts that were offered to Scorsese, *Alice* was the only one he read which offered him characters that interested him. In contrast to *Mean Streets,* which Scorsese knew would appeal primarily to an audience of young males, he deliberately tried to appeal to a broader group in *Alice:*

> I really wanted it to be a very commercial, entertaining piece because I think whatever messages they [the audience] feel towards people in the film makes them know a little more about themselves. I didn't want to cut it off in any way so we watched our ratings, we watched everything. I didn't care at all with *Mean Streets.* Every other word was fuck this, fuck that, mother fuck straight through. Offend everybody. It didn't matter. We even offend a few people in *Alice* [Macklin 1975, 16].

Alice was released during the resurgence of the women's movement during the early 1970s. Perhaps as a backlash to the women's movement, before the film's release there had been a scarcity of movies featuring female leads. Nevertheless, *Alice* is not a women's liberation film. Scorsese makes it clear that his interest in Alice lies in the fact that she's had liberation thrust upon her; it is not something she's actively sought out, and therein lies an important difference. He points out:

> I understand a person being taken away from the trap, not of her own accord, but by God's will. The finger of God comes down, the truck crashes. Because if she left the husband it would be a different story, and

Diane Ladd (*center*) and Vic Tayback (*right*). The overloaded mise-en-scène suggests an explosive situation. Flo is visually hemmed in by customers and her boss. Under pressure, Flo expresses her exasperation at demands from all sides. Although Alice had initially been repelled by Flo's bawdiness, here she can't help laughing at her colorful epithets. This is a pivotal scene because of Alice's reaction, creating a common ground for their eventual friendship.

> then I really wouldn't be interested in it. It would have to be a person thrown out on her own, out into the wilds, and that's the kind of thing that interested me about the whole piece (Macklin 1975, 15).

Alice is, however, a film of its time, and although its concern is not with women's liberation in the "correct" ideological manner, some of that spirit does pervade, especially in Burstyn's powerful performance. Pauline Kael called *Alice* an angry woman's film. She responded especially to the anger Burstyn expressed in her role as Alice. In trying to understand the motivation for this anger, Kael posits that the anger is unfocused; it was something that was ready to be expressed at a given time. She points out, "as in the angry-young-men British plays of the fifties and the angry-young-men American movies of the late sixties, you can't always be sure what the protagonist is angry about. The anger is resonant precisely because it hasn't a specific cause" (Kael 1975, 77). Kael also believes recognition of this anger, however inarticulate, is important: "Sometimes a person's anger and overstatement tell a bigger story than the person knows how to tell. The anger may derive from deprivation of the means to express oneself calmly, rationally" (Kael 1975, 77).

The anger Burstyn expresses may also have a much more concrete origin. It may simply stem from the outrage of repression that women have traditionally endured and, according to economic statistics, continue to endure. It has always been a man's world in worldly spheres: men have power, and women do not.

What is exceptional about *Alice Doesn't Live Here Anymore* is that it captures aspects of a woman's experience that other films never have, captures them truthfully, realistically, and compassionately. So often the character of Alice — in her anger and in her vulnerability, in her hopes and in her disappointment — mirrors the commonality of a woman's experience. In many ways, she expresses what it is like to be a woman. This is especially true in some of the smaller moments of the movie — the less showy scenes where witty dialogue and humor do not predominate.

For example, when David and Tommy walk into the diner to get some food to take on their fishing trip, Alice greets them happily. She proceeds to tell David about an exciting incident that just happened; however, he abruptly cuts her off, telling her to order the cheeseburgers. Hurt, Alice says nothing more and complies with his order. The fishing trip is cancelled a short while later because David's truck needs repair. Tommy and Alice both are disappointed. Tommy tells his mother about the cancelled trip and listlessly pours a can of tomatoes into a pot on the stove. Alice applies lipstick, ruminating, "Well, don't worry because tomorrow you're going to be twelve years old, fully grown. You can do whatever you want to — go fishing or get married." This scene recalls Alice and her husband, who also wasn't sensitive to her need for conversation. This situation — not being listened to and wishing to converse — is true to the experience of many women. This scene also shows the man as implicitly dominant. There is the tacit understanding that it is the woman's place to yield. Both Tommy, the child, and Alice, the woman, feel pouty here, perhaps with good reason.

Anger is a good way to control others, and it is doubly effective when expressed violently. Alice is terrified at Ben's maniacal actions as he lashes out at his wife, crashes through the glass door to enter the motel, throws his wife around, and threatens to cut her with a knife. In a similar situation, Alice, lying in bed, curls up in fear as she overhears a couple arguing and fighting in the suite above her. When David and Tommy fight later on, Alice cowers in the kitchen. Aggressive behaviors such as these are ways men exercise control over women. Whether it be yelling louder or pushing harder, men can exercise power over women and extort compliance. Usually, these aggressive behaviors effectively eclipse a woman's assertion of her rights.

Burstyn's performance also reveals Alice's "traditional" values — that is, stereotypically passive, "helpless" behaviors. Alice sports a new curly hairdo and a tight-fitting dress as she looks for work as a singer. As she approaches each club owner for work, she is soft-spoken, polite, and smiling, eager to please through traditionally feminine means. Although it is perfectly understandable that Alice should be frustrated to the point of tears at feeling the pressure of needing to get a job to support herself and her son and of enduring nothing but rejection, still it is her final crying that motivates Mr. Jacobs to give her a chance as a singer. A woman's crying often troubles a man and arouses his sympathy. Crying also provides an opportunity to try to help, to rescue as is the case here. Nevertheless, Alice's need is real, and her frustration is sincere. It is cynical and perhaps misogynist to coldly assume, as one critic (Michael Bliss) did, that Alice's motives are purely calculating. Mr. Jacobs sympathizes with her plight, and his concern and kindness are laudable. Yet the whole dynamic also has many traditionally male-female underpinnings.

Crying as a dramatic means of being heard or expressing desperation at feeling helpless is not an unusual situation for a woman to find herself in. Perhaps because of the cultural differences in the ways men and women are raised, women often have fewer avenues open to them and fewer means to get their needs met. Alice was anxious to please her husband, Donald, too. In typical domestic style, she made special dinners for him and fancy desserts to win his approval and appreciation. She does not seem to question these roles, nor does she seem uncomfortable with these behaviors.

Fortunately Alice has many other resources available to her. Her pluck, her sense of humor, and her dream all are positive attributes that distinguish her as an individual and help ease the way for her in life. Alice shows a healthy rebelliousness at the very outrageousness of some of the situations she finds herself in. When her husband hollers at Tommy and smashes china at the dinner table over the sugar and salt substitute prank, Alice throws her own temper tantrum, pounding on the patio door then opening it to express her frustration with everything, including the town she lives in. "Soccorro sucks!" she shouts petulantly. Similarly, when one of the club owners asks Alice to turn around as part of a singing job interview, she retorts indignantly, "I don't sing out of my ass!" and walks out on him.

Even under some of the most trying situations, Alice maintains her sense of humor, which is the essence of her appeal. When Donald bellows for Alice to turn down Tommy's music, she drolly remarks to Tommy, "How are we supposed to have a *meaningful* family relationship with him about to kill you half the time?" In fact, much of the relationship between Tommy and Alice is developed through their humor, playfully bantering about language and delighting in each other's wit. Finally, Alice's willingness to pursue her dream is a winning quality too. Though she is not particularly talented, her singing is special to her. Although in many ways Alice's life is disappointing and limited, this outlet for her romantic yearnings provides some comfort.

In contrast to the dark, rain-slicked New York City blocks of *Mean Streets, Alice* is a film of sunlight, roadside motels, and stretches of flat, open highways. Just as Scorsese captured, in realistic fashion, a sense of life in the neighborhood of Little Italy, he has also captured the look and feel of life in the suburbs and small towns of the American Southwest. From its rows of white stucco houses to its bars with cowboys, Scorsese provides a setting rich with the same attention to detail as his previous work.

Scorsese uses bright light in an especially effective way when he photographs Alice as she looks for work as a singer. When she enters the various bars, we experience with her the disorientation of adjusting from the bright sunlit streets to the darkness of the bars, just one of the small, sympathetic details Scorsese chooses to show us, one of the many discomforts of pounding the pavement, looking for work.

The credit sequence presents a homage to the studio-era women's pictures, serving as Scorsese's tribute to his predecessors. This sequence establishes the genre and the revisionist approach and also helps to reveal character. The script handwriting has a background of blue satin. The frame is masked off in the old 3-by-4 dimensions. On the soundtrack, Alice Faye sings the romantic tune "You'll Never Know," recalling the style of a 1940s woman's picture.

The opening shots place Alice, as a little girl, on a farm in the warmth of a red-orange sunset on an obvious studio set. Everyone and everything look idyllic, pastoral: the father doing chores in deliberate, graceful motion; a silhouette in lamplight through the window of the farmhouse. In fact, the set was actually from *Citizen Kane*, used in Kane's childhood scene. Like other film-buff directors of his generation, Scorsese likes old movies, and his films, like those of his fellow directors, are filled with loving homages to the classics. This is a different era, however. Although Scorsese loves the way old movies were made and greatly admires the old masters, he feels times simply have changed, "So, Hitchcock is dead, Ford is dead, John Wayne is dead. It's all over. We don't make pictures like these guys did" (Oumano 1985, 247).

Scorsese comments on this difference in his homage by adding some realistic touches to the warm, idealized scene. Alice's mother says roughly, "Alice Faye, you'd better get into this house before I beat the living daylights out of you." And Alice is a tough, determined little girl who curses defiantly, "I can sing better than Alice Faye . . . and if anybody doesn't like it they can blow it out their ass." Alice is nothing like the endearing, adorably bratty little heroines who came before her. Alice, with just a few distinguishing characteristics established, also emerges as an outsider, the type of character Scorsese makes movies about. Although Alice as an adult is an appealing character, as a little girl, she is harder to like, just the type Scorsese invites us to get to know.

The revisionist slant picks up in force and power as the camera reduces the farm image to a small square surrounded by a large black frame accompanied by a crisp modern-sounding drum and piano accompaniment. The camera quickly leaps forward twenty-seven years to show us what became of Alice, the little girl who dreamed of becoming a singer — better than Alice Faye. The camera scans the New Mexican suburb of Soccorro from an aerial view — past white stucco houses, palm trees, and hedgerows to find Alice's house. It peers into a window, through the bushes and treetops, to find Alice, clad in a pink ruffled housedress, working at the sewing machine and singing along to her son's blaring Mott the Hoople record. The jazz-rock piano accompanying the camera movement sets the tone of Alice's current life: not glamour, but not dreariness either. Rather, the tone of her life is upbeat, energetic, not completely conforming and dull.

There are shots in *Alice Doesn't Live Here Anymore* that evoke a mood, an intimate moment, shots of found beauty. For example, when Alice sits down at the piano to play and sing, the camera captures delicate details that add to the beauty of the scene — gathered curtains blowing in a light breeze, leaves on the boughs out the window, Alice singing a medley of romantic songs, her voice tentative, yet softly expressive. The poetry of this scene helps convey that Alice is in her own world here. We watch as she experiences the music she plays, art that envelops, delights, and comforts.

Another intimate moment is recorded when Alice and David drive home after a day's outing. In dark tones, Scorsese shows us a back view of Alice sitting next to David. She lights a cigarette for him and hands it to him. There are no words during this scene, just a brief shot of the love and peacefulness between them, a small tender moment.

The closeness of friends is shown in another small scene with Alice and Flo. In close-up, we see Alice and Flo in silhouette, sunning themselves. Both blond and fair and both with their hair pushed back, they almost look like sisters, fitting, because they are kindred spirits in this scene, sharing stories, feelings, and laughter. When the camera pulls back to reveal the barren, dusty street where they are seated, we are startled. This small, warm poetic scene originated in the most unlikely setting.

When Alice sings, the characteristic signature is a circular camera movement. Both at home while Alice is practicing and at the clubs while she is performing, the camera circles lyrically, underscoring her experience. The movement serves as a metaphor suggesting Alice's private rapture as she sings. Scorsese comments, "She's in her own world and all the camera sees is her, until it almost becomes like her mind. And every time she sings I felt it should be like that" (Howard 1975, 26).

Camera movement creates darker tones, however, with many of the handheld shots. The unsteady, handheld camera is often used to fore-shadow violent scenes to come. For example, when Ben violently throws his wife around and threatens to cut her, the scene actually begins with handheld shots of Alice talking to Tommy about Ben. Throughout the scene when Tommy asks his mother about Ben as she spreads peanut butter and jelly, wipes crumbs from the table, and cleans the range top, the unsteady camera movements foreshadow the dangerous events that follow.

In contrast to the episodic style of *Mean Streets*, *Alice* has a more conventional narrative structure. The events of the film center on what happens to Alice as she has a second chance thrust upon her. Like *Mean Streets* and most of Scorsese's other films, the storyline of *Alice* is also ragged in parts.

A focus of criticism of the editing of *Alice* has been the way Alice's husband, Donald, comes across on screen. With good reason, he has been criticized as being flatly represented. Critics felt he was dehumanized, too one-dimensional, too obviously the insensitive husband. Some even said Donald seems more like a stepfather to Tommy than a father. He is, as critic Judith Crist aptly put it, "a chowderhead" (Crist 1975, 64), and his "male" traits are exaggerated. Fortunately, there are small parts of Billy Green Bush's performance that show Donald as more than a composite male infused with traits that limit and frustrate women. At times, we also see Donald's goodness and tenderness. For example, at a dinner scene, Donald says the following grace, "Father, make us truly humble and thankful, for it is only through you that all good things come." Donald is also caring enough to embrace his wife when he hears her crying next to him in bed.

Some critics believe that the second half of *Alice*, the romantic storyline beginning with David, is more conventional than the first half, with fewer surprises and artistic risks. Furthermore, they find fault with the movie's ending, criticizing its too-cute restaurant quarrel and kiss, which are straight out of a screwball comedy—too pat with all the strings neatly tied up. By conforming to some of the conventions of the genre, Scorsese seems to have intended to keep the material lighter, more entertaining than *Mean Streets*.

He considered ending the film when Alice nods in ascent to David's request that they try to make their relationship work. After he showed various endings to friends, they recommended that he end the film as he did. Scorsese commented:

> The most important scene at that point in the picture is . . . the part
> right before he [David] turns around and says, "Please," when he says,
> "Gee I think I understand you. There's got to be another way." She's so
> touched she can't even answer; she sort of nods her head and that's the
> whole picture [Macklin 1975, 26].

The music in *Alice*, both the songs that are sung and the songs that
underscore the visuals, do much to reveal character throughout the film.
The romantic songs Alice sings, like "You'll Never Know" and "Where or
When," give us a sense of the stuff Alice's dreams are made of. Some of the
most lyrical shots in the film are when Alice sings, in her quiet and
tremulous style, the lyrics from 1940s films, all romance, hope, and the
promise of love.

Kris Kristofferson's persona suggests the image of the late sixties and
early seventies counterculture. The laid-back country tunes that his character, David, sings are a part of this image. Not only do they typify the songs
a rancher might sing, but also they help characterize a seventies leading
man. An outgrowth of the hippie movement of the late sixties and early
seventies, the disenchanted older segment of the baby boomer generation
sought escape in a simpler, less corrupted life in the country than the
tumultuous sixties had been. David's being a rancher and living out West
would have appealed to the audience of the mid-seventies. Furthermore,
folk music of the type made popular by Bob Dylan and Joan Baez in the
sixties and gentle folk rock, especially the music of Kristofferson, had
recently been very popular. In fact, country-western music, formerly enjoyed by a more narrowly defined audience, was then enjoying widespread
appeal. People were discovering country, and movies such as *Nashville*
(1975) helped promulgate the country style. David's simple country songs,
to which he accompanies himself on the guitar, had a rich subtextual meaning, thus contributing to the revelation of his character.

Scorsese felt that Tommy is the type of kid who would like the rock
and roll of a group like Mott the Hoople. Loud, cacophonous, and easily
offensive to adults, Tommy's taste in music also suggests character in a
striking and expressive manner. Scorsese points out,

> The choices of music came from the characters' heads. In other words,
> the kid listened to rock'n'roll because I felt this kid would listen to Mott
> the Hoople, Elton John, and Leon Russell. . . . The mother, on the other
> hand, listened to stuff like "Where or When," "I've Got a Crush on You,"
> "Gone with the Wind," etc. [Howard 1975, 25].

Music also works to evoke tone in various scenes. The drum roll, then
reverberating piano-jazz-rock which accompanies the camera as it scans
the hills and homes of a New Mexico housing development helps suggest

the tone of Alice's present life. Rather than quiet domesticity, the music announces saucily that here we'll find an ironic twist.

The quiet folk rock of Elton John's "Daniel" sets a gentle and peaceful tone as Alice and Tommy embark on their trip west to Monterey. This song underscores long shots of the open road, the sound of cars ripping along the open highway, and Alice and Tommy peacefully driving in the sunshine and catching the wind. The song complements the open forms of this scene and suggests its peacefully liberating feeling.

By contrast, uproarious rock accompanies Alice and Tommy's frazzled and frantic getaway from the motel after Ben's violent outburst. The noisy, dissonant music of this scene underlines the frenzied movements of Alice and her son as they breathlessly scramble to flee the motel.

The muzak of Mel and Ruby's Cafe provides a wonderfully ironic comment on the various actions there. On her first day of work, Alice moves awkwardly through the motions as she tries to find things, get coffee, clear dishes, and take orders. The diner is packed with customers. Cowboys and girls are everywhere. The din of clattering dishes and lunchtime chatter adds to her stress. Accompanying this madhouse of nervous tension is perfect-sounding muzak, nondescript, bland, and blissful as greeting-card poetry.

Later, when Alice and Flo leave the diner to talk privately in the washroom, Vera is left alone to tend all the customers. The situation soon escalates to a riotous level: Fights break out. Vera, crying, pours a pitcher of water over the heads of a pair of brawling customers. She then secures the front door with a chairback and turns over the sign in the window to close the diner. Meanwhile, the cloyingly sweet sound of muzak plays happily and mindlessly in the background. The muzak diminishes the violence and pandemonium of the scene. It also wryly comments on the scene, revealing its irony and providing humor.

Scorsese's sound effects often add meaning to the visuals. For example, in one scene, Bea is pinning Alice's dress, with a baby crying in the background and throwaway dialogue in the foreground. When Alice answers the phone and hears that her husband has been killed in a traffic accident, a jet plan roars overhead, piercing through the sky as this news shatters Alice's consciousness. She cries out achingly, "Oh no . . . my husband is dead. God forgive me," with honesty and depth of feeling. The sounds of this scene evoke its sadness and convey Alice's shock and grief.

The violence of several scenes is enhanced through the effective use of sound. Often it is the loudness of the violence that terrifies. When Donald bellows at Tommy and breaks the china at the dinner table and when Alice pounds on the patio door, the volume magnifies the action. When Alice overhears a couple arguing in the motel room overhead, the sounds—a woman being slapped, screams and verbal abuse, objects broken—are what frighten her. When Ben catches his wife, Rita, with Alice, the shattering glass and Ben's vocal rage make Alice stiffen with fear. When she and David fight after Tommy's birthday party, Alice's anger and David's frustration fill the scene with a counterpoint of needs unmet and misunderstood.

By contrast, understated, pure, simple sounds, or in some cases the lack of sound, characterize other scenes. Alice, driving in her station wagon and feeling bereft at not being able to find her son, stops the car to cry out her anguish. In close-up, we see her sitting in the darkness, the simplicity of the picture highlighting the feeling conveyed in the scene,

When Alice stops to talk with David as he shows her around his ranch, all that accompanies their talk is the sound of the wind. It softly complements the pastoral open spaces of nature and the peaceful time of sharing. Similarly, the contented silence of the car ride home that evening accentuates the harmony and love between them.

There is much humor in *Alice Doesn't Live Here Anymore*. It is the quality that makes the movie accessible and agreeable to a wide audience and that expands the narrow focus of a woman's experience. First of all, Robert Getchell's script is witty and full of one-liners. Much humor also derives from characters such as Alice, Tommy, and Flo, who have a sense of humor, and others, like Vera, who don't but are funny anyway. Alice and Tommy are bright, articulate characters. They exchange quips and enjoy playing with words. For example, they assume a literary posture when Alice comments on one of their motel rooms: "It's not fancy, but we like it"; Tommy assumes a similar voice when he comes to the restaurant after Alice finishes work: "I came to escort you home." At the restaurant one day when Tommy complains about being bored, Vera kindly offers him a book to read. "You can color in it," she adds. Precocious Tommy, however, looks askance at the title and comments dryly, *"The Bride Screamed Murder?"*

Alice is quick to see the humor when Vera introduces her father to Alice after work one night. Vera's father turns out to be a big, burly, leather-jacketed Harley rider. "I'd like you to meet my Daddy Duke," Vera says politely. Alice says she's pleased to meet him, but aside, immediately responding to the incongruity of a Harley rider as a father figure, she turns to her son and says jokingly, "Daddy Duke!" Later, when Flo offers to fix up Alice with someone, Alice says with a twinkle, "Well, I kind of had my eye on Daddy Duke."

Women made major contributions to the making of *Alice Doesn't Live Here Anymore*. Scorsese's associate producer, Sandy Weintraub; his editor, Marcia Lucas; his set designer, Toby Rafelson; and Ellen Burstyn, along with other female cast members, all contributed not only in their respective professional capacities, but also in helping Scorsese to tell a woman's story honestly. Scorsese admits, "In terms of motivation, I relied heavily on the judgment of the women I worked with. . . . There was a great deal of improvisation, and when a line or response rang false, these women were free to criticize and suggest alternatives" (Rosen 1975, 42). Writing was not actually done on the set. Scorsese consulted with Getchell, Ellen Burstyn, Sandy Weintraub, and others separately. Somtimes he would ask their opinion of a videotape. The various means of improvisation were kept apart, but in general the making of *Alice* was a greatly collaborative effort (Rosen 1975, 44).

As in *Mean Streets*, Scorsese used improvisation in a number of ways during the making of *Alice*. With *Mean Streets*, he instinctively knew if an improvisation was right. With *Alice*, he asked help from the women he worked with and listened to their advice. Scorsese explains:

> I wanted to make a picture that was as true to women as possible. I wasn't always sure what that was. Perhaps a line wouldn't ring true, and I would say, "Well okay, what would you say? How would you express that idea?" And then they would go through a whole improv—"Well, I feel this way, that way"—and out of all that, we might get one thought or bit of business. And that's how we all worked it out together [Rosen 1975, 44].

During the two weeks of rehearsal for the film, Scorsese videotaped improvisations. Parts of the improvisations were later written into the scenes by Robert Getchell, the screenwriter of *Alice*. Sometimes Getchell used the improvised dialogue; other times he would write a new scene altogether. A number of gems in *Alice*, however, came from improvisation. For example, Tommy's telling of the great gorilla story in the car and his saying, "I feel sick." Also, the kitchen scene with Alice and David was an added scene. Finally, the bathroom scene is the result of several improvs and rewrites (Macklin 1975, 17).

The performances in *Alice* reinforced the initial critical observation that Scorsese was gifted at eliciting strong performances from his actors. He notes that awareness of a character's reactions is essential to good performance. So is having a good script. Finally, Scorsese believes that excellent casting is "eighty percent of your picture" (Rosen 1975, 44). Ellen Burstyn chose Scorsese to direct *Alice* for her, and they both decided to cast the movie with the best talent available, well-known or not.

Ellen Burstyn's acting in *Alice* was admired, garnering kudos from nearly all of the critics. Clearly the plum role of the year and beautifully acted, *Alice* later earned Burstyn an Academy Award for best actress. Critics noted the realism of Burstyn's performance, the fullness of her character, and the sympathy she inspires in us as we watch. They also recognized the distinctive decision Burstyn made to portray Alice in her ordinariness, deglamorized and sometimes shown unflatteringly.

The flashy performance by Harvey Keitel and the less showy, yet exactly right performance by Kris Kristofferson also received rave reviews. Critics were equally impressed with Alfred Lutter's acting, especially the authenticity Lutter brought to his role, all the more remarkable because the realism of method acting is rarely seen in children's performances. Like the smaller roles in *Mean Streets,* many other roles in *Alice* were also lauded, recognized, and remembered by critics, especially that of Lelia Goldoni as Bea, Valerie Curtain as Vera, and Diane Ladd as Flo.

Alice Doesn't Live Here Anymore later became the basis for a successful television series. Scorsese's next project took him back to Little Italy in New York where he made a documentary about his parents entitled *Italianamerican.* This project was funded by a Bicentennial Award from the National Endowment for the Humanities, and it was to become part of a series called *Storm of Strangers* about immigrants to this country (Thompson and Christie 1989, 52–53). Scorsese's next feature-length film was *Taxi Driver.*

Taxi Driver

---

*Loneliness has followed me everywhere. My whole life. Every-
where. In bars and cars, sidewalks, stores, everywhere. God's
lonely man. — Travis Bickle, N.Y. cabbie in* Taxi Driver

Taxi Driver hauntingly renders the loneliness of Travis Bickle's life. It
is that feeling which lingers — the look of pain in Travis's glazed eyes as he
struggles to articulate the anxiety and despair he is feeling, brimming over
with anguish. Considered a critical masterpiece both in 1977 and now, *Taxi
Driver* is a rich work which has captured the imagination of many critics
who have suggested many orientations and interpretations of the film.
Some have seen Travis (Robert De Niro) as a monster, others as a victim
of a violent society and *Taxi Driver* as an indictment of America in the
1970s. Some have focused on Travis as mentally ill, others on Travis as victimized because he served in Vietnam.

 Taxi Driver was a labor of love for director Martin Scorsese, the script-
writer Paul Schrader, and many of the leading players. Contributing their
considerable talents at bargain prices to lure a studio to pick up the picture,
those involved felt committed to putting their best effort into this work.
The result was a movie rich in detail and subtlety, even richer after repeated viewings.

 A movie of fragments, *Taxi Driver* is hard to follow. Watching it is similar to reading a modernist work such as T. S. Eliot's "The Love Song of
J. Alfred Prufrock" or "The Wasteland." In fact, approaching *Taxi Driver* as a
modernist work is helpful to understanding and interpreting it.* As in other
modernist works, the feeling evoked in *Taxi Driver* is one of desolation and
despair. There is a pessimistic view of life, and a sense of futility permeates
the world of this movie. The expression of alienation and isolation, the

---

*For definitions of modernism and film noir, I have consulted and adapted from Pro-
fessor Louis Giannetti's* Masters of the American Cinema *(Englewood Cliffs, N.J.:
Prentice-Hall, Inc., 1981), pp. 421–22 and 240–43.*

dominant feelings of Travis and a major focus of the film, is the quintessen-
tial characteristic of the modernist universe.

Also like most modernist works, *Taxi Driver* is a work of complex form
with much irony, and its appeal, for many people, is more intellectual than
emotional. Cinematographer Michael Chapman's photography of the
urban landscape in *Taxi Driver* is typical of modernist art, which often
features urban imagery, especially as a symbol of decay in modern society.
The photographic style is often expressionistic and subjective. The film's
artistic allusions include the works of other directors, especially Fritz Lang
and Alfred Hitchcock. Finally, *Taxi Driver* is modernist in that it is an ambiguous work which lends itself to multiple interpretations.

Taxi Driver is a variation of film noir.* Like other Scorsese films, it
looks back to the past, in this instance through the use of many noir
elements. Also like other Scorsese films, the use of this element borrowed
from the past is highly revisionist. Films made in the noir style began during World War II and continued to be a dominant mode during the 1950s.
Film noir, or black cinema, was a style used in several genres, including
the deadly female (or *femme fatale*) cycle, the thriller, the crime drama,
horror films, and psychological dramas. Originally an outgrowth of the
1930s gangster film, film noir often featured tough, cynical characters who
were corrupt and exploitive of others. Although only a small number of film
noirs were actually horror films, the feeling evoked by noir is often truly
terrifying. Mired in anxiety and paranoia, film noirs feature a corrupt,
menacing universe where virtuous characters are powerless against the
forces of evil. Most scenes are set at night, and they usually feature
evocative black and white photography, often in high contrast, creating a
shadowy world which can be beautiful as well as sinister. There is an attraction and a repulsion to this world. The camera sometimes captures found
poetry in the night world and even its tawdriness is often rendered artfully,
arousing an ambivalent, voyeuristic response in the viewer.

Taxi Driver contains a number of these elements, but it also departs
from the conventions of film noir in significant ways. *Taxi Driver* is a film
about the world of night, and most of its scenes are dark; however, Scorsese
has added the dimension of color. In the forties and fifties film noir, the
external world was oppressive; here, the source of oppression and anxiety
is largely internal. Travis's enemy comes from within, from his own mind.
The subtitle of *Taxi Driver* could be the Age of Anxiety, and no doubt
Travis's anxiety mirrors our own as well as that of the 1970s. In contrast to
twenty-five years before, when the enemies of World War II were known
and clear-cut, there wasn't any specific reason to feel afraid or tense, yet
many were feeling an anxiety that seemed endemic of the times.

Ibid.

Isolated, lonely, and fearful, Travis (Robert De Niro) is the epitome of modern paralysis. Having few friends and no family in town, Travis works long hours hacking at night. However, even after a long shift of cab driving, he still can't sleep. During his off hours, he frequents Times Square porn theaters (*Taxi Driver*, 1975).

Taxi Driver is strongly reflective of the post-tumultuous 1960s and post–Vietnam War period. Political assassinations had ceased shocking the populace yet still aroused their fear. The relations between blacks and whites were angry and tense. Crime seemed, overnight, to have become random, frequent, and unprecedentedly brutal. Fear and alienation were experiences of the population at large, and a new vocabulary was sought to articulate the source of the free-floating anxiety so many seemed to be experiencing. Scorsese tapped into this social paranoia. His examination of Travis's oppression and alienation reflects the anxiety many people felt during the 1970s.

Taxi Driver chronicles the story of Travis Bickle, a twenty-six-year-old Vietnam veteran and former Marine. He is also a Midwesterner living in New York City. Fraught with worry, and lonely from too much solitude, Travis applies for hack work because he can't sleep nights. In anonymity, Travis taxies people during long twelve-hour shifts. However, he finds little relief from his insomnia and loneliness. After work, he still finds himself too wired to sleep. Typically, after his shift, he goes to porn houses. One day while on the job, Travis sees the girl of his dreams, a beautiful woman in white, who turns out to be a worker for Senator Palantine (Leonard Harris), a presidential candidate. The woman, Betsy (Cybill Shepherd), is bright, confident, and stylish. Unlike Travis, she is fully plugged into life. She has friends, interests, and fulfilling work. However, she also has a curiosity about people and experiences, even those involved in the seamier aspects of life. We, therefore, aren't surprised when Betsy becomes intrigued by Travis and is curious enough about him to agree to a date. Travis's intensity is disarming and intrigues her, though she is also swayed through sheer flattery. Travis is also fortunate enough to be charming in his initial encounter with Betsy.

The date, however, ends shortly after Travis takes her to a movie at a porn theatre. He is apparently so out of touch with mainstream cultural norms that he is uninformed about the protocol of dating. Feeling ill at ease and concluding that she had misjudged Travis, Betsy abruptly leaves the theater. Bewildered, Travis implores her to stay with him, offering to take her to another movie or anywhere else she would like to go. Travis later calls to apologize and tries to send her flowers. She returns the flowers and, after that first call, she refuses to speak to him. Hurt and angry, Travis stalks into Palantine headquarters, demanding to know why Betsy won't talk to him. Tom (Albert Brooks), Betsy's co-worker and friend, quickly ushers him out and summons a police officer. Dejected, Travis slips into a morose passivity. He grows more introspective, and his worries and tension grow as the grinding loneliness of his world bores in on him.

Travis finally passes over the edge when he decides to act out the frustration he feels inside. He buys himself an arsenal of weapons and undertakes a rigorous program of "purification" and self-discipline. He narrates in his diary, "The abuse has gone on for too long. . . . No more pills, bad food, destroyers of my body. Total organization from now on. Every muscle must be tight." He spends hours exercising and practicing at the target range, preparing himself for battle. Finally finding release for the torment inside, he fantasizes fighting his imagined enemies. "You looking at me?" Travis taunts his potential bully, as he looks in the mirror, imagining himself the hero, just like in the movies.

Travis eventually finds someone to whom he can direct his efforts. He befriends a twelve-year-old prostitute, Iris (Jodie Foster), who earlier had gotten into his cab asking him to drive off quickly, so she could escape from her pimp. Deeply offended by the moral depravity surrounding him, Travis determines to clean up the city, at least by helping this young girl. He tells her, "This is nothing for a person to do. You should be home with your parents."

Cybill Shepherd and Robert De Niro. Amidst the squalor of the New York City that Travis observes, Betsy is an angel of light. He writes in his diary about her: "She is pure. . . . No one can touch her." Putting her on a pedestal, he extols her virtues and worships her from afar (*Taxi Driver* 1975).

The first near-victim of Travis's new aggression is Palantine. Standing in a crowd gathered to hear the politician, Travis begins to pull a gun from his jacket to kill him. But his attempt is foiled by a Secret Service man who spots him. The motivation for Travis to kill Palantine, however, is ambiguous. Palantine's association with Betsy, who rejected Travis, is probably a factor; perhaps his jealousy of Palantine, as a happy person with a fulfilling life, also contributes to Travis's action; and finally, he seems to be semi-delusional at this point—he seems to have snapped.

Ironically, instead of inspiring contempt as a political assassin, Travis is later proclaimed a hero. Through a fluke of circumstances, he ends up killing gangsters instead of a political candidate. After failing in his assassination attempt, Travis directs his aggression toward rescuing Iris from her depraved life. In a gruesome bloodbath, he shoots his way to Iris by slaughtering her pimp, a timekeeper, and an unlucky john. No one apparently mourns the loss of these undesirables, and Travis's actions are interpreted by the press as heroic acts. He is acclaimed as the cab driver who bravely challenged criminals, helping a child-hooker return to her parents. Iris's parents write to him to express their gratitude for his heroic efforts to help their daughter. Ironically, in the final scene of the film, Betsy enters Travis's cab. She talks to him about his fame, apologizing with her polite interest if not her actual words. Travis looks greatly relieved at the close of the film.

> I know this guy Travis. I've had the feelings he has, and those feelings have to be explored, taken out and examined. I know the feeling of rejection that Travis feels, of not being able to make relationships survive. I know the *killing* feeling, the feeling of really being angry [Martin Scorsese quoted in Flatley 1976, 43].

Much of *Taxi Driver* is an exploration of loneliness. Travis writes in his diary, "All my life needed was a sense of some place to go. I don't believe that one should devote himself to morbid self attention. I believe that someone should become a person—like other people." As Pauline Kael insightfully pointed out, "Travis Bickle . . . can't find a life" (Kael 1976, 82). Watching *Taxi Driver* makes us aware of the importance of friends, of having people who love us and appreciate us, of having opportunities to express ourselves and to be heard, of feeling comfortable and belonging somewhere. It also makes us think of how difficult it can be to obtain those things. Social interactions can be complicated because they are governed by many unspoken rules.

Ostensibly, people might feel they couldn't relate to Travis, whose murderous actions clearly mark him as a deviant. Yet, as critic Jack Kroll points out, "What he's really got is an agony of the spirit . . . his pathology is really an extreme form of a common condition" (Kroll 1976, 82). Anyone who has ever felt he or she has said the wrong thing, anyone who has ever felt ill at ease socially, anyone who has ever felt lonely, anyone who has merely felt anxious as a result of spending the day at home having too much time to worry—can relate to Travis's experience on some level.

Travis is painfully shy and lacking in social skills. There is the sense that he has been raised by parents who abused him by ignoring him. He has

Robert De Niro (*left*) and Nat Grant. Travis worries about disturbing aspects of society such as crime and prostitution. Profoundly alienated, Travis has too much time alone to think, and eventually his anxieties spur him to action. Taking the law into his own hands, he kills a young man who was in the process of robbing a deli (*Taxi Driver*, 1975).

spent too many hours alone, and he seems to have had little experience articulating his thoughts or conversing with others. Although the other cabbies good-naturedly include Travis in the group and cheerfully joke with him, he doesn't know how to respond to them. Serious and self-absorbed, he doesn't know how to get out of himself and how to participate in the dialogue of the other cabbies. With the interviewer for the cab job, the Secret Service agent, and Palantine, Travis also appears insecure and ill at ease. Admittedly, many people might be nervous during encounters such as these, but for Travis, these occasions are times when he is especially awkward and insecure. He sports a goofy grin and makes inappropriate remarks, so apparently unaccustomed is he to conversing with others. At times, with Betsy, Palantine, and Iris for example, Travis reveals an intensity of feeling that signals that there is something peculiar about them. Travis seems to be talking of things so private, particular, and deeply felt that he lacks the vocabulary to express himself in the language of common experience.

There is much silence and passivity in Travis's life. In his cab, he spends long hours as a quiet observer of his city. Passengers enter and exit in anonymity. Working nights, Travis observes some of the worst of humanity, and thoughts of the perversities he sees frighten, worry, and sicken him. He watches a man being mugged and dragged off. He sees a young girl strong-armed by her pimp. He listens as a sick passenger narrates in gruesome detail a plan to kill his wife. Like a television screen, the windshield of Travis's cab allows him to see firsthand the depravity of society, the sick underside of humanity that middle-class suburbanites never have to see. After work, Travis watches films at the porn theatres at Times Square. At home, still a passive participant of life, he watches television. He is the picture of modern paralysis as he gazes at the tube, watching a couple argue about their relationship, revealing an intimacy that is far removed from his own experience.

Television is a drug, as addictive as the junk food, pills, and liquor Travis ingests. Seemingly stoned, he passively watches television and rocks the set back and forth with his foot. Travis pushes a bit too far, and the television crashes and breaks. Dazed by this occurrence, Travis says, "Damn," as he hangs his head, hurting not only from the loss of his most intimate companion, but also from the weightiness of his depression. He feels assaulted by the forces in his life—the criminals on the street, children who pelt his cab as he drives by, scummy passengers who disgust him. He also feels the weight of his own ineptitude. Travis is vulnerable, however, until his decision to empower himself.

For Travis, there has been a lifetime of pent-up rage and self-hatred. He is full of repressed anger towards women, towards black people, towards the system. The rigid, judgmental attitude he has towards people is a protection against his own fear, against his complicity with the system.

"All the animals come out at night . . . whores, skunk, pussy, buggers, queens, fairies, dopers, junkies . . . sick, venal," he writes in his diary. And yet the rage he directs at them is actually a form of his own self-hatred projected outwardly. Travis needs someone or something to blame. He needs an outlet for the anger he feels towards himself, so he directs his fury at the depravity he sees on the street.

One of the reasons Travis hates himself is the duality in his own nature. In spite of himself, he is both attracted to and repelled by the moral squalor of the night world. As if mesmerized by sex and violence, he stares at the people on the street. Although he may be only dimly aware of it, Travis is addicted to sex and violence. Indiscriminately, he will drive anyone anywhere, even in the worst neighborhoods. Although he is afraid of and sickened by some of the experiences he has had while hacking, Travis makes no active decision to protect himself or to modify his behavior in order to eliminate some of those dangers in the future.

When Iris breathlessly enters Travis's cab and pleads that he take off so she can escape her pimp, Travis pauses. He watches what is happening, as usual, from the rearview mirror. Perhaps a part of him wants to help, yet he does nothing. Like the impulse that motivates us to look at an accident as we drive by on the freeway, Travis wants to observe the horrid but exciting drama that is being enacted in the back of his cab. We wonder why he doesn't respond to Iris's plea and drive off promptly. Travis recognizes his guilt on some level and hates himself for it.

We see the same impulse in Travis when he is with Iris later on. She keeps trying to engage him in a sexual act, and he keeps refusing — but not immediately. Iris loosens her blouse and begins to remove it. She later unbuckles Travis's belt. Each time, there are at least a few suspenseful moments when we wonder if he will allow her to proceed. His refusal is morally decisive, but only after those moments of ambivalence.

Then Travis makes the decision to act. He finally finds an outlet for all of these pent-up feelings of rage. He also becomes delusional at this point, living half in reality and half in fantasy. Using what he has learned as a soldier, he decides to empower himself with weapons and to use violence as a means of solving his problems. Full of grandiosity and pretending to be Charles Bronson or Clint Eastwood, Travis struts and swaggers. He imagines himself confronting some thugs, "You looking at me? . . . Who the fuck do you think you're talking to?" With satisfaction, he vigorously asserts himself as he writes in his diary, "Here is a man who would not take it anymore . . . who stood up. Who stood up against the scum."

The photography of *Taxi Driver* captures the look of the city at night.

In many ways, the world of the night is a dream world which has seductive appeal. There is a feeling of isolation, and people who are drawn to working at night are often more comfortable with solitude than their counterparts during the day. According to Travis, night is when the misfits and deviants come out. However, working nights establishes a kinship with the night world, just by being there. The photography of *Taxi Driver* helps us to experience the city at night — the billows of smoke rising from the street, the colors of the cityscape blurred by the rain, looking like an impressionist painting through the windshield of the cab, the grey look of an empty street deep into the night, the reddish glow of neon lights reflected on the pavement of rain-slicked streets.

Scorsese also captures the particulars of Travis's world as he hacks from 6:00 P.M. to 6:00 A.M. The farebox, the cigar box of tips, traffic lights, and individual parts of Travis's yellow cab — the rearview mirror, a silver ornament, a side view of the cab — are shown in fragmented close-ups. Visually the city is reminiscent of the yellow smoke and fog of T. S. Eliot's "Wasteland," and we become enveloped in this world of garish urban landscapes through Travis's eyes. The smoke, red filters, and greenish distortions of light make the city look like Dante's *Inferno*. One minute it is mesmerizing and mysteriously evocative, the next, grotesque, like scenes from hell. Although Travis claims to abhor what he sees, he nevertheless finds himself drawn to this world. Compelled by his addiction to sex and violence, he steals glances at the activities of a prostitute and her client in the back seat of the cab. Travis is a voyeur of the night world, and he watches both in disbelief and in rapt fascination.

By contrast, the camera sometimes coolly observes Travis, tracking him and his environs with clinical objectivity, recording him as a case study. This type of photography is often a slow tracking movement, as if someone were observing the scene carefully — left to right — to take in the whole panorama, to piece together the clues. This panning movement is used first to survey the taxi garage. Next, it is used to detail Travis's apartment. We see the drab, shabby place where he lives — scattered newspapers and magazines, a cot, a naked light bulb hanging from the ceiling, bars on the windows. The same ponderous, thorough tracking movement documents the aftermath of the explosion of violence at the end of the film. Unflinchingly, the camera surveys the entire scope of violence — passing over blood-spattered walls, several guns, mutilated bodies covered with blood. The camera also documents clinically from a bird's-eye-view angle (directly overhead) Travis curled uncomfortably on his cot and the aftermath of the shootout, the results looking coldly detached and as distorted as the violent acts that are being recorded.

Although *Taxi Driver* is a narrative film, it can also be looked upon as an essay on modern life, as an expression and study of loneliness. Scorsese has this universality in mind as he works, "I want to communicate on the basic human level — sad, funny, violent, peaceful. . . . Sometimes I look at one of my scenes and I say, 'My God, look at that! A thousand things went wrong,' But then an emotion comes through, and I'm happy. That's where I am'" (quoted in Flatley 1976, 41, 43).

On the basic human level, it is easy to have compassion and empathy for Travis, and the camera work guides us to this response. For the most part, he is a quiet man. He easily fades into the crowd, like most of us. His sincerity is touching, many of his fears are like our own, and his basic loneliness is universal as well. When Travis is rejected by Betsy, he calls her to apologize, but she wants nothing to do with him. Visually, his loneliness and sadness are conveyed by showing Travis talking on a pay phone in the lobby of a building. We see him in profile, a semi-private position, and we hear his voice — quiet, sincere, and apologetic. After several moments, the camera moves to the right, past Travis, to an empty, white corridor, which serves as a metaphor for the loneliness and emptiness in his life.

Much of Michael Chapman's cinematography in *Taxi Driver* conveys Travis's view of the world and his thoughts and feelings. Some of the footage appears to have been taken through the cab's windshield and back and side windows. The human drama of night street life is conveyed expressively, in fragments. Crowds meander in slow motion. Hookers ply their trade. Travis's cab traverses dark, deserted streets. We experience all as he does. For example, we wince with fear along with Travis as he drives down the street, and, for no apparent reason, he becomes the victim of the violent actions of a gang of kids as they pelt his cab with eggs and rocks.

The camera memorably depicts Travis's loneliness and isolation when he stops to have coffee with some fellow cabbies. Subdued and withdrawn, he orders coffee, and, when the cabbies ask him how everything is going, he proceeds to tell them about a driver who was cut up in Harlem. One of the drivers remarks, "Fuckin' Mau-Mau land." Associatively, the camera then shows Travis's thoughts. He gazes meditatively at two black men who are sitting across the way in the restaurant, both in suits and hats, one dressed in black, the other in white. They look stern and tough; one wraps his fingertips against the counter menacingly. Worn out and self-absorbed, Travis puts an Alka-Seltzer tablet in a glass of water. The camera zooms in closely to the glass, picking up the sounds of the fizzling tablet. One of the cabbies, Doughboy (Harry Northup), tries to get Travis's attention. He speaks to Travis three times before he responds. We aren't surprised by Travis's lack of response, however, for the camera has followed his isolation and drift.

To try to reach out for help, Travis asks Wizard (Peter Boyle) if he can talk with him. He then follows Wizard out onto the street. In contrast to the bright light and white of the cafeteria, the street is dark and filtered in red. Once on the street, Travis sees a young black man stalking and clanking a chain that he carries with him. Travis stops and stares. After the man passes by, a gang of young kids taunt some prostitutes on the street, and the prostitutes quickly defend themselves and chase the kids away. Travis is inarticulate, and he gropes for the words to explain what is bothering him to Wizard. As we watch Travis gaze at the menacing and aggressive behavior on the street, we see a part of what torments him.

We also see some of Travis's happier thoughts and feelings conveyed visually. For example, when he watches Betsy enter Palantine headquarters, she seems to float through the crowd. Her hair softly swirling with a turn of her head, Betsy moves in graceful slow motion, visually conveying Travis's enchantment with her: "I first saw her at Palantine headquarters at 63rd and Broadway. She was wearing a white dress like an angel out of this filthy mass. She is alone. . . . They cannot touch her." Later when Travis is walking down the street to meet Betsy for their date, his feelings are again conveyed through the camera. Dressed nicely in a jacket and tie and sporting clean and shiny hair, Travis looks especially handsome. In slow motion, he is photographed walking down the street in a crowd of people, but in his own world. The crowd of people he walks among is blurred, and the visuals of this scene are underscored by soft, romantic music. Thus, both visually and aurally, we see Travis's oblivion to the crowd, full of anticipation about his date.

Since most of *Taxi Driver* takes place at night, those scenes containing light are particularly noticeable. For example, those featuring Betsy are almost always filled with light. A competent, well-adjusted individual, she is consistently shown in the world of daylight — at headquarters, at Childe's coffee shop, at the various political rallies. Travis's fellow cabbies also work nights, and they fit into the night world because each of them is a bit offbeat. However, it is appropriate that they too are shown in the bright lights of their late-night haunts. They are cheerful originals, content and accepting of each other's eccentricities and their lives as cabbies.

The eerie ambience and psychological tension so prevalent in the film were in part created by the soundtrack and musical score. Bernard Herrmann, the composer of the score for *Taxi Driver,* also wrote the music for psychological dramas such as Hitchcock's *Psycho* and *Vertigo* and Welles's *Citizen Kane.* No doubt, it was Herrmann's experience with and talent for conveying music suggestive of mood and nuance, especially those reflective of the underlying psychology of a character, that motivated the decision to employ Herrmann for the music for *Taxi Driver.* Although the score has been criticized as being too dramatic, it is also considered by many as richly evocative and effective for this film. Perhaps because Travis is so quiet and inarticulate, the music of *Taxi Driver* is especially significant in conveying not only detail and nuance suggestive of the environment of the film, but also important psychological information about the main character.

The musical score reflects the duality of Travis's nature. At times, it underlines his dark vision of the city as he prowls the streets of late-night Manhattan. This music sounds ominous, brooding, and foreboding. A variation of this music features a deep bass and drum beat which sounds unyielding, relentless, inexorable. This music expresses the fearful and sinister qualities of the city. By contrast, the score also features a soft, wistful, jazzy music which suggests the more positive connotations of the city, its romantic possibilities, those parts of the night world that fire the imagination. The city inspires this response in Travis too. Although he is inarticulate about this aspect of his experience, the romantic yearnings suggested by this music are clearly supported by both music and visuals.

The sounds of *Taxi Driver* also render the loneliness of Travis's life. First of all, there is the absence of dialogue. Both at work and during off-hours, Travis spends many hours in silence. He overhears or listens to his passengers, but he doesn't usually converse with them. The conversations he has with his co-workers are often awkward for him, and he participates only sparingly. Mostly, Travis listens. Both the visuals and the sound effects of *Taxi Driver* convey his lonely life. When Travis picks up a man and a prostitute, he overhears their conversation and does as he is asked. Meanwhile, the windshield wipers of Travis's cab thud relentlessly, an audible metaphor for the tension that is building up inside him. Camera and sound also capture the monotony of his life as featured in close-ups of traffic light after traffic light and close-ups and clicks of the farebox. The hours of silence and isolation compound the angst that builds inside him. Travis's diary is also an expression of his loneliness. He literally has no one to talk to, no one with whom to share his thoughts and feelings. Keeping a diary provides at least some outlet, some means of expression.

When Travis becomes interested in Betsy, the music associated with her is romantic — soft, wistful jazz, full of hopeful possibilities and promise. The city looks especially pretty during this time. At one point, the neon of several bars reflects a rainbow of colors on the pavement of the street, something beautiful from something tawdry. The image is complemented by the shot's romantic score. In another shot, the view from the windshield of Travis's cab is a lovely pattern of colored lights. Soft, romantic jazz accompanies these shots which occur between the time when Travis asks Betsy out and when their date begins.

At the start of their evening, a drummer with oil-slicked hair announces that he will demonstrate the Gene Krupa syncopated style, and he proceeds to do so with a rat-a-tat-tat. It was an interesting decision to feature this drummer and his music in that he both works as a metaphor and foreshadows what is to come. The garishness of his appearance predicts the seaminess to follow while the rapid percussion suggests Travis's excitement about his date with Betsy.

Much of the dialogue in *Taxi Driver* consists of talk about people on the fringes of society—about criminals, murderers, pimps, prostitutes. The cabbies discuss crime and how they protect themselves from it. Betsy and Tom flirt with one another while discussing the possible relationship between a newsstand man's missing fingers and dealings of the Mafia. Crime is a preoccupation not only with Travis, Betsy, and the cabbies, but it is also a large part of the political rhetoric espoused by the presidential candidate, Palantine. He states, "We the people suffered in Vietnam. . . . We still suffer from unemployment, inflation, crime, and corruption." Ironically, *we* the people—including the audience of *Taxi Driver*—are seduced by, drawn in, and implicated by those issues. They are our preoccupations too. Thus Palantine's words work on a deeper and more significant level than the surface plot. Also, ironically, Palantine's campaign slogan, "*We* are the people" naïvely assumes that the people are all healthy while the visuals of the movie reveal that many are not.

Although *Taxi Driver* contains far less humor than most of Scorsese's films, it does have some, which provides welcome comic relief. Travis tries to joke with people occasionally—with the interviewer at the garage, with Betsy—but, reflective of his difficulty with connecting with others, his jokes usually don't work. One that does, however, occurs when he tries to convince Betsy to have coffee with him at a coffee shop near headquarters. He assumes a muscleman's pose and tells Betsy that he will be there to protect her. She then laughs and agrees to meet him.

The basis for the relationship between Tom and Betsy seems to be the witty banter they exchange. Their humor is intellectual and sophisticated. Tom is funny and bright, full of spontaneous one-liners, and Betsy complements his personality with her own quickness and intelligence. Also, the subtext of their exchanges is sexual—they are always flirting with one another—which adds interest and liveliness to the quips they exchange.

Another character with a good sense of humor is Iris's pimp, Sport (Harvey Keitel). He is quick-witted and funny. It is another of the film's ironies that Sport, who is clearly morally repugnant as the pimp of a twelve-and-a-half-year-old girl, should have so much appeal. Full of energy and life, Sport is the antithesis of the stereotypical pimp. When Travis talks to Sport about seeing Iris, Sport teases him about looking like a cop and about not looking hip. Sport laughs and jokes around, "You're a funny guy, but looks aren't everything. Go on. Have a good time."

Finally, other characters who consistently provide comic relief are Travis's fellow cabbies. Wizard especially provides several good-humored scenes in the film. In Travis's first meeting with the cabbies, Wizard tells a wonderfully preposterous war story about pulling over on the Triborough Bridge to make love to a prostitute who had gotten into his cab. Wizard tells his cronies she said, "'It's the greatest single experience of my life.' And she gave me a $200 tip and her phone number in Acapulco." On another occasion, Doughboy mentions that in California, when two homo-sexuals break up, one of them has to pay the other alimony. Wizard looks struck by that fact for a moment, as he takes it all in; then he says, "Yeah. Well, they're way ahead out there."

The acting of Peter Boyle as Wizard was superior as were the perfor-mances of many of the other actors involved with *Taxi Driver*. Scorsese was particularly skillful in casting performers, like Boyle, able to look and act the part of various New York City types in the film—the deli owner who gets robbed; Easy Andy, the consummate salesman; the cop who prompts Travis to move along on the street; the taxi dispatcher; Iris's timekeeper. Scorsese himself is powerful as the intense, neurotic, obsessed man who plots to kill his cheating wife.

The more sophisticated urbanites, Albert Brooks as Tom and Cybill Shepherd as Betsy, also were well cast. Brooks brings an intelligence and wit to his performance that are enjoyable to watch. More subtly, Brooks also reveals nuances of Tom as the hapless underdog, which makes him all the more appealing. In his limitations and insecurities, Tom is like many of us. Shepherd is well cast as the confident upstate woman—pretty, flir-tatious, saucy, and bright. In addition to the beauty and charm she brings to the role, Shepherd realizes a full character, someone lively and in-teresting and full-dimensional, for her performance shows a range in-cluding not only humor, but also moodiness, not only surface charm, but also conviction and integrity.

The other female lead character, Iris, is performed skillfully by Jodie Foster. Foster actually was twelve and a half, the same age as her character, when she acted in *Taxi Driver*. Precocious and instinctive, Foster is con-vincing as the tough, cynical child-prostitute. In her relatively few scenes, she realizes her character in a considerable range of feeling and behavior—from tough-minded street smarts to vulnerability and softness, and from adult seriousness to childlike spontaneity.

Harvey Keitel, Iris's pimp, plays his role with power and bravura. As a pimp, he is, of course, a slimy character. However, perhaps surprisingly, Matthew also has a lot of appeal and charm. For example, the most tender scene in *Taxi Driver* takes place when Matthew and Iris dance together. He holds Iris close to him, strokes her hair, and reassures her warmly, gently that their love for each other is special. The scene is so powerfully evocative and sensual that we aren't at all surprised at Iris's surrender to Matthew's considerable charm. On another level, Matthew's vitality and humor make him a likeable character. Instead of being a dark figure, Matthew comes across as just a guy doing a job. Full of presence on the street, he jingles coins in his pocket, looks around brightly, and sings a song as he scouts out his territory from the stoop.

Travis was a considerable departure from Robert De Niro's last role in a Scorsese film (Johnny Boy in *Mean Streets*). Whereas Johnny Boy was rash, spontaneous, and showy, Travis is introspective, repressed. Physically, Johnny Boy's movements were loose and fluid; Travis's are contained and compressed. Johnny Boy was fast-talking and quick to respond. Travis doesn't speak much, and when he does, he is usually soft-spoken and slow to respond. While Travis reads his diary, his voice drones on, expressionless. Johnny Boy expresses himself openly, flamboyantly. Travis mostly reacts rather than acts, and his expressions are low-keyed and emotionally subdued.

Scenes in which De Niro responds with spare, minimalist details are some of the most memorable in *Taxi Driver*. His face shows the internal turmoil he feels, his vacant stare revealing the lack of direction and purpose in his life. Often some of the most moving acting in the film occurs simply through a look and the resulting feeling that is conveyed. In the restaurant, Travis's eyes brim with sadness and isolation as he watches an Alka-Seltzer tablet dissolve in the water glass before him. Later, in the street outside with Wizard, his eyes are glazed and his face reveals internal pain and anguish as he tries to share his feelings. Then when Travis drives down the street, enroute to kill Iris's pimp, his body language reveals a man wired, stiff, his face frozen with the realization of what he is about to do. There are also the many quiet, spare responses to those who know him like his fellow cabbies and the grocer at the deli where he shops. Travis responds with an unspoiled, happy look when Betsy talks to him in the cab at the end of the movie. Method actors try to become their characters, and it is that quality which comes across in much of De Niro's acting in *Taxi Driver*. We get the sense that truly De Niro has become Travis, responding, feeling as Travis would.

Surprisingly, *Taxi Driver* was a box-office success. Scorsese took many artistic risks in making this film — its downbeat subject matter, its alienated central character, its graphic violence — yet audiences related to the film. He seems to have captured and expressed what many in America were feeling at the time: the tense race relations, fear of crime, loss of faith in politicians, the view of the city as degenerate, and sense of drift and alienation. Scorsese won the Golden Palm award at the 1976 Cannes Film Festival for *Taxi Driver*. His next movie would be the musical *New York, New York*. Scorsese felt drawn to this script because of his affection for 1940s films and music.

New York, New York

Sometimes you're happy and sometimes you're sad,
But the world goes round. . . .
Sometimes your dreams get broken in pieces.
But that doesn't alter a thing.
Take it from me. There's still gonna be
a summer, a winter, a fall and a spring.
—From "But the World Goes Round" *New York, New York*

In a number of ways *New York, New York*, Martin Scorsese's fourth major feature film, is bigger than any of his previous works. He enjoyed the luxury of choice afforded him by the film's large budget. Also, in Francine and Jimmy's story, he expresses truths about the relationship between men and women, giving him the potential to touch a much wider audience than with his previous works. *New York, New York* is many things. It is a revisionist musical. It is a visually beautiful film, filled with colorful costumes and period details, poetic scenes and artfully composed images. A period film, it looks back with affection at the late 1940s and early 1950s. It explores the story of two very interesting characters. It is a love story, and it is a movie about intimacy.

People were surprised that Scorsese decided to make a musical. It seemed incongruous that the director of *Mean Streets* and *Taxi Driver* would decide to work with a traditionally light genre. However, his choice really isn't that surprising. Scorsese grew up during the 1940s, and he grew up going to the movies. Musicals, a genre he admires, were popular during this decade. Scorsese's other love is music, and it would be a natural for him to want to make a movie with music and about musicians.

Scorsese wanted to use many elements of the classical musical. The movie opened in New York, as did many of the old musicals. The rough outline of the love story between Francine and Jimmy falls along conventional story lines, except for the ending. The movie was made in a studio rather than on location. The basic plot deals with becoming a success in show business. The film is photographed the way the old musicals were, including wipes and montage sequences. It is a romantic movie with lots of sentimental music and features a musical within a musical as many of the old films did.

Although *New York, New York* adhered to conventions of the traditional musical, it departed from them too. Scorsese's version of the genre is highly revisionist, and his original style can be seen in many ways. No doubt these departures are some of the reasons *New York, New York* was received with such mixed reviews and why some people were startled by what they saw. Their expectations about the conventions of a musical were violated in some astonishing ways. They did not expect reality in a musical, and they were unprepared for the dark quality of *New York, New York*. Aptly, Scorsese has called his work a "film noir musical."

Stylistically, *New York, New York* is a blend of realism and formalism. Although Scorsese works within an artificial world, as do traditional musicals, he also adds a number of real elements. Scorsese explains:

> I took a lot of chances shooting in the style of the 40's taking the trappings of an old-fashioned musical and using studio interiors that are supposed to be exteriors. I wanted to set up a tension between a style that distances you from the characters and a drama that brings you close to them. By showing a modern relationship set in the old days, I was trying to show that things may not have been so different then [Flatley 1977, C8].

Scorsese's revisionism includes wise guys and con artists who are less refined than the characters in the 1940s musicals, less stylized and stereotypical. In fact, the crudeness and crassness of his characters can offend. In the raucous V-J celebration crowd, fights break out and guys look for a pick-up, hoping to get laid. Yet the tone is not shabby or judgmental. Rather, there is a feeling of fun and a sense of vitality. There is also an appreciation for characters who are originals. Other elements that are distinctly Scorsese's are the film's city humor, the featuring of a strong woman as one of the lead characters, the focusing on people who are outside of the mainstream, and the obvious use of improvisation in many scenes.

New York, New York is a love story focusing on Jimmy Doyle (Robert De Niro) and Francine Evans (Liza Minnelli), who meet during a V-J celebration. Jimmy is determined to find a date. One of the women he pursues is Francine Evans. One of the brightest and most humorous of the movie, this opening sequence goes on for twenty minutes. Jimmy never succeeds in picking up Francine.

By coincidence, Francine goes along to an audition Jimmy has in Brooklyn. There, Jimmy plays a nervous, energetic sax as hyped up as he himself is. During the course of the audition, Francine helps Jimmy get the job by singing along with him. They are hired as a boy-girl act. However, later that night, Francine's agent calls to tell her she is to begin a tour the next morning.

It takes some time before Jimmy can find Francine, but he eventually does. Soon they are both playing in the same band. Eventually they marry. Later, Jimmy takes over as bandleader. All goes well for a while. Jimmy's band is a success, Francine's talent is being recognized, and their relationship is a happy one. Then Francine becomes pregnant and wants to go back to New York to have the baby. Jimmy is distressed at the news, perhaps instinctively knowing that the band needs Francine in order to thrive.

Upon arrival in New York, Francine takes occasional singing jobs doing demos and commercials. As Jimmy suspected, a short while later the band sharply decreases in popularity. He decides to sign over the band. Upon returning to New York, he feels depressed over his loss. A few days later, he finds a job playing in a club in Harlem.

Francine's career begins to blossom. She is offered a record contract and brings her manager and a record producer from Decca Records to the Harlem Club to meet her husband and talk over the offer. Jimmy is embarrassed at their being in the club and feels diminished by his wife's success.

The next scene features Francine after she has given birth. Saying he just can't bear to, Jimmy doesn't even see the baby. An indeterminate amount of time passes during which Francine and Jimmy have separated. The next scene features Jimmy watching a movie, *Happy Endings,* starring Francine Evans, followed by a newsreel announcing that Francine Evans has returned to the States. Jimmy too has become a success. His song, "New York, New York," is number one on the charts, and he has just opened a club.

Jimmy attends one of Francine's performances and attempts a reconciliation with her. He asks Francine to meet him that evening. However, as Francine approaches the stage door, she has second thoughts and returns to the elevator. As she pushes the button, Jimmy instinctively realizes that she's changed her mind. He walks down the street without her. There is the bittersweet ending that, although they love each other, perhaps it is better that they are apart.

Clearly, Francine is a woman who is sure of herself and strong. Yet she is not particularly aggressive nor does she have a big ego, characteristics often associated with strong female leads. Feminine, competent, and loving, she is an attractive character. Scorsese has said about Francine, "The woman Liza plays is the kind of woman I like. She's driven and ambitious, with a brilliance all her own. You know from the very beginning, by her little looks and gestures, that she is not going to be the long-suffering, submissive wife" (Flatley 1977, C8).

As a fellow musician, she appreciates Jimmy's talent and his originality. She is also attractive, talented, and classy. Her singing is immensely appealing—full of vitality, feeling, and resonance.

Jimmy is a true original and a typical Scorsese character. The antithesis of the romantic leading man, he is unpolished, unrefined, and annoying, qualities that offend. Yet he also has a charm and a bravado that can be appealing to those open to his original style. Jimmy doesn't necessarily mean to offend. He simply lacks the social graces that would help make him more acceptable to others. Yet his originality also makes him an interesting character—full of surprises, vitality, passion—and fun to watch and get to know.

One response to *New York, New York* is that it contains elements of male chauvinism. Some strongly sympathize with Francine and feel that Jimmy dominates in the relationship. However, upon a second viewing, what is striking is how fair Scorsese has been in presenting both characters. Neither is a villain. As strongly as we might identify with Francine, it is also just as possible to sympathize with Jimmy. Scorsese points out,

> I'm a guy, and I understand the things beneath the chauvinism of Bobby De Niro's character. I see the vulnerability. He's trapped and frightened, like a child, and he doesn't know how to reach out. . . . I tried to be fair to both characters, because I love them both. They just never can get together; they're star-crossed, and that makes me sad [Flatley 1977, C8].

One of the most remarkable features of *New York, New York* is the truth of its expression of the relationship between men and women. Throughout the film, there are intimate scenes which accurately reflect the experiences of couples in a close relationship. We see tenderness, compromise, unmet needs, the dynamics of communicating within a relationship, joy, and heartache. All of this is rendered in a respectful way. This film is the work of someone who values loving relationships and knows their complex dynamics. Rather than presenting a love story in more stylized, conventional ways, Scorsese presents a relationship that mirrors those found in real life, a relationship full of contradictions. This element makes *New York, New York* a special film.

For example, the proposal and marriage scenes contain a number of privileged moments that reveal the intimacy of real-life love relationships. When Jimmy proposes to Francine, he is so original in his approach that she is caught completely off guard. Jimmy reads some poems that Francine has written about him, and he is so moved that he tells her to put her coat and shoes on and to come with him. In the middle of the night, they drive to a justice of the peace. Characteristically impulsive and off-beat, Jimmy appeals to the justice of the peace to marry them; he says they're in a bit of a hurry, he can't explain why. The justice of the peace and his wife agree, but Francine calls Jimmy aside. Astonished, she asks Jimmy, "You mean that was it? Your proposal? 'Come on. Get your shoes and coat on'?" "What's the matter with that?" Jimmy says defensively. Francine explains,

Liza Minnelli. Although *New York, New York* is a revisionist musical, it also adheres to many conventions. For example, it is a love story about musicians and their rise to fame. It uses photography characteristic of the musical, such as wipes as transitions and montage sequences to condense events. The story also takes place within the artificial world of studio sets. Furthermore, it features a musical within a musical. This shot is from one of the big production numbers featuring glittery costumes and a large cast of singers and dancers. The number, cut from the first release print, was later restored (*New York, New York*, 1977).

"Well, I just thought it would be different." Jimmy replies, "It *is* different!" Francine points out, "That's not the kind of different I had in mind. I thought it would be calm and pretty. You can't say it's pretty."

Jimmy proceeds to prove his love by offering to kill himself. He asks the cab driver to back up over him. Horrified, Francine tells the driver not to back up. Jimmy then gets down on bended knee and aggressively pleads with her to marry him. During this entire drama, both Jimmy and Francine are nervous, understandably feeling much emotion during such a major event. Jimmy's response is to take control and to be even more weird and manic than usual. Francine is so overcome with emotion that she becomes teary-eyed. When she finally agrees to Jimmy's proposal, she is feeling so much that she can't speak. She merely nods her assent.

In this spontaneous and humorous scene, there are several moments not shown in the typical love story. We see the vulnerability of being in love in both Francine and Jimmy. Francine is overwhelmed with conflicting emotions. Jimmy is vulnerable, too. He sincerely wants to marry Francine, and he feels hurt at being criticized about his proposal. We also see the dynamics of typical male/female roles but played out in atypical intensity. Jimmy's masculine anger and need to control are a powerful part of this scene. Francine eventually surrenders to the force of Jimmy's aggressive behavior. The range of emotions in this intimate scene is considerable — love, astonishment, embarrassment, disappointment, excitement, frustration, and joy.

There are many scenes that reveal the intimacy of love in *New York, New York*. During the argument that erupts when Francine tells Jimmy that she is going to have a baby, we see their closeness and love. There is the clashing of needs — Francine's to go to New York to ensure the health of her baby and Jimmy's concern over the implications of the loss of Francine to the band. There is the spontaneous clash of feelings — Francine's indignation about Jimmy's reluctance to agree to her going to New York and Jimmy's frustration at the loss of her talent. There is the immediate regret and making up after the argument, their embrace and reassurance of each other's love. Francine hugs Jimmy saying, "I just want you to be so happy." Typically, as it is with people who love each other, Francine feels distressed about any hurt she may have caused Jimmy, and Jimmy puts aside his concerns about his own self-interests for Francine's happiness.

Another intimate situation occurs when Jimmy loses the band and comes back to New York. Francine, hearing Jimmy playing the piano, gets up out of bed early in the morning to sit with him. In a contemplative scene, Jimmy plays the piano as a solace for the loss he is feeling. After some small talk, Francine asks if he'd like to talk about it. He doesn't want to. Francine says she understands, but Jimmy tells her she doesn't. Of course, Francine has a great deal of compassion for her husband, and she does understand the sadness of loss. Yet Jimmy may be right. Some may scoff at a man's feeling that he must be a successful breadwinner as a mere gender-influenced tradition. However, in the past this has been considered a measure of a man's worth and masculinity. Nevertheless, it is the portraying of a couple during this moment that is important. It is the expression of one partner's feeling depressed and the other's trying to communicate and understand that is significant in this scene.

When Jimmy and Francine argue over his playing nights at the Harlem Club, their argument reveals the bartering of needs that takes place in a close relationship. What is particularly striking about this scene is its fairness. Neither person is all right nor all wrong. Each has a valid point of view and, under these circumstances — which reflect the arguments of real-life couples — it is hard to hear the other side, what one doesn't want to hear yet must come to understand and accept. Francine complains that Jimmy isn't paying enough attention to her, that she needs his help, that she is, after all, six months pregnant. Wanting to be responsible, Jimmy is offended by her criticism and points out that the other musicians are married too. Making a great deal of sense, Jimmy tells Francine, "You see this sax? Do you want me to smash it against the wall? Because if I don't have this, I'm no good for you or anyone." There is the hurt of disappointment and the processing of needs that must remain unmet.

Communication between a couple also involves touchstones, sensitive areas that set us off, making us feel the tender areas where we're vulnerable. We're shown this aspect of a relationship during a dinner scene at home before Jimmy leaves for work at the Harlem Club. Jimmy asks Francine if she'd like to see Paul Wilson (Barry Primus) and the rest of the band when they appear in town. She eagerly agrees, then adds that she'd like to invite along her friend Ellen, whom she'd like to introduce to Artie Kirks, the record producer.

At the mention of the extra couple and especially Artie Kirks, Jimmy suggests that maybe Francine would like to go alone with them as a business outing. Perhaps Jimmy changes his mind about going because he feels unsettled at the thought of the other couple. They would diminish the intimacy and support that he and Francine would have in this awkward situation. Or perhaps it is the mention of Artie Kirks, the record producer associated with Francine's demo work, that makes Jimmy uncomfortable. Whatever the true reason, Francine responds immediately to Jimmy's feeling, carefully trying not to cause him more discomfort. She offers to show Jimmy a new baby outfit, but she changes her mind, showing him something that might soothe him more, the lyrics she's written to his song. As Jimmy leaves, Francine sees him off lovingly, eager to please, offering to change a lyric he had questioned.

Francine is less in tune with Jimmy's feelings when they actually arrive at the Up Club to see Paul Wilson. Outside the club, Jimmy realizes he's made a big mistake in coming. He tells Francine he just can't do it. Looking forward to seeing her friends and having already arrived at the club, Francine offers the reasonable compromise of just staying for one set. As sometimes happens, however, one person doesn't hear what the other is saying and doesn't realize the depth of the feeling underlying his or her words. This miscommunication causes considerable hurt and embarrassment.

Yet another intimate scene occurs when Artie Kirks offers Francine a record contract. Francine, her manager, Tony, and Artie go to the Harlem Club to discuss the offer with Jimmy. However, Jimmy is surprised by their appearance and embarrassed at the awkwardness of the situation:

Liza Minnelli and Robert De Niro. *New York, New York* is a film about intimacy. Instead of the usual boy-meets-girl love story with a predictable happy ending, Scorsese looks at a couple in a more realistic love relationship. In addition to the happiness, he shows us the sadness, loneliness, and vulnerability of being in love. In this scene, Francine tries to comfort her husband, Jimmy, who is grieving the loss of his band (*New York, New York*, 1977).

His wife has just been offered a record contract, and he is playing in a club in Harlem. When Artie and Tony leave, Francine sits and drinks, celebrating this happy occasion alone.

After a while, Francine goes up to watch the band. Jimmy plays, "Just You, Just Me" in a modest fashion, looking at Francine with some humility. She misreads his glance, however, and assumes he has invited her up on stage with him. As she walks up the steps, Jimmy briskly changes the tempo and song, musically distancing himself from her. Francine gracefully descends and begins to dance with someone in the crowd. A short while later, she leaves with the same gentleman. Jimmy storms off the stage and follows her. He jumps into his car only to find that Francine is hiding in the back seat. A huge argument ensues.

Gene Shallit called this scene the most real argument between a man and woman he'd ever seen on film. Nothing is held back. Francine accuses Jimmy of not caring, and he responds that he does care. All of their resentments, fears, and frustrations are aired. The worst of their thoughts gets verbalized. Yet this too is a part of intimacy, the sharing of such thoughts and fears. This profound vulnerability is a part of love, too.

Along with the camaraderie of a relationship, there can also be loneliness. Francine feels this in the hospital after her baby is born. Silenced and immobilzed by feeling, Francine has few words to say when Jimmy visits. She explains that she has named the baby Jimmy. Jimmy is overcome by the news, as though that fact added to the fullness of feeling that he's already having trouble managing is simply more than he can bear. With tears welling up, Francine hugs Jimmy, and they comfort and support each other as well as they can, both of them feeling fragile and vulnerable.

Finally, there is the image of loneliness and feeling of resignation at the end of the film when Francine decides not to meet Jimmy outside the theatre. There is the weightiness of loss in this scene. The final shots are nonverbal. The sadness and regret can be read from both their facial expressions. They love each other, but they will not get back together. In many richly meaningful ways, this relationship has been examined and revealed. As we watch, we too are sad at the bittersweet but right ending here.

Scorsese says, "I was born in late 1942. I remember the records and films of the forties from my early childhood. I wanted to relate what that music meant to me growing up and connect that with the reality of films. . . . New York on screen was more real to me than New York itself, even though I lived there" (Sterritt 1977, 22).

Scorsese's *New York, New York* was meant to be a homage to the old musicals. Having a large budget to work with, Scorsese was able to recreate the look and photographic style of those classic genre films, from employing a large cast of extras to using their traditional film language in the photography and editing. Scorsese points out, "This is a combination of all those places from movies of the Forties and Fifties. The color, the deco" (Hodenfield 1977, 43). Those who know the old musicals no doubt recognize many of the traditional film techniques that Scorsese used in the making of *New York, New York*.

For example, when Jimmy gets into Francine's taxi to go to his audition, Scorsese uses a horizontal wipe as a transitional device, pushing one scene off the screen and replacing it with another, thus moving from Jimmy's quick getaway from the hotel lobby to his leap into the cab. He also uses several montage sequences, a classical editing technique of overlapping and dissolving images, to condense the passage of time. Francine and Jimmy's celebration of the success of their audition, for example, features shots typical of a musical's montage—Times Square, neon lights of several clubs, their dancing, and champagne glasses—each shot dissolving into the next. Other montage sequences include Jimmy's search to locate Francine, snatches of Frankie Harte's band's tour, the decline of Jimmy's band, Francine's movie success, and Jimmy's success in the world of jazz.

Scorsese's *New York, New York* was also made using Hollywood back lots and sound stages. In contrast to Scorsese's usual on-location shooting, this movie, in keeping with the genre's tradition, was made entirely using artificial sets. Some of the sets—the hotel lobbies, Jimmy and Francine's apartment, even the street scenes—look less obviously like studio sets, whereas others—the forest and train station scenes—look deliberately artificial.

The opening of *New York, New York* has an impressionistic style. The sparkle of the V-J Day celebration radiates in the opening shots of the crowd at Times Square and at the party at the Starlight Terrace Ballroom. The movie opens in slow motion. A shirt is dropped out of a hotel window down to the street below amid the confetti in the air. The next shot is of the sidewalk and the spats of Jimmy Doyle, who is now out on the street, sporting his newly won Hawaiian-style shirt with the skyline of New York on it. Next there are overhead shots of the happy crowd at Times Square, the air filled with streamers and arms of people waving newspaper headlines. Above the noisy crowd and blaring horns, a radio announcer voiceover comments, "Times Square is wall to wall people for the greatest party ever. Times Square is happy, New York is happy, the United States is happy, and the world is at peace." From a high angle, the camera tracks Jimmy as he squeezes through the crowd, and the Tommy Dorsey Orchestra begins, "Pennsylvania 6-5000."

The good mood continues in the next part of the opening sequence at the Starlight Terrace, with its atmosphere of the 1940s era. The sequence begins with darkness, followed by a high-angled spotlight on Tommy Dorsey playing the trombone. Wearing wire-rimmed glasses and a well-cut blue suit with roomy trousers, Dorsey plays the smooth opening bars of "Moonlight Serenade." Again, there is darkness, followed by a spotlight on the drummer of the band, briskly tapping out another opening segment. The camera pulls back to include the whole band and the crowd, underscored by the orchestra's light, jazzy sound.

The camera seems to be enjoying the party, scanning the entire panorama, occasionally pausing to take in various visual delights — close-ups of Tommy Dorsey; a shot of the horn players standing in a row; shots of New York's silhouetted skyline, the backdrop of the ballroom; and long shots of the crowd jitterbugging. The musicians have the distinguished look of forties musicians — classy, mature, and manly. The crowd has the look of a Scorsese crowd. Photographed in a stylized manner, the crowd looks dressy and full of vitality. Most of the sailors, soldiers, and beautifully outfitted and coiffed women move with grace, but this crowd also includes a few drunks and fistfighters. Showcasing musicians whenever possible, the camera pans to a black trumpet player as he stands for his solo.

A striking quality about the mise-en-scène of *New York, New York,* in contrast to Scorsese's previous work, is that often there are self-consciously composed images, artfully staged pictures within the frame. Throughout the movie, there are many shots that are well-composed: Jimmy embracing Francine in a blue silhouette after they have talked over the news of the baby; the motel room Bernice and Jimmy share, which looks like an Edward Hopper painting; the orange sunset and muddy fall scene outside the roadside motel cottage where Jimmy signs over the band to Paul Wilson; many shots of Francine during her concert at the Starlight Terrace at the end of the movie; and the closing shot of the empty city street.

However, these shots are not merely ornamental as they are in some films, where directors add the occasional "poetic" shot — a picture of autumn leaves for example, providing an obvious crowd-pleaser, like typical commercial art. Scorsese seems to use these shots in several ways. First of all they are expressive of the abundant visual sense that the director has shown consistently throughout his work, adding another vehicle to his cinematic repertoire. They are also a part of the tradition of musicals — typically a beautiful genre — which Scorsese is trying to work within. Finally, they seem to be expressive of the way the director feels about the artificial world he is creating, art that, for him, is more expressive than reality. *New York, New York* is Scorsese's view of the 1940s and 1950s. It is his memory of the old movies and of his childhood, and it is a fusion of generic reality and personal experience.

Most of *New York, New York* takes place indoors, and many of the scenes take place at night. Usually the scenes are lit only by lamplight or other indoor types of lighting. The few outdoor scenes aren't terribly bright either; often the weather is rainy or overcast. This shadowed atmosphere is suggestive of the dark ambiguities the film is about. It is also a part of the allure of the night, with all its attendant connotations: excitement, glamour, glitz, and imagination.

Bright scenes stand in contrast to the cozy world of night, and they startle by their reality. Two brightly lit scenes are sadly ironic. When Francine is in the hospital, having just had her baby, the room is bright with hospital white. She still loves Jimmy, and he loves her, and the scene is very intimate and tender. Yet in this scene we sense that Francine has begun to give up on their relationship. At the end of the film, there is well-lit reality again, as Francine faces the stage-door exit and decides not to meet Jimmy. The light emphasizes the bright, glaring emptiness.

One of the most striking elements of Laszlo Kovacs's cinematography of *New York, New York* is the poetry of many shots. Perhaps it is the affectionate memories of the forties that prompted Scorsese to include this element in his work, or perhaps it is simply his way of seeing art as a part of life. Several small moments have this quality: From a stairway landing, Jimmy looks down at a couple doing a Fred Astaire and Ginger Rogers dance routine. Unexpectedly, we see a few moments of lyricism and grace on a subway platform. From a high angle, we see Jimmy playing his sax under a lamppost, another poetic shot. At dawn, Jimmy and Francine talk over the loss of the band. Jimmy plays his sax in front of a billboard for Paradise Park.

Two poignant scenes are Francine's listening to records and her recording of "But the World Goes Round." In contrast to the efficient editing of most movies, Scorsese takes the time to show Francine at home one evening while her husband is working. The camera scans the scene: a radio with a wooden mesh overlay over nubby fabric, 78 rpm records, an overstuffed couch, crinkly edged photographs, a *Life* magazine, and Francine lingering over pictures as she places them in a photo album. Listening to music, she is alone with her memories, thoughts, and feelings. Except for the record, this is a silent scene. Scorsese takes the time to show the experience of solitude, which he renders respectfully and sensitively.

The editing of *New York, New York,* is both functional and lyrical. Often, it is done in relation to music. For example, during the opening sequence, the V-J celebration, shots of Tommy Dorsey's orchestra and the individual musicians are intercut throughout the scene. The orchestra is not just a part of the scenery. Rather, it is a lead character of that scene.

When Jimmy tries to catch up with Francine after she's left on tour with Frankie Harte, there is a well-planned sequence of editing in which Jimmy's and Francine's separate movements are unified by the song "Once in a While." The scene begins with a high-angled shot of Jimmy playing "Once in a While" in a plaintive, mournful style, the lyrics of which are, aptly, "Once in a while, won't you try to give one little thought to me?" Next there is a dissolve to Francine singing "Once in a While," performing the song with Frankie Harte's band. Her singing underscores Jimmy hitching a ride to meet up with Francine. Another dissolve shows Francine, in another costume, singing the same song.

As this scene ends, the song "You Are My Lucky Star" begins, a faster, perkier, more optimistic love song that signals the reuniting of Jimmy and Francine. There is a dissolve to the wheel of the bus the band is riding in, followed by another to the back of the bus, another to Francine performing "You Are My Lucky Star," and finally one more dissolve to the parking lot of the Meadows, where Francine is just finishing the song. The editing and music of the montage, therefore, help show the relationship of Francine and Jimmy while condensing the narrative.

Several times, throughout the movie, Jimmy and Francine find themselves in awkward situations, in which they are trying to talk about something personal and private, yet others are nearby, very likely overhearing their conversation. The mise-en-scène works thematically to express the claustrophobia Francine and Jimmy experience in being overheard during intimate moments. It happens during Jimmy's audition in Brooklyn when the club owner overhears them arguing and during the scene when Francine is embarrassed at Jimmy's kissing her in front of the hotel desk clerk.

This awkwardness, along with comic touches, is especially apparent during the marriage scene. Francine interrupts the proceedings to talk to Jimmy. Startled at the realization that she's about to be married, Francine pulls Jimmy aside to express her hurt at Jimmy's abrupt, unromantic proposal. Feeling overcome by emotion at the situation, she also needs a moment to take in the whole experience. During this encounter, the justice of the peace and his wife watch the drama before them with interest, making an occasional editorial comment, "She's not sure." To show this added pressure at being overheard, the camera cuts back and forth between both couples. At one point, Jimmy, feeling the added stress, ushers the justice and his wife back into their house, telling them, "Please, just go back inside. We'll only be a minute." Of course, behind the storm door, they still observe with continued fascination.

A feeling of claustrophobia also occurs during Francine and Jimmy's argument in the green Buick over Jimmy's playing at the Harlem Club. During their talk, a couple pulls up next to them, gridlocking their space both physically and psychologically. Both Jimmy and Francine have individual agendas which clash with one another's, and the mise-en-scène, with another couple's hemming in Francine and Jimmy, shows this psychological roadblock. For a few minutes, the couples exchange words about the space, with traffic being blocked and horns honking adding yet more pressure to the situation. The camera cuts back and forth between the two cars. Jimmy and Francine can't even proceed with their argument until they finish arguing with the couple in the next car.

> The movie was a matter of recapturing in my mind a certain thing about the past, my memories of my uncles in uniform. I . . . remember the music. . . . One song was probably what made me make the movie. I used to play it over and over again. The song is an improvisation called "Love Letters." . . . You could take that love story and put it against the background of any time. Any period. It happens to be about the big bands because of my fascination over this record. I used to listen to it when I was alone [Hodenfield 1977, 41].

New York, New York's music is one of the most enjoyable aspects of the movie. Liza Minnelli's singing—certainly this film was made to order for her, providing a perfect vehicle for her considerable talent—is beautifully expressive here. To actually "become" a musician for this role, De Niro learned to play the sax. He was taught by Georgie Auld, whose playing we actually hear in the movie. The Big Band music we hear throughout is gently evocative of the forties era, a time of smooth, romantic songs, with simple, tender, upbeat, sometimes corny lyrics expressing love. It also adds meaning to the love story at the center of this film.

Sometimes the lyrics work in an obvious way in that they simply fit the occasion of the scene. Some of the lyrics of the first song Jimmy and Francine sing during his audition in Brooklyn are "You've brought a new kind of love to me." The lyrics to the song "New York, New York" are all about show business ambition, which both Jimmy and Francine have. Every word of "But the World Goes Round" tells of the emotional difficulty in having to accept the break-up of their marriage.

Sometimes the characters use music to express their feelings. Like many musicians, Francine and Jimmy are, to some degree, nonverbal people. Both are at their most expressive when they are playing or singing. Music is a real extension of them, a palpable means of expression. In a clearcut way, music is a metaphor for their respective personalities. Francine's style is smooth, classy, elegant, and easily appreciated by a wide audience. Jimmy's style is manic, eccentric, progressive, original, and appreciated by a narrower audience. In a more subtle way, music is simply a powerful means of expression for these characters. For example, Francine is hauntingly expressive during her singing of "But the World Goes Round." Both her performance and her facial expression are rich with meaning. Jimmy too uses music to express himself, as when he is upset at his wife's coming to the Harlem Club to sign a record contract. At first Jimmy's playing is quiet. He plays "Just You, Just Me," and the style comes across as a peace offering. When Francine starts to join him on stage, however, Jimmy is immediately distressed at her invading his territory. He then begins a contrasting, manic jazz piece to dissuade her approach. She immediately responds to his signal and turns around.

Francine's movie, *Happy Endings,* provides the opportunity to include singing and dancing in traditional musical style. A musical within a musical is also a typical element of the genre. Furthermore, *Happy Endings* provides an opportunity for Scorsese to comment on the typical musical. Surveying the genre from the Mickey Rooney–Judy Garland *Andy Hardy* musicals featuring the classic line, "I have an idea! Let's put on a show!" to the many backstage musicals of *Forty-Second Street* variety, we would find that musicals are usually about show business people. Typically, a portion of the movie is the characters' work. *New York, New York* is no exception. With *Happy Endings,* Scorsese provides a full cast of tap dancers, authentic fifties period costumes, and stylized choreography. The other typical elements are the rags-to-riches theme—through a lucky break, a struggling actress, in this case Peggy Smith, gets chosen for the lead of a Broadway play. She is an overnight success, and along the way she meets Donald, the man of her dreams. The other conventions are present as well: the chorus of adoring dancers; the obvious coincidence and artificiality; and the bigger-than-life hero who is handsome, polished, selfless, and romantic. They part but get back together at the end of the movie. *Happy Endings* also features a musical within a musical. The usherette, Peggy Smith, daydreams of being discovered and becoming a big star, and we watch her fantasy in musical form. She eventually awakens from her daydream, but the movie ends with the distinct possibility that her daydream could come true. In addition to being compelling visually, *Happy Endings* provides a splendid vehicle for Liza Minnelli to sing and dance.

However, *Happy Endings* is also at odds with the more realistic musical *New York, New York.* Its obvious stylization and artificiality contrast ironically with the more realistic style of Francine and Jimmy's story. Scorsese parodies the typical musical, reducing and mocking its conventions. Life is much more complex than how it was presented in the old movies. Donald came back to Peggy; the problem of being Mr. Peggy Smith became resolved somehow, and there was a joyous reunion at the end of the sequence. Francine will not experience such a happy ending in her life. Jimmy has real difficulties living in the shadow of his wife's success, and she will experience real loss and heartbreak in her personal life as she becomes a success.

The language of *New York, New York* is typical of its period. It is also reflective of the subculture it is trying to depict. *New York, New York*'s characters are musicians—nonverbal, creative, hip, street-smart people. The language of Jimmy, Cecil Powers, Tony Harwell, Frankie Harte, even Francine, who doesn't usually speak in this style but who understands it, is reflective of the musical subculture. Scorsese has said, "The life of musicians fascinates me; in a way, they are a subculture, like the Italians were in *Mean Streets* and the characters in *Taxi Driver*. They live their own kind of lives, they're on their own special wave length, and they have their own language" (Lindsey 1976, 11). An example of this language occurs when Tony gives Jimmy a message from Francine at the club in Brooklyn. Their conversation has a colorful style, and they clearly speak the same language. Throughout this interchange, Tony is aware of Jimmy's scam, and he good-humoredly plays along.

> Tony: Hey pops, are you Jimmy Doyle?
> Jimmy: No.
> Tony: Do you think you can communicate with Jimmy Doyle, the sax player?
> Jimmy: That depends.
> Tony: I have a very important missive for Jimmy Doyle.
> Jimmy: A what?
> Tony: A billet-doux.
> Jimmy: A billet-doux? (He jokes with the musicians.) A bob-bop a doo!
> Tony: Take it, Doyle. It's from Francine. She said she had a *wonderful* time!

Another aspect of the language of *New York, New York* is its humor, which seems to spring naturally from this milieu. For example, the opening of the movie, the highly improvisatory segment at the V-J celebration, during which Jimmy tries to pick up Francine, is humorous in the many approaches Jimmy tries and in his dogged persistence. After about a dozen attempts, Jimmy tries once again, "I guess a little small talk is in order." Exasperated, Francine retorts, "Can it get any smaller?" She then entreats Jimmy, "If you had any sense of a gentleman in you, you'd go away." Jimmy replies, "Do I look like a gentleman in this shirt?" Francine looks at the Hawaiian shirt, thinks a moment, then says, "Even a louse would go away."

Sometimes, within a scene there are sudden tone shifts. For example, during the emotional and intimate hospital scene, there are several light-hearted moments. In the midst of the scene, the emotional climax of the story, the humor provides some welcome comic relief. Jimmy begins to cry, saying that he can't see the baby, especially now that the baby's been named Jimmy after him. Francine is mildly startled at his response, and she looks at Jimmy expectantly. Though Jimmy is serious in what he is saying, he tells Francine of his feelings in a comic style, stopping at one point to blow his nose. Finding no tissues available, he uses the edge of Francine's bed sheet, explaining he doesn't want to use his only handkerchief.

There is also the language of love in *New York, New York*. Francine and

Jimmy's language is typical of people in a close relationship. Their communication often takes place at the feeling level. Knowing one another well, they each anticipate the responses of the other, and sometimes what is actually communicated is a shorthand with much said and felt. When Francine talks to Jimmy about going to the Up Club to hear Paul Wilson, for example, their conversation is very instinctive and elliptical, with Francine feeling her way through the conversation, sensing Jimmy's discomfort. In fact, Scorsese often shows us the limitations of words; there are other ways we communicate — tones of voice, gestures, looks, actions — that say much more.

In addition, there are the arguments that Francine and Jimmy have, which also are forms of communication, when unspoken resentments and stifled feelings are expressed. When Jimmy and Francine argue in the care outside the Harlem Club, Jimmy's resentment about the baby and his fears about his career come out. Mouthing the words that many women have spoken, Francine accuses Jimmy of only caring about his work and his interests and of not caring about her. And mouthing the words that many men have spoken, Jimmy keeps repeating that he does care, that's not the problem.

The screenplay of *New York, New York*, written by Earl Mac Rauch and Mardik Martin, underwent considerable revision, and in the end, an outline was used for the filming with much of the actual dialogue being created through a series of improvisations. Scorsese decided to keep much of the improvised fun of the opening scene, for example, and the scene goes on far longer than convention would normally allow. The surprise and freshness of improvisation can be felt especially in the marriage scene where several ideas, including the breaking of the glass and Jimmy's pleading with Francine to marry him, were added during rehearsals.

The spontaneity of improvisation is noticeable also in the short but memorable scene when Francine is trying to exit from a cab after being out late celebrating a successful audition with Jimmy. Trying to back out of the cab, Francine aims for the curb while she tries to break away from Jimmy's embrace. It is raining, and Francine finds herself standing without her shoes in a puddle of water at the curb. She says to Jimmy, "It's so late." Again, the scene goes on longer than convention usually allows with Francine continuing to try to break away and to reach the curb.

The level of improvisation in *New York, New York* also helps allow for the originality of some of the film's minor characters. Although the movie centers primarily on Jimmy and Francine's story, several of the film's minor characters are colorful and interesting portraits, for example, Artie (played by Lenny Gaines), who is a crass character. With a thick New York accent and many ethnic traits, some of them abrasive, Artie is a typical Scorsese type, not mainstream and not quite acceptable. However, Artie also has a shrewd business sense, and he is kind to Francine and Jimmy. He emerges fully here, although he is only in a few scenes.

Lionel Stander also gives a memorable performance as Francine's good-hearted and likeable manager, Tony Harwell. Stander particularly shines in the scenes when he delivers Francine's message to Jimmy and when Tony and Artie go to the club in Harlem to discuss Francine's contract. Georgie Aulde as Frankie Harte plays the part of orchestra leader with style and panache. Aulde looks and moves the part, a bit heavyset and manly. He talks the part too, speaking the slang of musicians and the lingo of the streetwise.

Liza Minnelli and Robert De Niro give meaningful performances in the lead roles of the film. What is particularly striking about the acting here though is the complexity of the performances. The feeling level that is rendered and the ambiguity and subtleties that are attempted are far richer than what is usually conveyed in a love story. Scorsese is delving into a realm of intimacy rarely conveyed in art. In commenting on the production of this film, Scorsese, De Niro, and Minnelli have all said how extraordinarily intense and emotionally demanding the experience was.

When we look back at the performances, what we often remember is the look and feel of a scene. In fact, it is frequently literally a look that conveys the emotional accuracy and richness of a scene. Some of these moments are when Jimmy is on the telephone after talking over his wife's record contract with Artie and Tony, the look of processing that uncomfortable event; when Jimmy is signing over his band to Paul Wilson, the look of vulnerability on his face as he watches the band members drive into the muddy fall sunset; when Francine spends the evening alone listening to records, the look in her eyes as she gazes into the mirror; and when Francine sings "But the World Goes Round," the look of sadness and strength as she sings. The richness and depth of the performances that were attempted in this film were ambitious, and the result is an intricate and unusually evocative work.

"I was extremely disappointed when the movie was finished because I had had a really bad experience making it. But over the years I've been able to see that it has truth to it. I still don't really like it, yet in a way I love it" (Scorsese in Thompson and Christie 1989, 72).

New York, New York garnered average box office receipts; however, generally it was not considered a successful film. Critical response was also tepid. From a later perspective, however, *New York, New York* has been regarded by some as an undeservedly underrated movie. As with other Scorsese films, initially it was hard for critics to know what Scorsese was trying to do. His work is often so revisionist and individualistic that, as with many artistic innovations, it is only later that critics have a more complete understanding and appreciation of it. One problem was the length of the film, originally four-and-a-half hours. It was cut down to 153 minutes, but that version left out important scenes, including the *Happy Endings* musical sequence. In 1981, the cut scenes were restored, and the film was re-released at 163 minutes. This version was later highly praised by critics.

Raging Bull

I put everything I knew and felt into that film [Raging Bull] and I thought it would be the end of my career. It was what I call a kamikaze way of making movies: pour everything in, then forget all about it and go find another life [quote from Scorsese in Thompson and Christie 1989, 77].

Raging Bull is both a disturbing and a beautiful film to watch. It is compelling, which is perhaps surprising, because it deals with a protagonist who is hard to like. The film is one of Scorsese's most tightly crafted works. It is also one of his most violent, poetic movies. Rich with complexity and ambiguity, this film offers no easy or obvious interpretation. Created in a strongly focused and instinctive way, *Raging Bull* attempts to capture aesthetically something about the intricacies and sadness of human experience.

Raging Bull chronicles the rise and fall of Jake La Motta, the middleweight boxing champion, for a brief period during the late 1940s and early 1950s. The movie opens in 1964 in a dressing room, where Jake (Robert De Niro) is rehearsing lines which he will recite as part of his act in a club in Manhattan. He is swollen with excess weight. He looks huge, misshapen. He smokes a cigar, his breathing seems labored, and the version of Shakespeare he recites is reductionist and crudely silly.

The film then flashes back to Jake early in his boxing career. It is 1941, at the Cleveland Arena, where Jake has just lost his first fight. Here Jake is lean and strong, in top form. Ironically, it looks as if he has won. He knocked out his opponent, and at the end of the fight, the referee has to raise the limp arm of the winner, seated in his corner. He is then carried out of the ring, while Jake, the loser, stalks the ring as though he were the victor. But Jake didn't win according to the Ohio point system. The opening fight scene introduces a major theme of the movie: *Raging Bull* is about a man who has great difficulty with compromise. He feels he must do things his way.

In the process of getting to know Jake La Motta, we also get to know the people who are important in his life. The film focuses especially on the relationship of Jake and his brother, Joey (Joe Pesci). Joey is exceedingly loyal. He is a loving and forgiving brother to Jake, and he is Jake's manager and best friend. While Jake can be difficult to watch, Joey is a comfort and a delight to get to know. He is the voice of sanity in this film. Although similar to Jake in some ways—Joey curses a lot, has a temper, engages in violent activity, operates by a double standard where women are concerned—he nonetheless evokes a feeling of safety because he is a decent guy. He forgives his brother's outbursts, recognizing at once the real source of Jake's angst: the strain of being a contender for so long, problems with his excess weight, worry over his wife's fidelity. With Jake's best interest at heart, Joey gives his brother sensible advice. Joey winces at the sight of Jake's physical and verbal abuse of Vickie (Cathy Moriarty), Jake's wife, and, sickened by this behavior, Joey speaks to Jake on her behalf. Affable and friendly, Joey also acts as a go-between for Jake in talking to Tommy Como (Nicholas Colosanto), the local Mafia don, about arranging for Jake to get a chance at becoming the middleweight champ.

Jake's relationship with Vickie is another concern of the film. She is strikingly beautiful. Jake admires her at first from afar and later wins her as his wife. He first notices Vickie at a pool, where she is sitting with others from the neighborhood. Vickie looks especially lovely with her platinum blond curls catching the glint of the sun's rays as she laughs and enjoys the company of the people she is with or sits at poolside dipping her legs in soft ripples of water. Jake is noticeably drawn to her and her unavailability, not only because of her exceptional good looks but also because she is friends with people Jake dislikes. This makes him long for her all the more.

Interestingly, Vickie's character is not developed much, except in relation to Jake. What we know about her is what Jake values in her. He adores Vickie. He puts her on a pedestal and is consumed with the idea that she might be unfaithful to him. Like a magnet, Jake, the epitome of masculinity, is sexually drawn to Vickie, his ideal of femininity, and she also seems to be drawn to him on this essentially sexual level. Vickie enjoys being worshipped by him. She seems to be a good wife. She is quiet and deferential, though not a doormat, and she handles Jake well, standing up for herself, but not succumbing to retaliation for the abuse she receives. Vickie loves Jake, and like Joey, she is loyal to him, forgiving his outbursts—his impatience, paranoia, and bad temper. She also enjoys and seeks out the attention she receives from those who admire her, a behavior which Jake finds threatening.

> Jake La Motta was a fighter, that's all . . . a streetbrawler. I would think that Jake thinks it's a movie about himself. But those who think it's a boxing picture would be out of their minds. It's brutal, sure, but it is a brutality

Martin Scorsese (*left*) and Robert De Niro. The fight scenes in *Raging Bull* are a blend of formalism and realism. Former middleweight champion Jake La Motta, upon whose story *Raging Bull* is based, worked for ten weeks with De Niro during the filming of the boxing matches. Scorsese sketched each frame of the fight scenes in *Raging Bull*. They are visceral, pulling viewers in, making them undergo the fight along with the boxers. The tight framing, close-ups, editing, and sound effects all work to make viewers experience the brutality of the ring, the power and pain of the punches, and the feeling of being punch-drunk (*Raging Bull*, 1980).

that could take place not only in the boxing ring, but in the bedroom or in an office [Quote from Scorsese, Ferretti 1980, 2–1].

The film can be approached as a revisionist boxer picture—the antithesis of such sentimental movies as *Rocky*. The movie is also a biography of La Motta. However, as with his other films, Scorsese's main interest is in character. Again, we get to know a character deeply, and again the person is an outsider. This is a universal as well as a particular portrait. Scorsese comments, "To call it a boxing picture is ridiculous. It's sports but it's something to do with living. Jake La Motta takes on the aspects of everybody" (Ferretti 1980, 18).

Raging Bull is uncomfortable to watch because it depicts Jake La Motta's life in such a visceral way. It shows us private elements of his life, especially his pain and anguish. He is an angry, obsessive, tormented man.

For example, La Motta is enraged at ways that life is unfair, and he is right. He is incensed over the match in the Cleveland Arena where he lost his first fight because he waited too long to knock out his opponent. Jake doesn't want to be controlled by the neighborhood Mafiosi, who control the fight game. Why should they reap the rewards when he is paying the price in pain? Yet without the help of these men, La Motta has no chance at a championship fight, and he'll have to endure beatings in the ring for several years trying to make it on his own. Jake is each of us at those moments when we are acutely aware of the injustices in life. He is us when we come to terms with our own powerlessness.

However, Jake is not about to admit powerlessness. He is egotistical and quick to anger. Lacking awareness, he blames his discontent on others and takes his hostility out on them. He especially victimizes those who love him. Never thinking about how his actions might affect them, he abuses them and pushes them around. *Raging Bull* is about bullying and its effects on relationships. It is about a megalomaniac determined to have his way.

Not all of Jake's troubles stem from his own willfulness, however. Some come from the cards he was dealt in life. Scorsese leaves vague the reasons Jake suffers from feelings of low self-esteem. It is interesting that Scorsese has the honesty and courage not to be reductionist in presenting why Jake is the way he is. We are introduced to him *in medias res*. We don't know why he is full of rage or why he is so ambitious. He has many strikes against him: he is poor, not very bright, inarticulate, uneducated, and lacking in social graces. Yet others in the film have a better life. Jake does not enjoy the fellowship and conviviality others share. It is, after all, a gift to be blessed with contentment, to have an easygoing personality which allows one to enjoy and to be at ease with others.

The sadness of La Motta's life is that he is not only a victimizer, he is a victim. Jake not only destroys others, he also destroys himself. His fury allows him little joy and contentment in life. He hears only his own voice, and his fears and worries torment him. Full of rage at both real and imagined threats, Jake is the author of his own discontent, the sower of the seeds of his own destruction. He suffers from his self-destructiveness. He has only a brief moment of glory as a champion. Soon afterwards, he loses everything. He finally pushes away those who loved him and were loyal to him. He ends up alone. His wife, children, and brother are gone.

Raging Bull is one of Scorsese's most spiritual works. It affirms the human condition and recognizes the beauty and mystery of life. It also has much to say about forgiveness. It is about the many ways people forgive each other their faults and love and forgive again despite unforgivable behavior. It is about the sadness and isolation of having pushed people too far once too often and of not being forgiven. It is about the loneliness of being right. It is also about the hardest type of forgiveness—self-forgiveness—of giving up being right and being at peace.

Raging Bull is a story of eventual redemption. Scorsese invites us to get to know a man who is hard to like, and he shows us behavior which is despicable. And yet, seeing all that we see, including those things that Jake could change, those he can't, and how he suffers as a result of both, the film's concluding biblical quotation is appropriate: "So, for the second time (the Pharisees) summoned the man who had been blind and said: 'Speak the truth before God. We know this fellow is a sinner.' 'Whether or not he is a sinner I do not know,' the man replied. 'All I know is this: Once I was blind and now I can see.'" (John IX: 24–26 the New English Bible).

Instead of presuming to know why Jake is the way he is, Scorsese treats Jake's story like a historical document. Shot in black and white, *Raging Bull* looks like a documentary, and in several ways it attempts the objectivity of this style of film making. It includes photos and footage of many of La Motta's fights and a storyline which includes important events and people in his life. *Raging Bull*'s structure is fragmentary, however. Conventional transitions are not provided, and viewers must actively participate in pulling together the materials for themselves and coming to an understanding of the meaning of what has been presented. Scorsese points out that this decision was deliberate:

> We did not feel a need for the old, cliched psychological structure. He hated his brother so therefore he did . . . that sort of thing. Why should anybody say anything came from anywhere? Reasons? We never discussed reasons. What we discussed was going back to the beginning, to basics and that's why one of our first decisions was to film in black and white [Ferretti 1980, 28].

In spite of the emotional heaviness of this film, there is something satisfying about its complexity, its messiness, and its humanity. It is a rich and full experience to get to know the characters in this movie and the lives they lead. It is refreshing that they are not typical movie characters who speak in well-written phrases.

There is a compassionate look at humanity here. Scorsese presents "real" working-class people, and he presents them nonstereotypically, very different from the way such characters are usually treated in conventional films and television sitcoms. They are not just genre types—predictable and one-dimensional. Scorsese confers dignity upon them. He also finds poetry in the lives of the characters he presents. He shows us a poignancy in their everyday lives.

The photography in this film at times recalls Imagist poetry in its simplicity and quiet mood. An example of this occurs when Jake and Joey are back in the Bronx after the fight in Cleveland. Joey talks with his friend Salvy (Frank Vincent) as they walk down the block where Jake lives. The camera takes in various snatches of neighborhood life: two women, seated on a stoop, talking with one another; a man selling vegetables; two women and a child talking to another woman; men talking to one another. There is a feeling of contentment about the scene, as though life were truly good then.

Scorsese has gone to lengths to present this time authentically. There has been real attention to detail, much more so than in the usual Hollywood nostalgia movie. What's more, the lives of the people are not trivialized. This is not gratuitous nostalgia or sappy sentimentality. The characters are sketched with a minimalist hand, and the result is a less-is-more feeling of dignity and respect for the characters whose lives he is rendering.

This same look at humanity is evident in the camera movement at the beginning of the neighborhood pool scene. The scene opens with a low-angle shot of some children who are climbing a fence. With a lyrical descending movement, the camera then sweeps down to the side of the recreation building and the pool where two boys jump into the water. The same respectful attitude towards neighborhood people and neighborhood life is also evident in the church dance scene, where people are dressed up in elegant forties styles, when attending a dance or nightclub was truly a classy affair.

The use of black and white for this film also suggests the 1940s because that decade is associated with film noir, a dramatic black and white style of photography. Scorsese used a high contrast film stock to make this movie, and he used the blacks, whites, and grays for specific purposes. This look recalls the boxer film. It also helps create a documentary feel and complements the objective narrative style Scorsese is using to tell the story.

The tone is often set from the atmospheric use of black, white, and gray. It is set by the gray look of the rain at the pool and on the sidewalk in front of the Italian social club, the fog of the opening sequence, and the thick cigarette smoke of the boxing ring. By contrast, the home movies section, which is in color, has a very different tone from the black and white. This segment records the happy times in Jake's life, whereas most of the film is sad.

The opening of *Raging Bull,* features Jake La Motta sparring in slow motion within the confines of the thick black ropes of the boxing ring. His head and body are covered by a hooded robe, making him look like a figure of death in a medieval play. The title of the movie, *Raging Bull* appears in small red letters to the right, but La Motta doesn't look like a raging bull here. The slow motion softens his punches, effecting a grace and lyricism

The lighting and mise-en-scène in this shot help to arouse our sympathy for Jake (Robert De Niro). Literally, with his head bowed, his body blood-spattered and spent, and his arms outstretched, he looks like Christ. The bright light from the top right of the frame also creates a haloed effect and softens the shot with light and shadow (*Raging Bull*, 1980).

as Scorsese continues to do throughout the film, aestheticizing the brutality and vulgarity of La Motta's life story. The black ropes cutting across the screen entrap La Motta. This symbol also figures tellingly as La Motta is entrapped not only by the violence of the ring, but also by internal violence. He is brutalized not only in the ring but also by his own inner torment.

The photography in *Raging Bull* often helps to reveal Jake's character. At times, for example, the camera shows us specifically how Jake views some events. Scorsese uses slow motion at several points to highlight how Jake views the action of a scene. For instance, after Jake has taken an interest in Vickie, he goes to a dance that she is also attending. Along with Joey, he purposely chooses a table where he'll be able to see her. Sitting at a table surrounded by girlfriends, she looks particularly radiant. She is wearing an elegant dress, and her blond hair is pulled back into a fashionable pompadour. As she proceeds to leave with some friends, Jake follows. Her movements during these segments are shot in slow motion, which underscores Jake's fixation with her. As though oblivious to all the activity around him — the people, music, bar, dancing — Jake is totally concerned with Vickie. Scorsese uses this slow motion camera movement several other times—all highlighting Jake's obsession with Vickie. It is used when Jake watches Vickie kiss Tommy Como on the cheek at the Copa, and it is used to highlight Vickie's movements as she sits sunning at the pool, slowly cooling her legs in the water.

We also get a strong sense of Jake's experience through the photography in the fight scenes. We get an insider's view of what it's like to be in the ring. Everything from the temporary blinding flash of camera bulbs whiting out our vision to managers hovering around the fighter in male support is included in our experience during the fight scenes. Blood spurting from cuts; close-ups of blows taken in the face; a bloodied sponge rung out over Jake's body; the sweat, smoke and sinew are almost palpable. Furthermore, the camera movement and editing during the fight scenes are like Jake's style of fighting—all punches and stops. The camera captures Jake's style of fighting, emblematic of his character. His style is tough, graceless, and determined. He boars in on his opponent, punching until his opponent surrenders. The cinematography captures Jake's fighting style with quick editing, camera movement, and close-ups.

The camera also shows us the cost of Jake's victories. In the ring, he typically takes an incredible amount of abuse, yet he perseveres with singleminded determination. For example, when Jake fights Sugar Ray Robinson (Johnny Barnes) to defend his position as middleweight champion, the camera shows us the physical and emotional agony that Jake endures. Jake hasn't kept in training, and his body is not in top condition. His steely determination is what keeps him standing and what helps him endure this most brutal of fights. Particularly punishing blows are slowed, highlighting the pain they inflict upon Jake. Jake can barely stand. He leans against the ring. Blood spatters on his legs which look thin, spindly, and vulnerable.

The photography of *Raging Bull* evokes the loneliness, emptiness, and sadness of La Motta's life. These feelings are not rendered sentimentally. Rather they express feelings basic to the human condition. Though we may not relate to Jake's particular problems, it is hard not to feel a kinship with him on a human level. His hopes, frustrations, struggles, disappointments— in a larger sense—are part of the human condition. Despite the sadness, there is also great beauty in life as it is rendered in this film. With all its sadness and disappointment, life is also affirmed.

Like the literary greats who have attempted to convey larger truths about the human condition, Scorsese uses a number of conventions from literature such as irony, poetry, metaphor, and symbol in this work.

For example, the opening 1941 fight at the Cleveland Arena contains excellent examples of Scorsese's irony. When the fight is over, La Motta's opponent, Reeves, is carried out of the ring while loser Jake swaggers about the ring playing up to the booing, restive crowd, incensed at the decision of the judges. Pandemonium then erupts in the crowd. A chair is tossed through the air, fights break out, and a woman who has fallen is trampled by the crowd. In the midst of this chaos, the referee's memory seems to be jogged. The national anthem customarily ends this sporting event. Dutifully, the referee signals the organist to begin playing, and he places his hand over his heart in reverence to the anthem, a symbol of peace and order.

Like literary greats such as Charles Dickens and F. Scott Fitzgerald, Scorsese freely uses poetry in his narration of Jake La Motta's story. There are many small touches of found poetry: a white curtain billowing in the background of two characters talking; a woman sewing needlepoint at the pool who provides a sense of the contentment Scorsese sees in living during this era; even the billows of smoke in the ring add a poetic atmosphere, reminiscent of Eliot's modernist landscape in "The Wasteland."

Other poetic shots are more overtly evocative. Some are simply lovely shots. For example, when Jake invites Vickie to his father's apartment, he and Vickie form a quiet, balanced picture with Jake at one end of the table and Vickie at the other, with bright window light at both sides of them. The minimalist design is a backdrop for the seeds of courtship which are sown. In a more somber scene, after Jake loses to Sugar Ray, in the fight before Ray enters the army, Jake sits alone, feeling sad, thinking over his loss. A few moments before he had mused to Joey, "I don't know. I've done a lot of bad things. Maybe it's coming back to me." As in *New York, New York*, Scorsese takes the time to show a character in solitude. Jake looks soberly reflective as he looks at himself in the mirror and soaks his hand in a bucket of ice water.

A poetry reminiscent of that found in Elia Kazan's films, a poetry of humanity and everyday life, especially neighborhood life, can also be found in this film. The truce scene is an example of this type of poetry. Several individual close-ups of small details set the scene: a sign, "Debonair Social Club Members Only"; a state of New York certificate on the wall; a coffeepot in a pan of water on the stove; a stack of coffee cups and saucers; an extreme close-up of a cup's handle and a saucer. Scorsese shows us small, graceful pictures. In style, these images recall the loveliness in the quiet simplicity of William Carlos Williams's Imagist poetry at the turn of the century. In mood, they recall the ability to fall in love with the small things that make up romance in life.

Another poetic device that Scorsese uses throughout *Raging Bull* is metaphor. For example, he frequently uses closed forms to convey the confinements of La Motta's life. Jake is typically pictured in the claustrophobia of rooms sealed off with firm boundaries. The confines of the neighborhood figure significantly: This is a movie about the Bronx, not Manhattan. Jake is free to rage and flaunt his strength within the boxing ring, but he later becomes a prisoner of the ring, fighting with fury, yet only shadowboxing for the title shot, as elusive as Sisyphus's hope of pushing the boulder over the top of the mountain. The thick ropes of the ring come to confine Jake both physically and emotionally as his worries mount: obsessions about becoming champ, about keeping down his weight, about doing things his way, and about keeping his wife faithful.

The picture of Jake trying to unscramble his out-of-focus television set is a perfect metaphor for Jake's mental state. Although Jake must defend his title the following month, his belly is swollen with excess weight, his breathing is labored, and he looks uncomfortable as he moves. Jake is the picture of someone who is out of control, physically and emotionally. While adjusting the set, he chews a hot dog and, sounding crazy and paranoid, he unrelentingly questions Joey about Vickie's fidelity, insisting that she's been unfaithful, possibly with Joey himself.

Perhaps the most obvioius use of closed form and metaphor is when Jake is in prison. Isolated and agonizingly remorseful, Jake literally pounds his head against the stone wall of the prison. Appropriately, this dark moment of the soul is shot with little light. Only Jake's head and shoulders are lit as he cries out, "Why? Why? Why? . . . Why did you do it? You're so stupid, so fucking stupid." All along Jake has been metaphorically hurling himself against a stone wall. He has insisted on doing things his way and imposing his will upon others. He has trampled on the conventional and spiritual rules that govern human relationships. He has also suffered the consequences of his stridency with others. Some have responded by merely keeping their distance. Others have been outraged and have challenged him in return. Saddest of all are those who once loved him and were loyal but finally, unwilling to take anymore, abandon him, too. Jake reaches the end of the line. He is alone, suffering miserably, friendless, and full of regret.

Yet another figurative device common to both literature and film is symbol, and Scorsese makes use of this device frequently in *Raging Bull*. Like Dickens who used atmosphere as symbol so effectively in *Great Expectations* and *Bleak House*, Scorsese artfully uses rain, fog, and smoke to convey meaning about La Motta's life and to add poetry to the rendering of his story. The fog of the opening sequence featuring Jake sparring in the ring provides a sense of the murkiness of Jake's story; this is not a story of crisp and clear black and white; it is all about the lack of clarity in shades of gray. When Jake throws the fight as he agreed to with the local mob, he sobs in remorse. In the ambivalence of the steamy atmosphere of the training room, he is comforted by his coaches, who sympathize angrily with his unmanly predicament. The look of the boxing ring—the setting in which the hard-edged brutality of this story takes place—is replete with the physical reality of punches and blood. The fight scenes especially give a sense of the male world in which La Motta's story unfolds, an unpretty world of sweat, steam, and smoke.

Rain, however, is used in a more tender way throughout the film. Associated with femininity, it provides a lyrical beauty as it softens the violent world in which Jake lives. Rain provides a respite from the productive business of life. It also typically accompanies sad and contemplative scenes, as though the world were stopping to empathize and underscore the events of life that cause us to pause and think. It also seems to provide an atmosphere of reflection and emotion. Rain pours down in front of the Debonair Social Club storefront, the setting for the truce meeting between Joey and Salvy, mediated by Tommy Como. The same rain introduces the next scene at the pool where Joey meets Jake to report the results of the meeting with Tommy. As thunder causes swimmers to run to the bathhouse for shelter, Jake ruminates about Vickie. Lost in his thoughts, he tells Joey, "I first met her here."

One of the most interesting and compelling aspects of *Raging Bull* is the way Scorsese uses music, language, and sound effects to complement the cinematography and to capture the abrasive, stormy conflict that is Jake's life.

Mascagni's haunting, lyrical music sets the mood of the film during the opening shot. A stark, solitary hooded figure, Jake jogs in place in slow motion within the ring. Set against the white of the canvas and surrounded by thick black ropes, Jake looks imprisoned by the ring. In contrast to this bleak scene, Mascagni's music is lyrical, delicate, poignantly melancholy. It softens the visuals and provides an emotional tone for the story to follow. This music is thematic and provides continuity throughout the film. It also works to blend the art and reality of *Raging Bull*.

During the home movie segment, when we see scenes of Jake's good years, we hear Mascagni's music once again. We see Jake's marriage to Vickie, scenes from winning fights, Joey's marriage to Lenore (Theresa Saldana), and other happy scenes. Mascagni's musical theme complements this segment's warm emotional tone and closeness of the characters. At the end of the sequence, the music softens and becomes gently melancholy, hinting at Jake's flawed character, his internal struggle, and his forthcoming downfall and defeat.

During Jake's middleweight championship fight, Mascagni's music expresses the poignancy of Jake's struggle and triumph. It also foreshadows his failure. In the ring, Jake functions with destructive abandon. He is on familiar ground and uses his pent-up rage to destroy his opponent. While visually the fight is seen as a form of violent art, the music softens the coarse, grinding impact of leather striking flesh. As the end of the fight nears, the music soars, rapturous and triumphant, adding to and punctuating the emotional climax of the scene, Jake's victory. As the music

Robert De Niro and Cathy Moriarty. Scorsese often casts actors who bring a rich subtext to their role. For example, many of the extras are characteristic New York types, people from the neighborhood, or people with ethnic characteristics, Jewish, Irish, Italian. In *Raging Bull*, Cathy Moriarty, a young model and an Irish Catholic from the Bronx, plays Jake's wife, Vickie. She brings many authentic details to her role as a neighborhood girl, including her accent, style, attitudes, and movements. It would be hard for someone without her background to imagine and act all of these traits. Ms. Moriarty was deservedly nominated for an Academy Award for her performance, which is rich, full, and sympathetic (*Raging Bull*, 1980).

expresses Jake's joy, it once again serves as a prelude to his impending fall.

While the music of *Raging Bull* affects us on an emotional level, much of the dialogue is purposely underplayed. Jake is not a verbal guy, and we are reminded of this through the use of muted dialogue. Many times throughout the film, actual lines of the characters are indiscernible as

Scorsese relies on the subtext to convey meaning. In other scenes, Scorsese has the actors use the real language of the violent urban setting he presents.

In the Bronx Italian neighborhood where Jake lives, streets are lined with buildings jammed up against each other. Throngs of people fill these buildings — standing at windows, sitting on stoops, and spilling out onto the sidewalk. In this tumultuous, jarring environment, shouting is the normal tone of voice. These people have been assaulted by sound since birth and have grown accustomed to the loud, dissonant cacophony that envelops them. There is ethnic music coming out of one door, and the beat of swing music coming out of another, a few doors down the block. Expressive threats and curses become a meaningful form of interpersonal communication as they establish a hierarchy of power in the family and in the neighborhood.

In view of Jake's character and the setting, the underplaying of the dialogue is fitting. Rather than using consistently clear dialogue, Scorsese frequently uses the subtext of a scene to provide the real level of communication. In addition to the incessant, intrusive city sounds and muted dialogue, Scorsese uses close-ups and careful framing to capture emotional nuances of the main characters.

For example, when Jake invites Vickie to his father's apartment, we hardly hear their intimate conversation. Instead, we are involved in the sensuality of the scene. The sense of the scene is one of light, calm, stillness, and controlled passion. Visually, the scene is photographed in open form with the windows providing light and framing the characters as they sit at the kitchen table. Vickie, fair and feminine, is shy and hesitant. Jake, dark and muscular, flirts with her in a playful, macho way. Although their lines are subdued and muffled, we sense Jake's strong attraction and Vickie's gradual acquiescence.

While Jake can be charming, his thin veneer of civility is always volatile. Underneath, he is explosive. The language and dialogue revealing his core come through unmistakably. His outbursts are loud, staccato, and argumentative. He frequently punctuates these outbursts with threats and profanity. Many times Jake reaps what he sows in these oral exchanges. The words "animal," "crazy," and "sick" are epithets frequently hurled at Jake, and, as such, emerge as significant motifs throughout the film.

For example, early in the story when Jake is arguing with his first wife in their apartment, a neighbor yells down from the apartment above, calling him an animal. Outraged by the insult, Jake opens the window and curses back at his neighbor. Later, when Jake is out of shape, Joey warns him that he can't eat and drink like an animal. This word "animal" is used frequently throughout the film by characters talking to Jake or about him. Many of the people Jake encounters in the film are disgusted by his behavior: the local Mafia, because Jake won't do things their way; Joey, because Jake is so thick-headed and won't listen to Joey's advice; and Vickie, because Jake treats her like a possession rather than a person.

These people are disgusted with Jake and, at the same time, are intimidated by his seething, volcanic rage. Jake does epitomize an animal, and he lashes out at everyone around him. His fears and insecurities grow into paranoia, and the motives of all others become suspect. He even begins to suspect the loyalty of his brother, who spends the early part of the film trying to help him. He does this by explaining Jake's behavior to others, apologizing for him, and acting as a go-between and a front man. Joey frequently tries to bring common sense to Jake's emotional irrationality. In one scene, Jake is concerned that he can never fight heavyweight because his fists are too small. Joey points out that it is crazy to be worried about something he can never change. Later in the film, when Jake confronts Joey about whether he has been sleeping with Vickie, Joey is completely caught off guard. He is astonished. He refuses to answer. He is outraged by the impropriety of the question. He tells Jake he is a "sick fuck, a sick bastard," and that his question is sick.

When Jake then accuses Vickie of sleeping with Joey, she is outraged and hurt. Jake keeps pushing her to admit infidelity. Finally, out of exasperation, she lashes back that she has slept with Joey, Salvy, and everyone on the block. She yells at Jake that he is a fat pig, selfish, a fool, and that he is sick. Jake immediately bounds out of the room and charges over to Joey's house. He breaks in and, in a fit of jealous rage, beats the hell out of Joey in front of his wife and children.

At this point, Jake's paranoia is full blown. Suspecting everyone of disloyalty and refusing to accept help from anyone, he begins to lose control over his life. He becomes overweight and out of shape, and he begins losing fights. His brother won't have anything to do with him.

Jake's life is falling apart. No longer able to win in the ring, he retires from boxing and opens a nightclub in Florida, but even this new venture is doomed to fail. Shortly after opening his club, Jake is arrested for serving a minor and is sentenced to jail. Vickie eventually can stand no more, and she leaves him. Thrown into a dark cell, Jake reaches his emotional bottom. At this point of the film, Jake's physical appearance has changed dramatically. He has put on weight and shows a large, protruding belly and a puffy face. He breathes heavily and looks uncomfortable when he moves. Slovenly and disheveled, he looks the loser he has become.

In his cell, Jake screams and bangs his head against the wall, crying out in anger and despair. Primordial sobs rack his body as he tries to understand his fate. "Why . . . you're so stupid . . . dummy . . . an animal . . . why?" In this scene, Jake seems to experience an emotional catharsis. All his anger and frustration find release in his wailing, sobbing outpouring of regret.

Near the end of the film, the story comes full circle to the opening shot of Jake rehearsing lines for his nightclub act. Here we see a different Jake. Alone in the quiet confines of his shabby nightclub dressing room, he rehearses his lines from the famous "I coulda been a contender" speech from *On the Waterfront*. Here, Jake is introspective. Standing in front of the lighted mirror, he seems to realize that he has managed to alienate everyone who was close to him, and this saddens him. He no longer exhibits rage, and, for the first time in the film, he seems to be in control of himself. Outside the doors of the dressing room lies another arena with a new crowd. Jake, having come to terms with his past, seems willing to go on and to make the best of his future. Although he is still by no means an endearing character, he does have hope.

While the dialogue and the language in the film are either muted and underplayed, or replete with curses, threats, and accusations, the sound effects allow Scorsese his most expressionistic use of sound.

Sound effects are used primarily in the fight scenes to increase the tension and to heighten the action. They seem to add to the visual violence. During the fight scenes, we are assaulted by the sounds as much as the visuals. Through tight, close-up photography of the brutal fights, filmed at times in slow motion, and the jarring, grinding, gasping sounds emanating from the contestants, we are drawn into the ring and made to endure the agony of both fighters. Each blood-spattering, sweat-drenched punch lands with a bone-jarring, resonant thud. Each agonizing body blow evokes a gut-wrenching groan from the unfortunate recipient. The sounds of the fight are heightened and discordant and underscore the close-up visuals. As the fight progresses, the ambient sounds of the arena are filtered out as the fight takes on a surrealistic quality. The camera zooms in on the fighters and isolates them in close-up, slow motion photography, revealing the punishing exchange of blows. During this sequence, the sound fades out at intervals, indicating the temporary mind-numbing loss of awareness caused by the shock and pain of leather striking flesh. We hear the labored breathing and the thudding heartbeats of the adrenalin-charged fighters as they stalk each other in ritualized combat.

Essentially, the sound texture of *Raging Bull* allows us to vicariously experience the life of Jake La Motta. We experience the violent urban setting of the streets, and through the use of assaulting visuals and sound effects, we become involved in Jake's fights. Our empathy for him stems not from sentimentality or romanticism, but from knowing the quality of his life.

Scorsese invested much creative energy into every aspect of *Raging Bull*, using it as a vehicle to express his own feelings which were similar to Jake's. Although a personal film, it was also a collaborative effort. When Scorsese was making *Alice Doesn't Live Here Anymore*, De Niro first gave him the book *Raging Bull* and suggested they make it into a movie. Mardik Martin wrote the initial screenplay, Paul Schrader later wrote a second version, and De Niro and Scorsese a third. Over a two-month period in the summer of 1977, Scorsese and De Niro talked over the film, completing their talks on the Carribbean island of St. Martin, where for two and a half weeks, they rewrote the script and developed the characters in detail.

De Niro prepared to play Jake La Motta for a full year. With La Motta as his coach, he trained as a fighter, working out every day. During this time, the rest of the film was cast. It was decided to use nonprofessional actors for some parts and to use actors who rely on instinct when playing a part for others. Scorsese believed that these actors would be best able to convey the realistic style sought for this film. Joe Pesci suggested Cathy Moriarity as Vickie. Originally from the Bronx, Moriarity had been working as a model in the garment district. Blonde, pretty, and Irish, she looks a great deal like La Motta's real-life second wife, Vickie. De Niro and Scorsese coached Moriarity, who had never acted before, helping her become the part of Vickie. Having a similar background to the real Vickie and possessing a gift for being natural and comfortable in the role (Ferretti 1980, 28), she brought much to her portrayal of Jake's wife. She is thoroughly convincing as a neighborhood girl, a good person, someone we like.

Joe Pesci admits his style of acting is unconventional. For *Raging Bull*, that style was what Scorsese and De Niro were looking for. Pesci commented, "I had made up my mind that I was through with acting. I couldn't work with most people. I'm not a disciplined actor. I work on feeling, and I couldn't find too many people who wanted to work that way" (Ferretti 1980, 28). Pesci also met La Motta's real-life brother, Joey; "I got to know, to feel the relationship he had with his brother" (Ferretti 1980, 28). Joe Pesci is remarkable as Joey. He is especially strong at conveying emotion. Some of his memorable scenes are the vulnerability he shows after Jake batters him in the practice ring for allowing his Mafia-connected friends to visit at the gym; his look of pity and compassion, even after their falling out, as he watches his brother lose a fight on television; and his look of disgust and astonishment when Jake accuses him of sleeping with Vickie.

A film about emotion, *Raging Bull* succeeds because its actors convey feeling so well. Essentially nonverbal people, the characters communicate much through facial expression and body movement. For example, Moriarity is especially convincing when she shows Vickie's suppression of feeling. She is the picture of the torment of repressed feelings in the scene before Jake's championship fight. After being married to Jake for several years, she knows she had better think before saying anything or making a move. Even so, Jake is unpredictable. Something could set him off, resulting in a slap anyway. Sitting in the hotel room before Jake's title shot, Vickie looks like a hothouse fllower. She can't even order what she'd like for dinner without Jake's interference.

De Niro won an Academy Award for best actor for his role as Jake La Motta. When considering the bulk of his work with Scorsese, one is struck with how diverse and separate have been each of his roles. Each character thinks, talks, even moves in an entirely different way from the others: Johnny Boy has staccato and fluid movements; Travis Bickle's are plodding and heavy; Jimmy Doyle is mercurial and manic; Rupert Pupkin's movements are precise and measured; and Jimmy Conway's are powerful and menacing. Jake La Motta's movements are muscular and determined. Noteworthy too is the depth of feeling conveyed in De Niro's performance, which is especially moving during Jake's more vulnerable moments, for example, when Vickie packs to leave him, when Jake is talking on the phone trying to get money for bail, and when he is arrested and put in prison. When Jake's rage subsides and he has achieved some peace of mind and has begun to treat himself in a more kindly way, De Niro's acting is remarkable in how he conveys the emotional nuance of this change of character.

Raging Bull is a complex work noteworthy for many reasons, some of which are its memorable characters, visual style, music, acting, and humanity. Along with *Taxi Driver* and *GoodFellas*, it is considered one of Scorsese's finest works. In addition to De Niro's Academy Award for best actor, Thelma Schoonmaker also won an Academy Award for best editing for *Raging Bull*. Recently, in a critics' poll, it was voted best American movie of the 1980s.

King of Comedy

Rupert to Jerry: "Why didn't you listen to the tape when I asked you to? I mean it wasn't that hard, was it? A few minutes of your time to listen to something I worked on my whole life?"

King of Comedy is about someone who desperately wants to be given a chance. It's about fame at both ends of the ladder of success. Scorsese explores fame from the viewpoint of one who desperately seeks it and from another who has achieved fame. Unlike most of Scorsese's previous works, which delve deeply into character, the main interest in *King of Comedy* is in ideas. In fact, the film can be interpreted more fully if thought of as an essay on fame. Through virtually all of the elements of the film — its tone, plot, character, setting, music, and use of satire — Scorsese explores the dynamics of fame, especially in show business. He shows us the power, luxury, shallowness, and loneliness of fame.

King of Comedy tells the story of Rupert Pupkin (Robert De Niro), a pedestrian man in every way except one — his obsession with talk-show host Jerry Langford (Jerry Lewis). One night outside Langford's stage door, Rupert seizes an opportunity to assist his idol in escaping a flock of his frenzied worshippers. In return, Rupert implores Langford for an audition to his show. Annoyed but resigned, Langford acquiesces. Rupert is thrilled. His dream has come true. Not wasting a second on doubts, Rupert is filled with fantasies of stardom on "The Jerry Langford Show." He imagines himself as Langford's crony, his pal. Then Rupert turns reality around: In awe of Rupert, Langford now implores him to be on "The Jerry Langford Show," and Rupert reluctantly assents.

Eventually, Rupert finds out that Langford's invitation to audition was only a ruse to escape his cloying grasp. However, Rupert's disappointment only fuels his determination. He and another Langford fan, Masha (Sandra Bernhard), determine to kidnap Langford for their mutual benefit, he for airtime on the show and she for time to romance Jerry. Amazingly, the kooky scheme works. Rupert gives his monologue on the Langford show, and he even gets to watch himself on T.V. in front of Rita (Diahnne Abbott), a girl he's liked since high school. Of course, he is also arrested immediately afterward. But he uses the time in prison to work on his comedy routine and to write his memoirs. Ironically, at the close of the movie Rupert is about to perform on television again.

This film is different from Scorsese's previous works in several ways. The plot is straightforward and clear, unlike the raggedly plotted works of his earlier efforts. Another departure is that there is less emphasis on character. Other Scorsese films are essentially character studies; narratives are loosely structured, with emphasis on the complex emotional makeup of the protagonist. Here, the characters are more one-dimensional. Finally, the tone of *King of Comedy* is also cooler and more intellectual than Scorsese's other works.

There is also a coldness in the entire mood created in this film. One of the very few sunny scenes occurs when Jerry walks buoyantly down the street, joking along the way with a cabbie and some construction workers. However, minutes later, the scene turns sour. A disgruntled fan curses him for not taking time to talk to her nephew on the telephone, and Masha spots Jerry and begins a high-speed chase which motivates Jerry to leap through traffic to his office building. Overall, the tone of the film is more remote and detached. Unlike the warmth of Scorsese's earlier films, many of which are rich in period and setting detail — the forties of *New York, New York* and *Raging Bull*, the seventies of *Alice, Mean Streets*, even parts of *Taxi Driver* — this movie is like a piece of modern art, worthy of admiration, yet containing little with which to connect emotionally.

The film also lacks warmth because there is very little friendship, unusual for a Scorsese picture. There are only brief moments of warmth — Rupert's familiarity with the other fans outside Langford's show and with the receptionist who greets him on his rounds as messenger — but very few. Rita is not really a friend because there is no real connection between her and Rupert. Theirs is a relationship of expedience. There isn't the warmth of Charlie and his buddies, Alice and her friends Bea and Flo, and the brotherly love of Jake and Joey. Like Travis Bickle, Rupert and Jerry are utterly alone, utterly alienated from their fellows.

All of Scorsese's previous works have dealt with a character who wants very much to succeed: Charlie, who wants to do good works while also becoming a success in the neighborhood; Alice, who wants to be a singer; Travis, who aspires to rid the city of moral depravity; Francine and Jimmy, who both hope for musical stardom; and Jake, who wants his shot at the middleweight boxing championship and who later seeks a show business career as well. Here Rupert wants so desperately to be someone, to have ten minutes of fame on "The Jerry Langford Show" that he's willing to kidnap Langford and later pay the price by going to prison just to have his chance. As Rupert figures it, "Better to be king for a night than schmuck for a lifetime."

The title *King of Comedy* is an interesting choice of words because Rupert wants to be a *king* of comedy. The expression is common, but it is also telling in this case because the famous in this country are worshipped like royalty. In Rupert, we see how important it is to *be* someone, how one is defined by what one does for a living. It's unacceptable to be a messenger or a janitor or a waitress. In our competitive society, where one is expected to move up to the next class, even those who have no talent or inclination for becoming educated for higher status jobs feel the necessity to advance, to reach the top. Increasingly, people feel ashamed of more humble stations in life.

Scorsese is working in a genre of sorts, but this show biz story is so radically revisionist that its original is hardly recognizable. A dark work, it is the antithesis of an old classic movie, in which a chorus girl gets her big break when she fills in for the ailing star. In the traditional story, there was always hope. Here the walls are impenetrable, and the odds of success are a million to one. Even more discomforting, Scorsese shows us the degradation and humiliation involved in trying to break into this arena. There is no innocence or charm in this modernist version of trying to make it in show business. Unlike the romantic yearning of the old show-biz movies, this story is harsh reality, all high-tech and no heart. No one is remotely interested in a newcomer.

It's uncomfortable to watch Rupert's struggle. Scorsese captures his desperation with shocking honesty. The agony of Rupert's effort, his frantic elbowing and pushing his way to the top isn't inspiring, it's embarrassing. Scorsese shows the humiliation and demoralization. As Jonathan Swift pointed out in *Gulliver's Travels*, one must do his share of leaping and creeping to curry favor with the king. So it is with Rupert, who, when he introduces himself to Jerry, is so nervous he can hardly speak. Scorsese shows us the lack of dignity in Rupert's trying to talk to Jerry, his fumbling over words, quickly trying to explain, convince. He shows us Rupert's degradation and vulnerability, hoping to be listened to, to be taken seriously. The person with the power to make his dream come true is Jerry, who sits in judgment, coldly, unsympathetically. This is one of many acts of humiliation that Rupert endures: the humiliation of the receptionist's asking him to wait outside, the security officer's escorting him out, Rupert's trying to go back in to see Jerry, Miss Long's asking him what he's doing there, and his being thrown out of Langford headquarters and not being taken seriously be anyone. He must endure sneers, condescension, and mockery from everyone—from his mother, Rita, Jerry, Miss Long, the cameraman, the FBI agent.

Every door is shut in Rupert's face at one point or another. These humiliating rejections aren't supposed to happen. They negate the American dream, the mythology of which tells us every boy can be president and a

Robert De Niro and Jerry Lewis (*center*). Scorsese shows the down side of fame in the character of Jerry Langford. In this scene, Langford is literally trapped by his fans who worship him. Langford's fame is lonely, too. He is rude and suspicious and seems to have few relationships with others. Ironically, although he is surrounded by people, he is alone.

lucky girl can be an overnight sensation just by being discovered sitting at the counter at Schwabb's drugstore. *King of Comedy* shows us how hard it is to be heard, makes us ruminate on how mortifying it is to be on the outside and not even have a chance at success.

Who would purposely travel this minefield of rejection, hurt, and humiliation? Those who have low self-esteem; the disenfranchised; the shy, who've been on the sidelines all their lives and who, finally, seek an audience who'll listen to them; and the outsiders, people who don't comfortably fit with the mainstream of life and who have a desperate desire to achieve the admiration of others. Rupert and Masha fit the category of outsiders, perhaps more obviously than Scorsese's other alienated characters. In this sense they echo Scorsese's previous concern with telling the story of people whose lives are not chronicled in typical movies. Rupert and Masha prefigure Scorsese's characters in *After Hours*, a veritable collection of oddball types, more extreme than those of *King of Comedy*.

Rupert is an unlikely candidate for the next king of comedy. Not because he has a silly name, or because of his dopey gags (like his wallet-sized card with a picture of Pride wax and Joy dish liquid which he offers to show people as his "pride and joy") or because everything about his life is ordinary—his nagging mother, dull friends, boring job. He is unlikely because his talent for comedy is average too. There is nothing in his stand-up routine to distinguish him, to interest others, to make him deserving of notice or recognition.

Rupert wants to be the next Jerry Langford, and he has put all his energy into mastering the cliches of the job of late-night talk-show host and comedian. Putting remarkable drive and determination into pursuing his goal, Rupert's mimicking his idol shows a great deal of energy and elaborate attention to detail. From his style of dress to the cut of his hair, Rupert mimes Jerry with slavish devotion. In his basement, Rupert practices being Jerry in an impressive look-alike Jerry Langford–style living room set. He literally walks through the motions of being a talk-show host and comedian. To an imaginary audience, Rupert rehearses his comedy routines. The tired banalities and shallow chit chat of celebrities plugging their latest recording, movie, or club engagement that make up the menu of the talk show format are art to Rupert. He has lovingly memorized all the cliches: there is no freshness, no spark of talent, no wit.

What does distinguish Rupert, however, is his fanatical single-mindedness, not only in his mastery of the mechanics of the Langford show but also in his drive to succeed. In fact, Rupert has several qualities that help him in his quest. He is willing to persevere to the point of obnoxiousness. Admittedly, perhaps it takes a pushiness and steely determination to become famous, even a willingness to go to preposterous lengths. The mental dimness that blinds Rupert to the tawdriness of the Langford show also helps him to miss the smirks, sneers, and putdowns of those around him. Rupert is surrounded by cynics: No one listens sympathetically. However, because he seems to be thick-skinned and impervious to criticism whether subtle, veiled, or blunt, the lack of support doesn't seem to bother him. He has incredible defense mechanisms. Rupert remains an idealist and a romantic. He has dreamed about Rita since high school and still has dreams of marrying her. Even the terminology he uses—he hopes to be a "king of comedy" and he wants to make her his "queen"—reinforce his romanticism.

Rupert is hard to like. Scorsese treats him ambivalently, stressing his lack of charm, yet also showing us a reason to sympathize as well. Rupert has the potential of touching an audience, a wide-range one at that— anyone who has ever wanted to be taken seriously and anyone who has wanted to be treated with dignity and respect by those with power. He is anyone who has ever been unemployed and has had to endure the humiliation of talking to one of the smug employed, who behave as though they've never had to look for work themselves. Rupert is one of the downtrodden in society, one of the little people, the unempowered, which includes a great many people.

There are a number of qualities in Rupert that invite an audience's sympathy. Being heard matters greatly to him. In fact, it is likely we might have more compassion for Rupert on second viewing. After all, this is a story about the triumph of a little guy. With imagination, one might even view the story as a cynical, updated, highly revisionist version of *Mr. Smith Goes to Washington*. When Rupert sits in the reception room of the Langford offices, he nervously maintains his perfect appearance while he gazes up at the ceiling, making small talk with the receptionist about the efficacy of cork for soundproofing. The picture of Rupert clinging to a payphone, protecting its potential ring, shows his yearning, how much this phone call matters to him. Rupert also connects with viewers in his need to be vindicated. This is especially true in the wonderful satire in which Rupert's high school principal admits how wrong everyone was about him. In addition to arousing our sympathy, Rupert's dream of becoming a talk-show comedian also makes him interesting. His aspirations and his romanticism make him more than an ordinary man.

Despite her bizarre behavior, Masha also elicits sympathy, especially during the "romantic" dinner scene. Even though her fawning over a tied-up T.V. celebrity is grotesquely funny, her outpourings of affection are sincere. Masha, a romantic like Rupert, sings to Jerry as though she were in an old musical. There is an innocence and a childlike quality to her love. Her recitation of details about her life, the loneliness and emptiness, is touching. Even with an oddball, one-dimensional character like Masha, Scorsese adroitly adds shading, revealing her humanity in a slight but important way. We get to know some of the underpinnings of her fanatic and neurotic behavior. There is something sad in Jerry's complete lack of response to all her gestures of love.

Like thirteen-year-old groupies, both Masha and Rupert are obsessed. They stand outside Langford's stage door, mount photographs of him on the walls of their homes, and can recite details about his career and private life. Thoughts of Jerry give their lives excitement; plotting to actually meet him and to become a part of his life is a palpable fantasy. We smile at such thoughts and dreams in prepubescent teenagers. In adults, however, such obsessions are considered aberrant, dangerous. Instead of creating lives for themselves, perhaps dating, marrying, pursuing careers, at least establishing relationships with others, Rupert and Masha put all their energy into their infatuation with media celebrities. Masha and Rupert are two of a kind. And like teenage siblings, they compete and squabble.

Rupert and Masha's rivalry, however, is harmless compared to the bullying that apparently goes on at the corporate level in the field of entertainment. Imperious Jerry Langford is rude to everyone from his producer, Bert Thomas, to his butler, Jorro. Actually, compared to Jerry Langford, Rupert fares well. At least he's polite. However, Rupert's courtesy and

Left to right: **Robert De Niro, Jerry Lewis, Diahnne Abbott.** Television creates a false intimacy between onscreen celebrities and the viewing public. Celebrities share their thoughts and experiences, while communicating feelings of warmth, humor, and goodwill. It is as if these celebrities are our friends. However, in real life, there are strict boundary lines, and although it feels as if we're on a first-name basis with these people, we are strangers. In this scene, Rupert, along with his friend Rita, has invaded the privacy of his hero, star Jerry Langford, by coming to Langford's home uninvited (*King of Comedy*, 1982).

reasonableness get him nowhere. Later when Clarence McCabe, the writer, behaves reasonably and courteously, he also gets no results. The way of kindliness and compassion is anathema to those who have achieved success and fame. Egos are enormous, frosty, and disdainful. Underlings aren't considered to be human beings with feelings. They aren't important and are treated accordingly. If one is powerful, he has apparently earned the right to behave rudely to others. Jerry snarls at his producer; Miss Long sneers at Rupert; and Tony Randall barks at the cue-card girl. Part of the reason why Jerry is too furious to speak during the kidnapping and why he is utterly outraged at seeing Rupert appear on his show is that Rupert has usurped Jerry's power.

Scorsese hints that Rupert won't be much better when he achieves fame. Rupert hardly behaves with humility when he calls Jerry Langford's office from an office friend's telephone. Enjoying her envy and respect, Rupert behaves haughtily in return. Likewise, the moment he has a chance to audition for Jerry, he doesn't even want to be seen with Masha. Exploitation is permissable, and loyalty and honesty aren't allowed to interfere with one's self-interest. Rupert takes money from Masha to get her letter to Langford, but he shows no loyalty to her in actually trying to deliver the letter. When Rita apologizes to Jerry for walking into his house uninvited, Rupert quickly distances himself from her. Similarly, Rita's behavior is exploitive at Jerry's summer home. She takes liberties that are inappropriate for a guest, snooping around the house and helping herself to whatever takes her fancy. She also slips a small decorative item into her purse, just after she has shamefacedly apologized for coming to Langford's house uninvited.

Although Scorsese treats Jerry fairly, giving us an idea of why he is so hardened and self-protective, the picture of Langford is, overall, an unflattering one. During the kidnapping, when Jerry explains the pressures of his life to Rupert, his defense should arouse sympathy, but it doesn't. What comes across much more vividly is his coldness, his inflated narcissism, and his anger. His bullying of underlings and his disdain speak far more powerfully than his tepid explanation. Jerry's violent behavior, his grabbing the gun and shooting the fake bullets at Masha's belly and then slugging her, is an unsurprising expression of his anger and self-centeredness. In fact, there doesn't seem to be a soft side to Jerry—no humility or humanity—and, ironically, little humor—no ability to laugh at himself or take himself less seriously. In achieving fame and fortune, he seems to have paid a high price, cutting himself off from being vulnerable and enjoying the lighthearted areas of life.

Another aspect of fame that is shown is its loneliness. In the world of outsiders, we see Rupert, someone who has no time for friends, except for friendships of expedience. All his efforts are in the service of his own ambition. In the world of the insiders, those who have achieved fame and fortune, Jerry feels the need to build walls, literally and figuratively, to protect his privacy. We see how angry, cold, and distant fame can make people. Jerry is alone in his luxurious, moneyed world. He has no loved ones around him, no relationships with others. He has just fans, people distant from him, people he must keep at a distance.

The world that is depicted here is a cold, lonely, glass-and-chrome, soundless environment of hushed tones, distance, and alienation. There is much artificiality in the look of the film, the contrivance of the plot, and in the range and behaviors of the characters. There is not much that is warm, human, sane, or normal. There are few morals in this world, and Scorsese adds nasty touches lest we think anyone is immune from self-seeking. Even former high school cheerleader Rita, who seems to be a decent, albeit cynical, person, steals from Jerry Langford; and Rupert, who is supposed to adore Rita, spurns her to ingratiate himself with Jerry, "What does she know? She's a girl who works in a bar."

Unlike formalistic photography, rapid camera movements, and highly stylized visuals seen in Scorsese's earlier work, the camera work in *King of Comedy* is spare, minimalist, classical. The camera is more static; the cinematography doesn't call attention to itself. In the past Scorsese has used the camera lushly, passionately, to create images of feeling and poetry. Here, however, in collaboration with cinematographer Fred Schuler, he uses the camera in a manner as cool and dispassionate as its subject matter. Stylistic decisions reinforce the theme of the movie. In keeping with the film as essay, the style is dryer, more cerebral.

There are a few characteristic techniques: Scorsese again uses slow motion to show Rupert's fixation with Jerry when Rupert observes Jerry exiting through the stage door. We can also see Scorsese's style in the handsomely mounted opening freeze frame, which reveals his sense of art and irony. It isn't entirely clear whether the wall-sized black-and-white photo of an audience, before which Rupert can practice his comedy routine, is real or a representation of another of Rupert's fantasies. This technique is reminiscent of the opening of *Alice*; Rupert's photo audience gets smaller as the camera pulls back revealing a growing rectangular frame of white space. Overall, however, the camera work is a departure from Scorsese's previous films; it has a very different look and feel. Nonetheless, it is characteristic of Scorsese to be experimental with each film, and he later uses some of the elements of the camera style of *King of Comedy* in later works, *After Hours,* and *The Color of Money.*

The world of those who have achieved success and fame is depicted as cheerless and lonely. As Jerry enters his apartment, he walks through a shiny chrome door. The camera tracks the emptiness as he enters his suite. A high-angled long shot reveals a large, quiet, orderly environment decorated in squares and rectangles of furniture in beiges, white, glass, and chrome. The color scheme is reminiscent of the icy neutrals of Woody Allen's *Interiors,* where a character's wearing a red dress is a shocking intrusion into the restrained and repressed atmosphere. Langford's entertainment center features three television screens; his only company is his dog. Langford's country house echoes the same look. Likewise, the offices of the production company of "The Jerry Langford Show" have a chilly, modern look: decorated in white and beige, it is an environment of hushed tones and high technology. The receptionist sits in a rounded white work station that looks as if it could fit into the decorating scheme of the Starship *Enterprise*. No messy human clutter or emotions are permitted to pollute these pristine settings.

Outside the world of Jerry Langford, there is more coldness and artificiality. Manhattan looks overcast and uninviting. Grays and greens are featured mostly in the city shots, and the buildings have a stark, modern, and efficient look. Just across the Hudson River in New Jersey, we find

Rupert's house, located on an ordinary-looking street. However, in Rupert's basement, we find a treasury of the bizarre. Here, Rupert has ballooned his fantasy into lifesized replicas of reality. He has set up his own late-night talk-show television set, equally as artificial looking as Jerry Langford's. It contains life-sized cardboard cutouts of Jerry Langford and Liza Minnelli, "guests" on "The Rupert Pupkin Show."

In addition to the artificiality of Jerry's and Rupert's haunts, other settings go beyond the artificial to elements of the grotesque. During the seduction scene, as Masha waltzes languidly towards her beloved Jerry, the rooms are lit by dozens of candles. A few minutes later, we are treated to a bird's-eye view of their romantic dinner for two: candelabra, fine china and crystal, gourmet food, and a revolver. The object of Masha's affection is literally a prisoner of love, for Jerry is tied to his chair by a mound of thick white tape. (Scorsese here adds a little editing pun as he cuts to Inspector Garrity saying, "Suppose we tape him at seven.") Poor Masha also looks hideous instead of lovely. Her plain features haven't been enhanced; in fact, her application of ruby-red lipstick all over her voluptuous lips has made them look even larger. In close-up, Scorsese captures the moment when she puckers them seductively for Jerry, who is inches away, terrified.

Some of Rupert's fantasies are equally ludicrous. He excitedly dreams of the acclaim and acceptance with which he will be warmly greeted once Jerry has heard his tape. In Rupert's fantasy, Jerry is so consumed with envy that he begs Rupert to tell him how he does it while grabbing him by the neck and shaking him back and forth, so excited and enthusiastic is he over Rupert's talent.

The world of the film is peopled with various shades of weird. In the opening scene, all of the fans wait eagerly outside Langford's stage door. Women in scarves, transfixed, walk through the crowd, yearning for Jerry, worshipping him, their movements looking almost biblical with devotion. There is something pathetic about the oddball types that make up the crowd of fans.

Like the visual style of *King of Comedy,* the use of music is also more restrained and less formalistic than in previous Scorsese films. Typically, Scorsese uses music vividly. Here, however, there seems to be a deliberate holding back, a stark austerity. Much of the background music is comprised of subtle blues piano interludes that sometimes end, introduce, or occasionally underscore various scenes. The accompanying music for "The Jerry Langford Show" and, later, for Rupert's television appearance, is nondescript, typical of that genre of entertainment. Generally, the music does not distract us from the cerebral experience of the film.

On a rare occasion, the music does directly underscore the visuals and contribute to the exploration of the phenomenon of fame. The opening scene is a prime example. When Jerry tries to enter his limousine and discovers Masha, clawing, cloying, and ravenous to embrace him, he quickly exits to the throng of ecstatic fans clamoring to be near him. When Rupert seizes the opportunity to assist Jerry, pushing the fans back to protect him, Scorsese freezes the frame at that moment. Masha's hands are slammed against the window of the limo and cover Rupert's face, which is just outside in front of her. With mild irony, Scorsese underscores the freeze frame with a smooth, blues version of "Come Rain or Come Shine." The fans' unyielding, loony loyalty is expressed in the words of the song, "I'm gonna' love you like nobody's loved you come rain or come shine." The opening music in *King of Comedy* also works more subtly, suggesting the mood of the movie. Ray Charles's singing of "Come Rain or Come Shine" is punctuated by a somber-sounding chorus, subtly casting an ominous mood over the scene to follow.

The same counterpuntal irony occurs again in the scene in which Rupert, fraught with anxious hope, clings to the phone in the Times Square area, waiting for Jerry to return his call. In the background, Frank Sinatra, singing "Fly Me to the Moon" croons mellifluously, "You are all I long for, all I worship and adore. . . . I love you."

There is a meaningful use of doubles in language and behaviors in the film. For instance, Rupert and Masha show they are on the same level in the way they put down one another. Rupert says to Masha that he's embarrassed to be seen with her because he has a real relationship with Jerry, "no fantasy world." Of course he has no real relationship, only a sad false hope, and the relationship with Jerry he play acts at home in his basement is pure fantasy. Later, when Rupert is thrown out of Langford headquarters, his denial is so great — and his fantasy so strong — that he insists he was not thrown out; furthermore, he even claims to have been invited to Jerry's house for the weekend. Masha retaliates telling him, "You're a constant embarrassment."

One of the qualities of the script of *King of Comedy* is that it has captured the banality of talk-show banter. Talk-show formats follow a set routine and have a similar ambience: the opening monologue, sidekick put downs, jokes with the bandleader; the backdrop curtain and guests lined up on the couch; the show business mutual adoration and shallow chit chat before the promotional purpose of the guest appearance. For Rupert this outlet is perfect. Rupert talks and thinks in cliches. When he shows his autograph book to Rita, for instance, every comment about the stars is common show-biz gossip.

Where the script is especially original and inventive is the use of Rupert's fantasies. His dreams of fame are so real for him that he seems to slip into them as a normal course of action. Sometimes he also has trouble distinguishing his fantasies from reality. Whereas his real life is dull and predictable, his fantasies are full of excitement and hope. Furthermore, even though Rupert's fantasies may not be our own, we can understand his wanting to be a success in life. The most unassuming of us has an occasional flight of fantasy whether it be a daydream of a moment of glory or a full-blown just-wait-and-see.

Rupert's first fantasy is triggered as Jerry walks up the steps to his apartment after Rupert has asked if he can audition for Jerry's show. Rupert feels this audition will automatically bestow upon him the success he craves. In the fantasy, Jerry is the supplicant. He begs Rupert to take over his show for six weeks; he wheedles, cajoles, entreats. In real life Rupert has just suffered the indignity of asking a favor of Jerry. In Rupert's fantasy, Jerry must humble himself to ask a favor of Rupert. Not only is this fantasy thrilling, it also serves as a useful coping device for Rupert's having to endure the awkwardness and humiliation of the exchange he has just had with Jerry.

Rupert's second fantasy occurs immediately after he gives his audition tape to Miss Long. Again, there is a parallel to real-life events that have just occurred. Rupert has been polite, but persistent and assertive with Miss Long about knowing the specific time when he can expect to receive feedback on his audition. In his cartoon-like fantasy, Jerry again exchanges places with Rupert. Here, Jerry is pushy, manipulative, and obnoxious. Doggedly trying to find out the secret of Rupert's success, Jerry pleads over and over again, "How do you do it?" So enamored of Rupert's talent is Jerry that he literally becomes slaphappy, shaking and grabbing Rupert while pleading for an answer. Once again, this fantasy is a satisfying walk into the sunset of happy endings. Rupert's talent has been recognized by someone famous, and success in his career will now be assured.

The third fantasy, which occurs just before Miss Long informs Rupert of their appraisal of his tape, is the ultimate success fantasy. In this daydream, Rupert is a guest on Jerry's show, where he is warmly welcomed not only by Jerry but also by a mystery guest — Rupert's former high school principal. However, his principal is now a justice of the peace, and he has been invited on the show to marry Rupert, the king of comedy, to his queen, Rita. For Rupert, who loves all the trappings and corniness of late-night television, this, of course, would be the classiest of recognitions. The best part of the fantasy, however, is when Rupert's principal apologizes to him: "We'd like to apologize and beg forgiveness. In high school, no one thought you'd amount to a hill of beans, but we were wrong. We'd like to apologize and beg forgiveness for all the things we did to you, and we'd like to thank you for the meaning you've given our lives." The grandiosity of the fantasy is silly, but the scene works wonderfully as satire. Accurate and entertaining, it is one of the memorable scenes of the movie, appealing to the Rupert in all of us.

Overall, *King of Comedy* is a dark, somber work with snatches of comedy which come more from the New York City–type characters than from Rupert, an aspiring comedian, or from the genre suggested by the title. Although the title *King of Comedy* suggests that it is a comedy, the film is not especially funny. It has snatches of humor, less so than other Scorsese films, but little comes from Rupert, except perhaps the running joke on his name which gets translated as Pumpkin, Bopkin, and several other variations. More frequently the sources of humor are darker. Masha's neuroticism during the kidnapping and the absurdities of her romantic dinner with Jerry are examples of the black humor of the film. Masha flings a wine glass to the floor, demonstrating the extent to which she is willing to go in her efforts to please Jerry. She ruminates happily, "I just want to put on some Shirelle's. I want to be black. Wouldn't that be insane? Know who I wish I was tonight? I wish I was Tina Turner. Just dance into the room. Ooo-oooh!"

The ironies of the film also contribute comic elements, although their source is cynical and dark. Flanked by security guards, writer Clarence McCabe explains to them, straining to be reasonable, patient, "I told you. I wrote a book. It's called, *The Vanishing Siberian Tiger*. I spent two years in Russia and two years in China researching that book." Garrity responds suspiciously, "Two years in Russia. Two years in China." To which McCabe retorts in exasperation, "Right. Does that make me a Communist now too?"

Many times, however, the humor comes simply from the city types that populate the movie. Scorsese captures the wit and humor of New Yorkers. The T.V. director (played by Scorsese), Inspector Garrity, the cameraman, and Rita all contribute funny lines to the film. Excited over having just met Jerry, Rupert tempts Rita, "Guess who I was just with?" She answers archly, "Your shrink?" Poor Rupert is teased again when he enters the Langford studio. No doubt, the cameraman found himself unable to resist.

Rupert:	Hello. I'm the King.
Cameraman:	The what?
Rupert:	The King.
Cameraman:	Oh. What can I do for your highness?
Rupert:	Really, I'm the King.
Cameraman:	Oh yes sir. Your dressing room is backstage. Your throne is right in there also. You'll recognize the door. There's a half-moon. A couple of stars.

The casting of minor characters in this film is memorable. Characters like the receptionist at Langford headquarters, Inspector Garrity, and the security guard linger in one's memory long after seeing the film. Their performances come off as unstudied and unplanned. Scorsese seems to have selected them with care for innate characteristics that make them right for the film. As a result, they often emerge as full characters, much more than just actors giving expression to lines written on a page of script.

Many factors about Garrity's performance, for example, make him interesting, and not just as a stereotypical Irish cop. As he often does, Scorsese makes instinctive and original choices in casting, often selecting actors with personality or style, though not in the usual Hollywood sense. He then motivates the actors to show what he saw in them, capturing them at precise moments when they show that characteristic style best. A good example is the little ethnic details in the character of Garrity—his rugged Irish mug, his huskiness, his sure movements, his speech, e.g., his warning to Rupert, "You better not try to go anywhere or I'll break your friggin' ankles." His tough, in-control style, and even his reassurance to Rita as they watch Rupert on television make Garrity spring to life. In fact, he is a far more interesting and full character than the protagonists of many average feature films.

The receptionist is another character who is especially well cast. Competent, pleasant-looking, and showing no signs of imagination or artistic interest, she is precisely the person to be the receptionist at a famous person's office. The security guard, another small part, was also ideally cast. Practiced at handling people, the guard acts the part minimally and convincingly. He is practical with the fans: "All right. Give me the books. Give me the books" and polite at the door, "I'm sorry sir. Your name is not listed. Only authorized personnel are allowed to enter." He was actually played by someone who is a security guard in real life.

Other parts were also played by a mixture of veteran actors and people who live their movie roles in real life, like Fred De Cordova, producer of "The Tonight Show," who played Bert Thomas, producer of "The Jerry Langford Show." The entertainment executives are another example of inspired casting as was Shelley Hack as Miss Long, whose grace, charm, self-confidence, and efficient, capable style make her the perfect choice for Langford and Thomas's assistant.

Jerry Lewis does a splendid job personifying a Johnny Carson type. He contributes important elements to the unsympathetic character of Langford. A brilliant casting coup, Lewis provides a very fine and brave performance.

Sandra Bernhard, known primarily as a stand-up comic, also gives life to the character of Masha, a rich but lonely and plain-looking young woman. She is strident and passionate in her movements, funny in her neuroticism, and amusing to watch in her spontaneous and studied expressions of love for Jerry.

Robert De Niro and Shelley Hack. There is an inherent lack of dignity in yearning for recognition and having to implore someone to listen and take you seriously. People in authority have great power over those who have none. So much rides on their openness, judgment, and mercy. Rupert personifies the humiliation and degradation people must often endure to be heard, to be given a chance. In this scene, Jerry Langford's assistant, Miss Long, mildly but skillfully rejects Rupert, one of the many metaphorical doors that slam in his face in this film (*King of Comedy*, 1982).

Robert De Niro, in yet another completely different role in collaboration with Scorsese, here gives a notably more restrained and minimalist performance. He keeps Pupkin's defenses up at all times; it is not as easy to connect emotionally with Rupert as it is with other characters he has played. As annoying and offbeat as they often are, his other characters have moments when they more clearly reveal their vulnerabilities. Rupert's guard comes down occasionally in his enthusiasm and apparent naivete and in his role as victim when he is put down and teased. Overall, however, whatever motivates Rupert is well hidden.

King of Comedy did not fare well at the box office. Its dispassionate, essay style and striking contrast to previous Scorsese works generally puzzled audiences. Later, critics Gene Siskel and Roger Ebert would recommend *King of Comedy* as an underrated film that probably goes unnoticed on video store shelves. They admitted that they did not fully understand or appreciate *King of Comedy* when it was first released, how-ever.

Scorsese's next film was to be *The Last Temptation of Christ* but cost and timing were to prevent him from starting work on this film for some time. From among several scripts, Scorsese chose *After Hours* as his next film.

After Hours

Now she's the one in the Mr. Softie truck who's trying to kill me. They're all trying to kill me. I mean . . . I just wanted to leave my apartment, maybe meet a nice girl, and now I've got to die for it?—Paul Hackett, word processor in *After Hours*

After Hours is a low-budget independent film. Scorsese decided to direct it after the filming of *The Last Temptation of Christ* fell through four weeks before production was to begin. He had very much wanted to make *Last Temptation*. To channel his disappointment, he decided to make another film. His lawyer at the time, Jay Julien (the lawyer in *King of Comedy* who's suing everybody), offered him the script of *After Hours*. The script had been written by Joe Minion, a student at Columbia University. Scorsese liked almost everything about it.

After Hours chronicles the adventures of Paul Hackett (Griffin Dunne), a young computer operator, who goes to Soho late one night for a date with Marcy (Rosanna Arquette), a pretty young woman he met earlier that evening in a coffee shop. However, this harmless, hopeful decision results in a string of unusual and frightening experiences. Nearly everything that could possibly go wrong does. The evening begins inauspiciously with Paul's losing his money, a twenty dollar bill, which flies out the window as the cab careens downtown as though it were in a movie car chase. Paul next finds himself a stranger in a strange land as he meets a collection of oddball types who turn out to be not only quirky but also dangerous. By the end of the night, he is literally running for his life. A vigilante group has taken to the streets, searching every building for him. They are out to kill him because they think he is a local burglar who has outraged the neighborhood by committing multiple burglaries in the area. Paul escapes, literally, through the vehicle of a lucky coincidence. The real burglars steal Paul, who has been disguised as a paper-mache work of art (in the style of sculptor George Segal), place him in the back of their van, and drive him uptown where he falls out of the truck in front of his office.

After Hours is a notable departure from Scorsese's previous work.

Griffin Dunne and Rosanna Arquette. Appearances can be deceiving. In this scene, Marcy strikes up a conversation with Paul in a midtown restaurant. She is very attractive and appealing. She flirts with him artfully, establishing a connection by flattering him with a comment on the book he is reading, *Tropic of Cancer.* **Dreamy, feminine, she piques his interest and invites him to call her for a date. Charmed by her, he does call but later finds that she is very disturbed.**

First of all, there is little to suggest that it is a personal film. In a PBS documentary, Scorsese commented passionately about film as a means of expression: "Films are not film to me. They're life. That's the idea. . . . Especially . . . a film that reaches a certain kind of truth. You learn. [It's] like reading a certain philosophy or trying to practice a certain philosophy."

In the most interesting of Scorsese's movies, a viewer can easily discern the truth of that quotation. In all of the films discussed so far — *Mean Streets; Alice Doesn't Live Here Anymore; Taxi Driver; New York, New York; Raging Bull; King of Comedy* — Scorsese has clearly made films that attempt to convey a kind of truth. Accuracy, depth, compassion, risk-taking are all characteristics of Scorsese's films up to this point. *After Hours* doesn't fit this category of film. It lacks the depth and richness of Scorsese's previous work.

The photography takes us into a New York with elements of gothic. The camera work, by cinematographer Michael Ballhaus, is captivating and suspenseful, capturing New York at 2:00 A.M. with steamy, spooky, deserted streets. Combining elements of suspense and horror, *After Hours* is a black comedy with neurotic and sometimes sick humor. Interestingly, this brand of humor has a definite audience, though viewers who delight in *After Hours* are not necessarily those who usually appreciate Scorsese's films. *After Hours* is basically a one-idea movie. Nevertheless, it is well-done and entertaining.

The characters are part of the fun. A hallmark of Scorsese's films is that they focus on an outsider as the protagonist, a person hard to like and someone most directors wouldn't make a movie about. With a coy irony and jokey inversion, Scorsese has carried this idea to an extreme. Rather than focus on an outsider struggling to fit in, here the joke is that mainstream likeable Paul is an insider struggling to fit in surrounded by outsiders.

Paul is a yuppyish sort of character. He has a good job, nice clothing, and a pleasantly appointed apartment. He is easygoing and polite. His main problem is loneliness, an emptiness in his life which comes across as a vague feeling of discontent. Bored with the dull conventionality of his own life, Paul feels ordinary and is in awe of the highly individualistic styles of the arty types in Soho.

Typically middle-class, Paul is open to getting to know diverse people and to having new experiences. This quality allows him, against his better judgment, to make a date in the middle of the night to meet Marcy. Open-minded, eager to please, and lacking street smarts, Paul is often slow to respond to his feelings, which often warn him about people, places, and circumstances.

There are several signs that Paul should rethink his decision to go down to Soho, but he misses them. When he calls Marcy, she tells him that she's had a terrible argument. She is also noticeably upset and vulnerable. Assuming a basic healthiness and normalcy, he sympathizes and glosses over the situation. When Marcy tells Paul he should come downtown to see her, he hesitates because of the late hour; nonetheless, he agrees. Although Marcy is staying with her friend Kiki Bridges (Linda Fiorentino), she tells Paul that Franklin will be on the nameplate and that Bridges is crossed out. This detail piques Paul's curiosity, but he doesn't ask about it.

On the way downtown, the hair-raising taxi ride is a flag-waving premonition. When Paul arrives, Marcy, curiously, is out. She's picking up a prescription at an all-night drugstore. It turns out to be an ointment for burns, a subject that makes Paul queasy. Still, he isn't discouraged.

In fact, instead of heeding the odd signals of this adventure, Paul embraces his new experience. Kiki is tired and sore from dipping paper-mache, so she asks Paul to help. He is delighted. Feeling like a real Soho artist, he offers her a massage, though making such an offer to a perfect stranger is probably out of character for him.

Paul meets many unusual people as his adventure in Soho unfolds. Charming, fragile, and vulnerable, Marcy is attractive to Paul, and he looks forward to their late-night date. Later, however, Paul feels uneasy with Marcy for several reasons: her mysterious burn ointment prescription and books about burn patients; her mood swings; and her disjointed, peculiar conversations. At one point she mentions her husband in Turkey, whom she only knew for three days and to whom she writes every day. Naturally she doesn't like to talk about it.

Marcy is staying with Kiki, a sculptress. Kiki, another attractive woman, wearily applies paper-mache strips to her sculpture. Outfitted in a black bra and jean skirt, she turns out to be kinky in several ways. First, her cool, abrupt style is disconcerting. She doesn't even speak to Paul when he enters the loft. Her line of conversation is also unusual. When Paul compliments her as having a great body, she answers, "Yeah, I know. Not a lot of scars." She backs up her statement adding, "Some women are full of them. Not me." Paul, mildly startled, merely comments, "I'd never have thought of that." Later, Paul goes back to the loft to tell Kiki her sculpture and television have been stolen. When he rings, he is horrified to find that Kiki has been bound and gagged. He quickly works to untie the knots, but when he does, she just laughs. Paul might then understand Kiki's previous comment for she and her boyfriend Horst like engaging in sado-masochistic rituals.

When Paul seeks shelter in a local bar, he meets the cocktail waitress Julie (Terri Garr), Miss Beehive 1965, who loves the 1960s and who surrounds herself with memorabilia of that decade. Charming and likeable, she invites Paul into her apartment and tries to befriend him by offering to listen to his problems. However, Julie's personality is not as easygoing as it seems. Apparently, beneath her sunny exterior she is very sensitive and emotional. When she assumes Paul has taken a condescending tone about her daytime xeroxing job, she becomes deeply offended and defensive, radically shifting moods. When Paul brushes aside Julie's present, a bagel-and-cream-cheese paperweight, she vows that he'll be sorry. Feeling spurned, she later hangs posters with Paul's picture as the Soho burglar.

Yet another dangerous female is Linda (Catherine O'Hara), the tough cookie who drives a Mr. Softie truck. Again, Linda seems normal. She shows distress at having injured Paul with a taxi cab door, and she offers to dress his wound. Once up in her apartment, Linda too shows her eccentricities. She prevents Paul from making the phone call he's asked permission to make by calling out various numbers while he dials, a prank she finds so hysterically funny that she repeats it. Then she aggressively insists that Paul remove his shirt so she can dress his wound. She reads from a bit of newspaper stuck to Paul's arm that a Soho vigilante group pummelled a man to death the previous night because they suspected he was a burglar. She dramatizes as she reads, obviously relishing the horror of the incident.

Linda Fiorentino and Griffin Dunne. *After Hours* **takes place in Soho where many New York artists live. There, eccentricity is the norm. Bored with the dull conven tionality of his life, word processor Paul Hackett is at first fascinated by the bo- hemian types he meets in Soho. Casting off his middle-class sense of propriety, Paul offers to massage sculptress Kiki, who's comically at ease being semi-nude in front of a stranger. Paul later discovers that one of Kiki's oddities is her penchant for sado-masochistic rituals (**After Hours**, 1985).**

Then she offers to remove the paper by burning it off, at which point Paul tells her he's had enough, and he's going to walk home. She then shifts back to kindness, offering to give him a lift in her Mr. Softie truck. Once outside, however, she spots one of Julie's posters, tells Paul, "You're dead, pal," and blows a whistle alerting the vigilantes to his whereabouts.

The last woman Paul meets in Soho is June, also an artist, but so ap- parently sane and normal that, surrounded by all of the eccentric per- sonalities in Soho, no one usually notices her. Paul is physically, mentally, and emotionally spent by the time he meets June. With no pretensions or artifice, he humbly explains his dire straits and appeals to her for help: "I wondered would you care to join me for a drink . . . just talking. I'm having a really, really bad night and I can't seem to find anyone who would just

Griffin Dunne and Terri Garr. *After Hours* features a cast of oddball characters. One of them is Julie, a cocktail waitress who hates her job and who apparently is in a mental time warp. The movie takes place in 1985, but for Julie it is still 1965. She listens to Judy Collins's "Chelsea Morning" and to the Monkees. She wears mod fashions, white go-go boots and mini-length dresses. She sports a beehive hairdo and maintains a backup supply of a dozen cans of Aqua Net hairspray. Julie is warm and kind, but she is also neurotic and overly sensitive. In this scene, she suspects that Paul has taken lightly her kindness and hospitality. She feels used. Later her method of seeking revenge has serious and potentially deadly consequences (*After Hours*, 1985).

sit with me without yelling at me or something. I obviously wouldn't approach you in this state were it not so unusually intrigued. Well there. I've bared my soul to you."

Feminine and ladylike, June listens to Paul and asks nothing of him. They enjoy a quiet, calm dance together. June not only seems to be a gentle and kind person, but she proves actually to possess those qualities. She offers to help Paul, and she does with no thought to her own self-interest.

Naive, Paul at first is attracted to the peculiar types of Soho. He seems to be enamored of the mystique of these people on the fringes of society. They seem hip, interesting. Later, Paul discovers firsthand that, in reality, they are merely self-absorbed. He also finds that, instead of being deep, they simply lack basic social skills. Moreover, he realizes that their mystique, their self-possession, stems more often from narcissism than from artistic vision.

The storyline of *After Hours* is filled with inter-related plots. Following the convention of the well-made play, the tightly crafted script makes use of threads of the plot that are later picked up and woven into the fabric of the storyline. Ironies and coincidences abound. Motifs such as keys, burns, Paul's inadvertently offending a succession of people, seemingly kind and friendly people turning crazy or dangerous, unexpected incidents causing delays, twenty dollar bills, burglaries, bagel-and-cream-cheese paperweights, and papier-mâché life-sized sculptures all repeat and figure prominently in the script.

For example, Paul loses his only money on his way down to Soho. Losing money by having it fly out the window of a cab as it careens down the street is funny and odd to begin with, but Paul's having no cab fare not only infuriates the cab driver, but also keeps Paul stuck in Soho. Coincidentally, the subway fares have gone up at midnight, and when Paul tries to take the train, he finds he has only ninety-seven cents when he needs a dollar fifty. Later on, Paul removes a twenty dollar bill stuck to Kiki's papier-mâché sculpture to use for cab fare so he can finally go back uptown. By incredible coincidence, however, he gets the same cab driver. Full of self-righteous revenge, the cabbie grabs the twenty from Paul's hand and retorts, "See how you like it!" as he speeds away.

Gene Siskel has called *After Hours* one of the most uncomfortable comedies he's ever watched. On a first viewing, the movie is both frightening and funny. On a second, one can relax and enjoy the film's humor. *After Hours* is easier to like than other Scorsese films, perhaps because many enjoy the film's offbeat black humor, which is neurotic, urban, and contemporary. Much of it stems from Paul's reactions to people, places, and things he encounters. He is an everyman of sorts. Odd is normal here, and we identify with Paul as he makes his way through the labyrinth of after hours in Soho.

At least initially, Paul consistently responds politely, calmly, and in an understated manner to the surprising people and events he encounters. When Marcy tells Paul about the paperweights her friend Kiki Bridges is selling, he says mildly, "Bagel-and-cream-cheese paperweights. Really?" As the cab driver zooms downtown, Paul comments, "No hurry!" as he grasps a strap to steady himself as he slides across the back street. As he watches Tom (John Hurt), the bartender, pound and kick the cash register to open it to get the subway fare, Paul suggests, "Do you have a key for that?"

Much of the humor comes also from the characters' eccentricities. One of Marcy's quirky qualities is that her conversations are marked by sudden reversals and tone shifts. She tells Paul the gruesome story of a six-hour rape she once endured. But a moment later she admits, "Actually I slept through most of it." Julie's sixties obsession provides comic relief from her mini skirts and go-go boots to her dozen cans of Aqua Net hairspray and her record collection. To set the atmosphere, she begins by playing a perky Monkees record for Paul. However, when she finds that Paul is depressed, a gracious hostess, she plays "Chelsea Morning," a more reflective, sensitive selection. Pepy, the burglar, reveals a quirky irony in his plight when he says, "The first thing I ever bought! Someone rips it off." One of the funniest moments of character humor occurs when Paul, exasperated and worn out, runs down the block, kneels down in the middle of the street, looks up to the sky, and says, "What do you want from me? I'm just a word processor for Christ's sake!"

After Hours opens with a bravura camera movement. As though on a roller skate, a quickly moving camera tracks down the aisle of a busy office and halts at its target: Paul Hackett, word processor. Camera work that calls attention to itself is the characteristic style of this film: well-designed mise-en-scènes; the use of the moving camera, varied camera angles, and many close-ups; Hitchcock-style editing; and evocative lighting and sets.

A captivating, gothic-looking shot occurs when a low-angled camera follows Paul and Marcy as they walk along a foggy, rain-slicked street to a late-night diner for coffee. Other atmospheric shots also occur outdoors on the wet, deserted Soho streets. Unable to take the subway uptown, Paul runs through the pouring rain, a couple of blocks later finding the warm, inviting red glow of a bar's neon lights. When Paul enters the bar, the camera tracks around it, encircling all of the action to be seen from an elegant couple dancing to the bartender and the cocktail waitress in miniskirt and beehive hairdo. (This same camera movement was later used in *Dirty Dancing* when Baby observes the resort staff's late-night dancing. This film also paid homage to Scorsese by opening with the Ronette's "Be My Baby," the opening song of *Mean Streets*.)

As with the above tracking shot, a number of the setups are from Paul's point of view, giving us a sense of his experience. The sideways shot capturing the water cascading over Paul's face as he washes up, trying to refresh himself, trying to stay awake, reminds us of the physical toll this night is taking on Paul. Close-ups also figure prominently in this movie. Small important details — clocks, keys, death-mask faces — are magnified through close-ups.

Hitchcock used associational montage to reveal character and plot and to involve the viewer in the film (Giannetti 301), and Scorsese uses this same technique, especially for the thriller aspects of *After Hours*. For example, trying to leave Julie's apartment, Paul reassures her that he *will* call. One of the mousetraps around Julie's canopy bed snaps shut, and a close-up shows the caught animal. The cutting between these two shots shows why Paul is a jangle of nerves. We aren't surprised when moments later, he barks at Julie, knocking out of her hand the bagel-and-cream-cheese paperweight she offers him as a gift. Scorsese admits that Hitchcock was an influence in the camera style of *After Hours*:

> *After Hours* is to some extent a parody of Hitchcock's style. Over the years his films have become more emotionally meaningful for me. By the time I realized he was moving the camera, it was over and I had felt the effect of the movement emotionally and intellectually. So if you take the scene in *After Hours* when Paul is running with the invitation in his hand—there's a shot of a hand with the ground below—basically this refers back to the moment in *Marnie* where she's holding the gun and going to shoot the horse. When I first saw *Marnie*, that shot remained in my mind and I kept going back to watch the whole two hours just to see it again. I loved the feeling of it. . . . [Thompson and Christie 1989, 101]

The classical music which underscores the opening of *After Hours* is bold, forceful, and connotative of the kind of arty films that are targeted to appeal to yuppies. (When this music is resumed at the close of the film, there is a relief in hearing it as order is restored, and we are reassured by this familiar, traditional sound.) The next sound we hear is office noise, after which we hear a string classical piece which resonates the tone of Paul's life. It is a sad, plaintive piece which complements the empty, quiet, lonely shots of Paul in his apartment. Although his surroundings are well-appointed and tasteful, decorated in a contemporary look of beiges and white, they don't seem to cheer or comfort Paul, who seems discontented as he restlessly switches channels on his cable box. He is knocked out of his listlessness by the crazy cab ride with its blaring, lively Latin music which increases in tempo and volume as the ride progresses.

The score which accompanies much of the action in *After Hours* helps set the mood of the film. Suspenseful and mysterious-sounding, bleeps dash up and down the scale, sounding both curious and cautious. The modern synthesizer sound is also appropriate for a neighborhood at the vanguard of artistic taste. The oldies that are played in the bar, however, have an inviting familiarity and add to the warm atmosphere of the bar, which offers Tom a dry, safe place, at least for a while. The final song played in the Berlin Club, "Is That All There Is?" is appropriate not only because it picks up the burn motif of the movie, but also because of its wry, questioning message.

The acting style in *After Hours* is also a departure from other Scorsese films. The other movies (except *King of Comedy*, which is not an in-depth character study like the others) feature highly improvisational acting, resembling the method acting in a Kazan or Cassavetes film. The aim is for an authenticity and truth not usually found in the typical feature film. With comedy, this acting technique comes across differently. Probably Scorsese worked the way he usually does with actors, encouraging their improvisation and including various suggestions in the final version.

Griffin Dunne's performance as Paul Hackett is low-keyed and natural as he responds to all of the odd people and events of the evening. The wistful look on his face as he glances around the office while one of his computer trainees talks of artistic ambitions is one memorable example. Rosanna Arquette brings a soft, waiflike vulnerability and a romantic femininity to her role as Marcy. Terri Garr's modern mix of warmth, humor, and a touch of neuroticism make her an appealing character. Her sixties obsession, with all of its paraphernalia, also adds to the fun. Linda Fiorentino is strikingly attractive as Kiki, and she adds a likeable charm to her oddball character. Catherine O'Hara is frightening as the mercurial ice cream vendor, who starts off as kind, but who also has pronounced streaks of macabre and toughness. John Hurt gives a powerful, full performance in the rather small part of Tom, the kindly, passionate bartender. Full of feeling, Hurt is a convincing and memorable presence in each scene in which he appears.

After Hours was a modest commercial success, and it helped revive Scorsese's career. Scorsese also was awarded the best director award for this film at the Cannes Film Festival in Europe, where his work has been consistently well received. Scorsese next directed a segment in the horror genre for Steven Spielberg's television series *Amazing Stories*. He then took an acting part in Bertrand Tavernier's *Round Midnight*. Shortly after completion of the filming of *After Hours*, however, Paul Newman called Scorsese to ask him if he would be interested in making a sequel to *The Hustler*. Scorsese was interested, and his next film would be that sequel, later titled *The Color of Money*.

The Color of Money

Eddie: "There used to be 35 balls down there. . . . This isn't pool. This is like handball or cribbage. Straight pool you had to be a real surgeon. It was all finesse. Now everything is nine ball because it's fast. Good for T.V. Good for a lot of break shots. Oh well. What the hell. Checkers sells more than chess."

Vincent: "But the thing is even if it's just for bangers, everybody's doing it. Everybody's doing it. . . . Lotta guys doing it, but only one guy can be the best."

The Color of Money isn't a sequel in the usual sense. A viewer doesn't have to have seen *The Hustler* or have any knowledge of it to understand this related movie. Rather *The Color of Money* tells another story about the main character of *The Hustler*, Fast Eddie Felson, twenty-five years later.

Similar to *After Hours*, *The Color of Money* is a minor work. It is also a fine movie and enjoyable to watch. Vincent Canby called it a Cadillac among the fall movies of 1986. It is a very polished film and made with the same directorial confidence as *After Hours*. It has excellent craftsmanship—superb photography, well-written dialogue, a vivid soundtrack, inspired casting, and fine performances. It is also a mainstream movie, made for Disney and produced with the intent of appealing to a mass audience. Although not a box office smash, it was a commercial success, and it earned Paul Newman a well-deserved and long overdue Academy Award for best actor. *The Color of Money* is a minor work, however, because it lacks the complexity and depth of Scorsese's mature films. Also like *After Hours*, *The Color of Money* was not a personal film for Scorsese like his earlier movies. It also doesn't take the artistic risks that so often characterize a Scorsese film.

The Color of Money picks up on Eddie Felson (Paul Newman) in 1986, twenty-five years after he retired from pool playing. Eddie has become a prosperous liquor salesman. As the story opens, Eddie is talking to his girlfriend, Jazelle (Helen Shaver), a bartender, about stocking an excellent but cheap imitation of top-shelf whiskey. Although Eddie no longer plays pool, he occasionally backs other players with his money. One such player, Julian, interrupts Eddie's conversation to ask for money to pay Vincent (Tom Cruise), a flaky kid who cares more about the game than the money. A short while later, Vincent's powerhouse break shot arouses Eddie's interest.

Eddie invites Vincent and his girlfriend Carmen (Mary Elizabeth Mastrantonio) to dinner where he interests her in the possibility of making real money with Vincent's pool playing. Within a couple of days, the three of them go on the road to make money by pool hustling for six weeks before a tournament in Atlantic City. Loving to play and thriving on being the best, Vincent hates losing on purpose, even though it means winning in the long run. Eddie teaches him through the school of hard knocks, letting Vincent experience the consequences of his actions. By the end of the movie, Vincent, now a consummate hustler, outshines his teacher.

Along the way though, Eddie decides he wants to play pool again. He gives himself a second chance at doing something he loves. He gets glasses, starts swimming, and practices long hours to sharpen his game. When he goes to Atlantic City, he is is fine form. He wins several matches and is scheduled to play Vincent in the quarterly finals. However, Vincent, now an even better hustler than his teacher, throws their match without Eddie's even knowing it. At the end of the film, Eddie has convinced Vincent to play him and to give him his best game. The story ends optimistically, with Eddie realizing he may lose, but excited enough at playing again that he looks forward to still other matches, even if he doesn't win this time.

The characters in *The Color of Money* don't look, act, or communicate the way middle-class people do. Rather, this movie is about people who acquire and wield power in a different way. It's about bookies and pool players, people like Charlie and Michael in *Mean Streets*. Its characters are all defenses, practiced at manipulating through stony looks and tough talk. They are also very instinctive, intuitive, and acquisitive. As Eddie puts it, "The guy with the most is the best." But pool excellence, he says, is not about excellent pool. All the greats were "students of human moves."

One of *The Color of Money*'s interesting focal points is how it renders this segment of society. The dialogue, costumes, atmosphere, and characters have all been detailed vividly and accurately. Again, Scorsese shows us a segment of society that is outside the mainstream. The protagonists are people many viewers ordinarily would not get to know. These characters are presented fairly, fully, and nonjudgmentally.

Interestingly, the same sort of rendition was achieved in director Robert Wise's 1961 version of *The Hustler*, but the depiction of that era is a remarkable contrast to the updated version. The smoky black and white *Hustler* suggested a more tawdry atmosphere peopled by an older, more

Left to right: **Paul Newman, Tom Cruise, and Mary Elizabeth Mastrantonio. Although *The Color of Money* was a sequel to a well-known film, *The Hustler*, and although it featured two big stars, Paul Newman and Tom Cruise, it was first turned down by Fox studios before being picked up by Touchstone, the adult division of Disney Studios. Scorsese has always been well regarded by critics, but his movies, in general, are not mainstream. Arty and individualistic, his films have sometimes been profitable, but rarely box office hits (exceptions are *Taxi Driver, The Color of Money*, and *GoodFellas*). Movies are big business, and to continue to work, a director often must hustle to get a film made (*The Color of Money*, 1986).**

hardened crowd and characterized by rigid rules and rituals and heavily reflective of the more repressive society of that period. Overall, the tone is more downbeat in the earlier movie. *The Color of Money* is less bitter. It has more vitality, passion, and holds out more hope and possibilities for success.

The story centers on Eddie, Vincent, and Vincent's girlfriend, Carmen. Handsome, mature, and charming, Eddie is an attractive character. With a lifetime of experience behind him, he is smooth and skillful at getting what he wants. In spite of his machinations, it is hard not to like him because we also see his integrity, honesty, and humility.

Vincent, by contrast, is young, artless, and inexperienced. He's softer and more middle class than his tough, street-smart girlfriend. Vincent is a

Paul Newman (*left*) and Tom Cruise. The young people of each generation often differ radically. The young people of the fifties and early sixties, young Eddie Felson's generation, were expected to mature quickly and to assume adult roles in their late teens and early twenties. They dressed more formally and at least acted the part of adults. Young Eddie Felson was callow but a different type of hot shot than Vincent. In *The Hustler*, young Eddie was hapless and inexperienced, up against a hardened older generation with a streak of cruelty. Young Vincent, by contrast, is a part of the generation raised in the age of Rambo, Nintendo, video games, and shopping malls. Soft and immature, Vincent is a part of a more prosperous, suburban generation that has a long period of adolescence, often not marrying or taking on adult responsibilities until their late twenties or older (*The Color of Money*, 1986).

1980s kid, a product of the suburbs, brought up in the age of Rambo movies, video games, and shopping malls. Full of boyish vitality, he is what Eddie calls "an original" and "an incredible flake." Imagining himself a Ninja warrior, Vincent struts around the table between shots, spinning his cue stick like a martial artist. And just as Eddie sensed, Vincent attracts the unwanted attention of the other pool players, who are "killing each other to get at him."

Carmen is a commanding third main character. In Scorsese's films, there is always at least one important female. Typically, she is a strong character, interesting and intelligent. Carmen is pretty, bright, and hardened. She has gone through life using her good looks and sex appeal as the source of her power. Cunning and committed to her own and Vincent's self-interest, she cannily uses her intelligence to steer Vincent to success.

Beyond pool, some of the areas of interest in *The Color of Money* are the transformations that occur in the characters and its focus on the contrast between the younger and older generations in contemporary society.

During the course of the film, Vincent loses his innocence and Eddie regains his. At the beginning of the film, Vincent is a naive kid who works at a toy store, Child World. Money isn't a concern for him. A hot shot pool player, he simply loves to play. Under Eddie's tutelage, Vincent grows up, becomes more tough-minded, and learns how to showcase his talent for big profits. At the beginning of the film, Eddie is a practiced businessman. Reaping profits from liquor sales is easy for him. "It's tired," he explains to Vincent.

During the course of the film, Eddie changes from a man of talk to a man of action. He begins with the jaded viewpoint that Vincent is crazy to forgo the chance to win money just to play a game of pool. With a hustler's gift of gab, he speaks with assurance. In a surprising turn of events, however, Eddie changes roles. He trades his role of teacher for that of student. He rediscovers the joy of the game, of playing excellent pool for the thrill of competition, for the chance to be the best.

In recent years, the trend has been that youth is worshipped. Society values those who are young, strong, and physically at their peak. By contrast, the position of older people often lacks dignity. Physically, they have declined. At a certain point, older people are also devalued economically.

An interesting aspect of *The Color of Money* is that it highlights the advantages of maturity. Whereas youth is characterized in this film by passion, exuberance, and inexperience, maturity is associated with intimacy, depth of experience, and comfort. One of the interesting side stories of *The Color of Money* is Eddie's private life and his relationship with Jazelle. They share a closeness that is characterized by gentleness, discretion, and elegance.

There is an irony in Vincent and Carmen's youthful arrogance at the start of the film. Scorsese highlights the lack of dignity in being older when Eddie talks to Vincent about the days when he was playing pool. It is inherently undignified for Eddie to have to prove that he knows all he does. Although older people have a lifetime of experience behind them, society doesn't confer status upon them. In *The Color of Money*, Eddie and Jazelle make this time of life look attractive, a time of distinct advantages, something to look forward to. The vitality with which Eddie pursues playing pool once again is also an appealing development of this theme.

Stylistically, *The Color of Money* is splendid. It is a polished film with an elegant look. Scorsese obviously put much thought and creativity into this effort. In fact, rather than invest great personal energy into character or theme, as he did in his more personal movies, Scorsese seems to have focused his creativity on stylistic elements in the making of this film. In a documentary on Scorsese made for PBS, he commented on how enjoyable it was to make *The Color of Money*.

> It was a lot of fun working with Paul Newman, Tom Cruise, and Mary Elizabeth [Mastrantonio], and all that and also Helen Shaver. We had a great time. And especially the camera. We had a great time with the camera moves. And the tracking shots and the cutting. The look. That kind of elegant look we were trying to get with the sliding camera.

The screenplay was written by Richard Price, a novelist whose works have often been compared to Scorsese's films. However, the script was also a collaborative effort. It was later revised and rewritten according to suggestions that emerged through a series of meetings with Scorsese and Paul Newman, a distinguished film director in his own right.

The screenplay captures the language of fast-lane types, full of allusions to sex and money, and bloated with ego. Eddie hooks Carmen's interest at the bar when he offers to play Vincent for five hundred dollars instead of twenty dollars per game. Practiced at hustling, he one-ups her in a friendly way at her own game. Later, in a roadside restaurant, Carmen replies to Eddie's explanation about why he no longer plays pool, "If you can't cut the mustard, you can still lick the jar." Eddie tells her no one's ever asked for a refund, to which she tartly responds, "Not yet." Driving in his plush Cadillac with Vincent and Carmen a captive audience, Eddie teaches them, "It ain't about pool; it ain't about sex; it ain't about love. It's about money. The man who has the most is best." Carmen then taunts Eddie, "Are *you* the best liquor salesman?" Full of swagger, Eddie boasts, "You bet."

The script also captures the associative quality of the thinking and style of speech of these types of characters. When Eddie asks Carmen what Vincent sees in her, Carmen replies obliquely, "Vincent's the best." She then coyly relates the story of how they met at the police station, where Carmen and her old boyfriend had just been arrested for breaking into Vincent's parents' house. She also proudly comments on her locket, garnered from the spoils of the burglary, "Vincent says his mother has one just like it." Elliptical, intuitive, and unschooled, the language of the screenplay accurately captures the speech of the types that frequent pool halls and bars.

Furthermore, care was obviously taken in creating and writing the dialogue for each individual character. A wide array of interesting, colorful types are drawn in the film. Again, Scorsese enjoys focusing on characters who usually aren't featured in movies, at least not with this level of vividness, individuality, and realism. This script provides finely drawn characters, each with an individual voice. It also provides a much more accurate representation of the speech of such characters than many movie scripts.

The photography of *The Color of Money* is flashy and stylish. In contrast to the static, low-keyed camera style of *The King of Comedy*, the photography of *The Color of Money* is noticeable and lively, commenting freely and colorfully on the action. There is the sense, overall, that Scorsese simply had fun with the camera in making this movie. He captures the exciting life of the characters with quick and showy camera work. For example, he photographs the grill of Eddie's Cadillac from a low angle as it roars down the highway, showing Eddie's puffed-up ego as he brags to Carmen that he's the best liquor salesman. The montage sequence shows the fun Eddie, Vince, and Carmen are having while hustling in poolrooms on the road: Vince, wearing glasses and looking inept and naive, then pocketing his winnings while sporting a goofy grin; Vince, high on success, taking a shot of whiskey along with his winnings from a stoned, slimy blue-jeaned competitor; Vince, Eddie and Carmen smiling as they take their winnings and run with unhappy losers at their heels.

Scorsese has a myriad of creative ways to photograph the many shots of pool playing in the movie. He captures all the breakshots and the trick shots requiring an expert's skill. He uses close-ups, quick cuts, and camera moves which catch the action on the table. To keep our interest during the montage and to add sparkle and variety, he uses fast motion, accompanied by the clicking sound of the balls as they slide into the right pockets of the table. When Vince shows off at Sheckie's, the camera follows his flashy show-off moves with a watchful eye. Warily, we see the action as Eddie does. When Eddie walks out, disgusted at Vince's lack of self-control, we know why Eddie, irritated, walks out on him.

Sometimes the camera simply finds what is lovely. A part of life in the fast lane is the desire to live luxuriously: dining in fine restaurants, wearing expensive clothes, and driving fancy cars. The camera focuses on a restful, balanced mise-en-scène as it shows a close-up of Eddie and Jazelle lying on satin pillows with warm, golden tones. The beauty and sense of security and intimacy of the shot illustrate the theme of the benefits of being mature. The camera glides elegantly with Jazelle and Eddie as they slide across the dance floor of a ballroom with a richly appointed decor of crystal chandeliers and brocade wallpaper.

The camera captures the flat, wide warehouse look of Chicago and its plain, barren, wintry landscape in sunlight. When Eddie talks to Carmen, sitting within the confines of his plush red leather seats, Scorsese captures the crisp, Chicago fall day with a reflection of a tree's branches in shadow against the window of the car.

The camera work is particularly fine as it shows Eddie's decision to play once again. Eddie is seated slightly above eye-level of the pool table and gazes speculatively at the game. There are several dissolves from player to player to pool table superimposed over Eddie's face as he mulls over his decision. Time passes. Against a medium shot of Eddie gazing at the pool table, the game looms large literally and figuratively. Before this, Eddie was a man of talk. After this sequence, he becomes a man of action. In the ensuing shots, we see Eddie's ascent to pool mastery once again.

From the lonely, moody instrumental underscoring Eddie's practice scenes to the blues tune with howling bass strings which adds atmosphere to Eddie and Vince's first match, the music in *The Color of Money* adds vitality to the film. Like the film's stylish photography, it comments on the action and shows us the excitement and allure of life in the fast lane.

The music remarks on the action when, for example, hotheaded and unthinking, Vince goes to Sheckie's to hustle. He doesn't stop to think of the strategy Eddie has outlined for this poolhall. Against Eddie's advice, Vince hot shots. Instead of trying to earn the most money possible, he plays without shrewdness or calculation. High on his own performance, Vince grins broadly while he dazzles his audience with his extraordinary pool playing. He prances around the table with his own version of fancy footwork, a voodoo-style dance, drunk on the experience of the crowd gathered around him to watch. The background music to this scene is "Werewolves of London," a song with a prominent beat and lots of spirit. Like Vince's joyful abandon, its vocals tell a tale of adventure and excitement, punctuated with bellows of "Wha-hoo! . . . Werewolves of London!"

The music comments in a similar way during the montage sequence. While Vince, Carmen, and Eddie are enjoying a string of successful hustles, "Tell Me Nothing" plays noisily in the background. The cocky, carefree lyrics and the happy, spirited twang of guitars complement the pictures of the three having fun and the click of balls on pool tables. In Atlantic City, when Eddie enters the grand ballroom filled with pool tables, the experience is underlined with cathedral music, suggesting that this is where Eddie worships. For him, it is a holy place.

In addition to adding to the action of a particular scene, the music often infuses the film with vitality, an attraction of this lifestyle. For example, the picture of Vince, Carmen, and Eddie as they cruise down the highway, the camera set at low angle to emphasize their power, suggests the excitement and promise of the adventure of being on the road. The music accompanying this shot is jazzy, loose sounding, free-spirited. Likewise, from Jazelle's bar in Chicago to the smoky poolhalls they stake out along the way to Atlantic City, the music played in the bars they frequent is abundantly atmospheric. The songs are electric and enveloping, tough, rebellious sounds which welcome its patrons.

The performances are first rate in *The Color of Money*. The lead characters provide fully realized, interesting performances, and the minor characters are especially well-cast and acted. The acting style, however, is different from that in previous Scorsese films. Scorsese used different methods than he usually employs when working on this film. He noted, that Paul is "the kind of actor who doesn't like to improvise that much on the set, so that everything was rehearsed beforehand. We did it the way he suggested, which was to take two complete weeks to work with the actors in a loft" (Thompson and Christie 1989, 108). By contrast, other Scorsese performances have qualities often associated with method acting: the privileged moments, surprising authentic details, and a looser, freer style.

Scorsese's directorial hand is evident in the fine performances, however. For example, Scorsese made suggestions to Mastrantonio which contributed small, but important details that helped define her character. Once he said to her, "You raised your eyebrow. Don't raise your eyebrow" (Pond 1986, 40). Journalist Steve Pond, who interviewed Mastrantonio, commented, "With Scorsese, she talked about how to portray someone who is simultaneously manipulative, defensive, and impassive. His solution: Don't do anything."

In fact, it is the facial expressions, the looks of characters in given scenes, that are most memorable in the fine performances of the film: Newman registers a range of facial expressions with Vincent at Sheckie's while he plays pool. He also shoots the way Eddie Felson would twenty-five years later. Somehow the older Eddie, seasoned, successful, and handsome, has even more appeal than the charming but callow younger Eddie. Especially on repeated viewing, the depth and subtleties of his performance become apparent.

Cruise also turned out a superior performance, stretching his acting range considerably over his previous work. He shows us Vincent's flakiness: boyish and innocent, full of energy and impulse, so completely himself that he unselfconsciously flaunts his pool talents and reveals innocence with many of his remarks.

Mastrantonio gives a noteworthy performance as Carmen. Another of Scorsese's strong female leads, she gives a commanding performance as the street-smart, pretty girlfriend who prizes Vincent and who helps engineer his success. She's at her most memorable when she's tough and confident, for example, when she gloats as she tells Eddie the story of how she and Vincent met and when she smolders as she answers with rancor Vincent's suspicion because she was out for a long time getting cigarettes.

Finally, the casting and acting of the considerable range of minor characters add a great deal to the film. Scorsese has filled the poolrooms with interesting players, so accurate and particular that it would take

An important part of acting is conveying character through bodily gestures, movements, and facial expression. In this shot, Paul Newman reveals the essence of Eddie Felson's character at the beginning of the film: shrewd, closed, self-satisfied. Here he first observes Vincent, smug and street-smart. He sizes up Vincent's naivete and artless, amateurish attempts to hustle with his pool talent (*The Color of Money*, 1986).

considerable imagination to select them. Duke (Steve Mizerak), Eddie's first opponent and someone who knew Eddie in his heyday, is a tall, slender gentleman who offers Eddie a drink as he orders another Drambui and potato salad. Other authentic types include Grady Seasons (Keith McCready), wearing a silky 1970s shirt with red polyester trousers, and Orvis, who says in a look the life experience he's had in the years he's spent in poolrooms.

The Color of Money was Scorsese's first commercial success following *Taxi Driver*. Scorsese noted, "The industry is now run by businessmen and if I want to continue to make personal films, I have to show them I have some sort of respect for money, and that it will actually show on the screen" (Thompson and Christie 1989, 114). In deference to the business aspects of movie making, Scorsese's pattern seems to have been to alternate attempting to make more commercial films with more personal ones. His next film, *The Last Temptation of Christ*, held little commercial promise, yet it was a film he had long dreamed of making.

The Last Temptation of Christ

When I was asked [by a studio head] why I wanted to make this film, I replied, "So I can get to know Jesus better."

In a way all my life I wanted to do that: first I was going to be a priest, but it didn't work out. . . . I felt that maybe this film would make me feel a little more fulfilled. Their reaction was very sweet, but they didn't want that answer. They wanted to know how much money I wanted to spend [quote from Scorsese in Thompson and Christie 1989, 120].

Scorsese first became aware of Nikos Kazantzakis's novel *The Last Temptation of Christ* when he was a student at New York University. However, he did not read it until he was given a copy by Barbara Hershey and David Carradine, actors in Scorsese's 1972 movie *Boxcar Bertha*. Scorsese was given the opportunity to direct this low-budget exploitation film by Roger Corman after he had seen and liked Scorsese's first feature-length movie, *Who's That Knocking at My Door?* a precursor to *Mean Streets* but done in a more autobiographical, arty, and film-student style.

Scorsese liked *Last Temptation* so much he took years reading it, completing it in 1979 (Thompson and Christie 1989, 116). He found Kazantzakis's focus on the human side of Christ very meaningful. He had always wanted to make a film about Christ (Thompson and Christie 1989, 117). Of course, there would only be a very small audience for such a work, and there would be no financial reward. It would be a labor of love.

For several years Scorsese planned to make *Last Temptation*, doing a great deal of research and surmounting many obstacles to make this film. First, he asked Paul Schrader, author of *Taxi Driver,* to write a screenplay. Schrader wrote two drafts of a script, closely based on the novel but condensing the long work to movie length. Over the next few years, with Schrader's permission and giving him credit for the screenplay, Scorsese was to write eight more drafts of the script (the last two along with Jay Cocks). Also in preparation for the film, he spent years studying previous biblical films based on the gospels. In the early 1980s, he secured studio

Willem Dafoe. Like virtually all of Scorsese's films, *Last Temptation* is a revisionist version of a genre. Unlike other Biblical films, *Last Temptation* focuses on Christ's humanity instead of on his divinity. In fact, his divinity is de-emphasized. Here Christ is a real human being who feels loss, uncertainty, anguish, and heartache. This shot of Christ in the desert shows his loneliness and vulnerability during a time of preparation, trial, and testing (*The Last Temptation of Christ,* 1988).

backing from Paramount and plans got underway for the film. Paramount later cancelled the project.

   Scorsese still had hopes of making the film at a future date. He continued to research the project while trying to find funding and persevering to get the film made and shown. When *Last Temptation* was cancelled in 1983, he began to subscribe to the *Biblical Archeology Review,* which he

This shot shows Christ's strength ambiguously. Holding a rock in each hand, Christ (Willem Dafoe) boldly challenges the Jewish law dictating that a woman who commits adultery be put to death. He also looks strong as his body forms the shape of the resurrected Jesus on the cross. However, Christ is placed towards the bottom of the frame, a diminished position of power. Visually, instead of surmounting his challengers, he is dominated by them and the rocky landscape (*The Last Temptation of Christ*, 1988).

studied for much of the film's art direction (Thompson and Christie 1989, 138). Scorsese approached and was rejected by every major studio until Universal showed interest in the project.

When the film was finally under production, it became the object of a furious protest by fundamentalists and other religious groups who considered the film's interpretation of Christ's story blasphemous. Scorsese spent hours with the press explaining his motivation and his artistic vision of this work, while also maintaining his right to individual creative expression. He pointed out, "Fundamentalism is not the state religion in this country" (James 1988, C11).

Clearly, Scorsese very much wanted to make this film. He hoped to make a religious film that would touch people as the Kazantzakis book had touched him. To this end, he had spent years thinking through the project carefully. Although Scorsese's efforts to make *The Last Temptation of Christ* were sincere, the result is a flawed work. Ironically, all the study, decision making, and personal meaning invested in the making of this film alienated viewers. Many of the artistic decisions are disconcerting. They often distance rather than enhance the viewer's spiritual experience. Much of the film simply comes across as just too weird.

> Later, looking at what we'd shot and constructing it in the editing room proved to be a very emotional and loving experience. I don't really look at my own pictures when they're finished, but on this one I had to look at screening after screening, and every time I see it I'm moved by the idea of trying to find out how one can live like that. How can one really live with this concept of love? I try but I don't purport to be able to do it myself [Thompson and Christie 1989, 130].

Scorsese found making *The Last Temptation of Christ* very rewarding. For example, he admired Willem DaFoe (who played Jesus) because of his willingness to take risks. Scorsese says, "It was a therapeutic experience to be able to sit with Willem and look at him as Jesus, to have lunch with him and argue with him, and then create this fantasy" (Thompson and Christie 1989, 130).

Admittedly, Scorsese's main point comes across well. He does motivate viewers to think about Christ's humanity and the sacrifice he made for us. Even viewers who don't particularly care for *Last Temptation* freely admit that this point is a clear and profound one. The Christ of this film is indeed very human, full of weakness, self-doubt, and ambivalence. Also, this is perhaps Scorsese's most violent film. The mental and physical torment Jesus suffers, both before and during the Crucifixion, is graphically presented. The emotional suffering Christ experiences is also emphasized. Unfortunately, except for this main idea, much else about the film is very distracting. Scorsese admits, "We took so many risks that there was bound to be something that people were not going to like" (Thompson and Christie 1989, 127).

Scorsese decided against using poetic language in *The Last Temptation of Christ* even though the translation of Kazantzakis's work is written in a poetic style. He comments, "We wanted a straightforward representation of speech, anti-poetic in a way" (Thompson and Christie, 1989, 128). It is easy to understand why one might assume anti-poetic language would be more direct and meaningful for a contemporary audience. Also, one might assume poetic language is just another convention of biblical epic films that needs to be altered to be powerful for the viewer. However, there are all kinds of poetry. Moreover, poetry is not only fitting for the grand subject of a biblical epic, it is also a potent language. One need only compare the language in a first-rate poem and a novel to know how intense and

Left to right: Martin Scorsese (wearing sunglasses), Barbara Hershey, Willem Dafoe, Harvey Keitel. Like directors who worked under the old studio system, Scorsese has a cadre of actors with whom he's worked on several pictures. Some of them are Robert De Niro, Harvey Keitel, Joe Pesci, David Carradine, Barry Primus, Lenny Scaletta, Murray Moston, Harry Northrup, Catherine Scorsese (the director's mother), Jodie Foster, Mardik Martin, Diahnne Abbott, George Memmoli, Steven Prince, Frank Vincent, Charles Scorsese (the director's father), Margo Winkler, Rosanna Arquette, Barbara Hershey, and Michael Powell. Barbara Hershey first worked with Scorsese on *Boxcar Bertha*, when she first gave him a copy of *The Last Temptation of Christ* (*The Last Temptation of Christ*, 1988).

purposeful poetic language can be. Ironically, the ordinary, plain language in *Last Temptation* is flat, limited, and ineffectual.

Scorsese also felt that the use of British accents would not be effective for American audiences. He felt such speech would trigger the response, "Great, it's another epic,' and [viewers would] know they don't have to think because it's safe." He deliberately chose to violate a convention of the biblical genre in order to give new meaning to his film. He wanted to use American voices and to use a variety of accents (Thompson and Christie 1989, 127). The resulting clash of accents, however, is diverting. More importantly, having the characters talk street style makes the story seem too local and provincial for the wide-reaching and profound implications of Christ's story. Also, although in New York it may not be a problem, in the rest of the country there are many stereotypical connotations to New York accents that diminish the audience's focus on the story.

Like the language and accents, the casting also has a contemporary quality. However, instead of adding immediacy, the actors simply work against the effectiveness of the film. Rather than suggesting the universal and larger-than-life as did the characters in other biblical films, these characters come across as insubstantial, particular, and insular. For example, it is reductionist to have the apostles cast as small-minded, spineless men. John the Baptist, Judas, and many others are too much New York provincial types to be convincing as biblical characters. It is hard to imagine Jesus's uncertain, timid style as one that could convince the street toughs that are his audience. Instead of being able to relate better to these characters, viewers are more likely to be less able to identify with them.

Scorsese made several other decisions that not only are startlingly revisionist but also detract from the spiritual focus of the film. Usually, for example, Scorsese's gift for recreating time period and setting is richly evocative and meaningful to his audience. Here, however, the details are often jarring. Few of us know what the holy lands actually looked like and how society actually behaved during that time period. In *Last Temptation*, for no explicit reason, there are weeping, wailing, screeching naked women in the background of one scene. Men kiss one another on the lips (which may not be unusual, but it is rarely seen on screen, much less in a biblical picture). Crowds behave primitively. These authentic details are also juxtaposed with contemporary character types and language. Mary Magdalene has a 1980s cornrow hairdo, and her body is covered with tattoos. The soundtrack contains odd music. The landscape often looks like a cinematic version of Salvador Dali's work. Jesus literally removes his heart. The wine they drink at the Last Supper turns to blood. Sometimes the film seems silly, as when the lion appears in the desert and talks to Jesus.

Some of the decisions are not only distracting, they are also offensive. Many people were disgusted by the showing of Jesus's making love on screen. Also, it was repulsive to a number of women to have a snake (woman) to be a devil temptress and later to have the devil appear in the form of a little girl, saying such things as all women are the same. It is ironic that Scorsese changed this character because he anticipated controversy, "In the book ... the angel at the end was a little Arab boy, but I felt that brought connotations and we'd have difficulties. People would get upset and it would get in the way of what the film's really about" (Thompson and Christie 1989, 143). It is also odd that Scorsese, who has been extraordinarily sensitive and respectful towards women, would not anticipate that this decision might incense a great many people.

However, perhaps one of the biggest problems of the film is the weak character of Jesus. It is hard to imagine that people would follow this man.

His humanity and frailty are emphasized to the exclusion of any presence, dignity, or inner strength that would lend him credibility. This Jesus is simply too neurotic, tormented, and unsure of himself to be not only mortal but also divine. He resembles Charlie in *Mean Streets*, who also doesn't do wrong, although some people see Charlie's actions as motivated by fear instead of virtue.

Although *Last Temptation* was meant to motivate the viewer to think of spiritual concerns, there are too many strange elements which detract from the movie's message. Instead of focusing on the story, viewers are conspicuously conscious of artistic choices. They are, therefore, focusing on form instead of content, having to put more than the usual effort into trying to suspend their disbelief.

Ironically, many of Scorsese's other films are much more spiritual works. There is a loving look at Charlie and his friends in *Mean Streets;* understanding of Jimmy Doyle in *New York, New York;* sympathy for Travis in his loneliness and alienation in *Taxi Driver;* and compassion for Jake La Motta in his powerlessness in *Raging Bull.* The very fact that Scorsese tells the stories of these outsiders, people who are hard to like, people for whom success and happiness in life do not come easily, has profound spiritual implications. He also tells their stories in a full and deep way with humor and empathy.

Sometimes the things we really care about are so personal that we cannot communicate their significance to others. This may have been the case for Scorsese in the making of *The Last Temptation of Christ*. Artistic trademarks associated with Scorsese — authentic rendering of time and place, effective revisionist genre, and interesting character studies — are all present, but the mix does not work well in this film.

New York Stories

Paulette: [about her painting] "Tell me what's here. What's here?
             Will I ever be good?
Lionel: "You're young yet. I love you."
Paulette: "Love me? You just need me around. Sometimes I feel
             like a human sacrifice." — argument from a scene in
             "Life Lessons" in New York Stories

Scorsese's next venture was a collaboration with film makers Woody
Allen and Frances Ford Coppola. Each contributed a short movie to a work
entitled *New York Stories*. Scorsese's segment, "Life Lessons," was loosely
based on "The Gambler" by Dostoyevsky and the diary of the author's mis-
tress and protégé, a writer named Apollinaria Suslova.

"Life Lessons" focuses on the parasitic relationship between a suc-
cessul Soho painter, Lionel Dobie (Nick Nolte), and his apprentice,
Paulette (Rosanna Arquette). Theirs is an obsessive-compulsive union
punctuated by stormy love-hate outbursts. Mostly, it is an exploitative relationship. Lionel needs Paulette so that he can paint. She's an object of sensual beauty to him, and their addictive relationship, fueled by her fiery
outbursts, pumps his passion to paint. Theirs is the most claustrophobic
relationship of Scorsese's work. As the movie starts, Paulette wants to break
off with Lionel. She is impatient with her artistic progress and feels unsup-
ported by Lionel. He won't tell her if her work is good. She is also full of
fury at being the focus of Lionel's passion. She tries to escape his clutches,
but he stalks her every move. At a party he even closes her in a room to
hide her away from someone who takes an interest in her.

Nolte is unctuous as the self-serving artist. Round-bellied, sweaty,
paint-splashed, he doesn't fit the romantic notion of an artist. Rather he
bears the Scorsese imprint of a leading man because he is not the typical
likeable protagonist. Arquette as Paulette is young, blond, willowy, feminine, and attractive. However, her angry outbursts, though understandable, make her hard to like, too. At times, it is even difficult to understand
why Lionel is so obsessed with her.

Of course, he is not really in love — in the positive sense. He is merely driven. Enmeshed, he needs her (or someone to replace her) to the extent that he is victimized by his own dependency. He is helpless when it comes to his relationship with Paulette. And she exploits this neediness as the only way to get back at him for using her. After a particularly infuriating incident, she tells him to prove his love by kissing a cop. He does. Then he looks back to where she was standing, but she is not even there.

Scorsese uses the camera boldly in "Life Lessons." In fact, much of the pleasure in watching the film is the artistry of its camera work. It is a movie about an artist, and it has been made by an artist who has used his cinematic paintbox and brushes to create expressionistically on his own canvas. Using techniques that call attention to themselves, like irises, close-ups, slow motion, quick cuts, zooms, high angles, and superimpositions, a large part of the experience of "Life Lessons" is the camera style.

Music also fills every frame, informing each one as powerfully as do the expressive visuals of the film. At the opening, Procol Harum blares from Lionel's paint-smudged tape player. Music is Lionel's muse as he agonizes over his canvas, which at first is painfully empty. Then, motivated by the inner anguish of his break-up with Paulette, Lionel fills the canvas with passionate strokes, applying layers of thick paint in a discordant color scheme. At one point, "Like a Rolling Stone" blasts while Lionel is painting furiously. Paulette shouts to Lionel to turn the music down, but he is completely absorbed in his work. The camera cuts back and forth between Paulette and Lionel. As she watches, her expression changes to a knowing smile, as she observes Lionel, a master, in intimate union with his true love.

In their final argument, Lionel poses what he obviously feels is a ludicrous proposal. He asks Paulette if she'd like him to just stop painting and be a nice person. His next remark is shot through with irony. Incredulously, Lionel accuses, "You think I just use people!" Paulette doesn't waste a word trying to tell him the obvious. In the final scene, a hostess who is serving at Lionel's opening touches his hand, hoping to bring luck to her painting. Lionel gazes at the pretty young woman before him. In a minute yesterday's obsession with Paulette is eclipsed by this new fascination. The hostess is thrilled to accept his offer: room, board, a small salary, and life's lessons. The circle is complete.

Popular both with critics and with the general public, Scorsese's was the best received segment of the three. His next movie, *GoodFellas*, probably his most widely seen and highly praised work to date, was to be an even greater success.

Nick Nolte and Rosanna Arquette. In "Life Lessons," one of three short films comprising the film *New York Stories*, Scorsese explores the dynamics of a self-serving claustrophobic relationship between two artists. Lionel Dobie feeds on the agony of love. In love with his own misery, he uses the angst of his stormy relationship with Paulette to jump start his creativity. In love with sensuality and visuals, he also likes having a pretty girl around. Paulette, however, is full of rage at being manipulated and exploited (*New York Stories:* "Life Lessons," 1989).

GoodFellas

For us to live any other way was nuts. Those goody good people who worked shitty jobs for everyday paychecks and took the subway to work and worried about their bills were dead. They were suckers. No balls. If we wanted something, we just took it. If anyone complained twice, they got hit so bad, believe me, they never complained again. It was all routine. You didn't even think about it — Henry Hill, narrator of *GoodFellas*

Picture three groggy men in a car driving during the middle of the night. One hears a thumping sound from the trunk. They pull over and, with grim awareness, all stand at a distance from the sound. The driver cautiously opens the trunk and stands back. Inside, a bloody, presumed dead, body convulses. One of the men savagely stabs a large chef's knife into the body several times. Then the other man, with stony determination, steps up and fires several shots into the still-twitching body. As the driver closes the trunk, he comments, "As far back as I can remember, I always wanted to be a gangster." The camera freezes him in medium shot. Then Tony Bennett warmly croons, "You know I'd go from rags to riches." The movie title *GoodFellas* appears in red against a black background. Then other credits zoom by, emblematic of the fast-lane life this movie will depict.

Shot through with irony, brutality, and realism, this bravura sequence arrogantly and cagily opens *GoodFellas*, an original among Mafia films and one of Martin Scorsese's finest movies. In this film, we are guided through the world of the Mafia by gangster Henry Hill (Ray Liotta). While being informed by our articulate narrator Hill, we become drawn into cinematography loaded with ambience and detail. Underscoring the visuals are songs that evoke period, mood, and tone.

GoodFellas chronicles Hill's experiences over nearly three decades. It takes us from Henry as a young boy, yearning to be one of the guys who hang out at the cab stand across the street from his family's apartment to Henry in his thirties, living on the edge, dazed and frantic, high on coke, and finally, to Henry in the cold empty aftermath, the dull reality after he has left the life.

Young Henry Hill thought being a gangster was "better than being president of the United States." When he was young, Henry worked as an errand boy for the mob, an apprentice, learning "every day how to score. A dollar here, a dollar there." The older gangster, Paul Cicero (Paul Sorvino), Paul's brother Tuddy (Frank DiLeo), and Jimmy Conway (Robert De Niro), were father figures and mentors to him. The 1950s Mafia scenes, the period when Henry is growing up, are characterized by warmth and friendship.

The 1960s is also a "glorious time." The wiseguys are "all over the place," and this decade is also a time of fellowship, prosperity, and goodwill. Henry comes of age during this decade. He meets and marries his wife, Karen (Lorraine Bracco), and they have two daughters. Life is good. They have plenty of cash and closets full of clothing. They have close friends whom they see often. They eat good food, frequent nightclubs, and live exciting, fast-lane lives.

In the 1970s, however, the good life begins to sour. Henry starts to be unfaithful to his wife, and the jealousy and hurt tear Karen apart. Killings, a way of life, become more frequent and require less justification. In this decade the loyalty and friendship among the wiseguys, cultivated over many years, are betrayed and abandoned.

Jimmy, Paulie, Henry, and others go to jail for several years. Afterwards, although there is the appearance of unity, it is every man for himself. Henry now both uses and sells drugs, and eventually he is arrested. He decides to turn state's evidence and join the witness protection program. Jimmy and Paulie go to jail. At the end of the movie Henry is free but bored with his new, dull, straight lifestyle.

GoodFellas is one of Scorsese's most highly crafted, richly textured works. It joins the ranks of *Raging Bull* and *Taxi Driver* as an artistically significant film; moreover, it transcends those works in its accessibility. *GoodFellas* is a culmination of Scorsese's work to date: It has the artistic unity, compelling visuals, and technical mastery of *Raging Bull*. It shows boldness of purpose in charting new territory like *Taxi Driver*. It shows his most inspired use of music since *Mean Streets*. It tells a story in a characteristically Scorsese style — according to instinct and feeling — along with the tighter crafting of traditional narration found in *After Hours* and *King of Comedy*.

Although *GoodFellas* is heavily plotted, its interest, like other Scorsese films, is in character and relationships. Like *Mean Streets, Alice Doesn't Live Here Anymore, Taxi Driver* and *Raging Bull, GoodFellas* has warmth and fellowship. However, these other character studies have a different emphasis from *GoodFellas*. They probe deeper, conveying the character's motivation with emotional accuracy and sympathy. *GoodFellas* is also a character study, but it is about mean, unscrupulous people. Scorsese has always had an interest in meanness and toughness, and such characters can be found throughout his work: Michael in *Mean Streets,* Ben in *Alice,* Jake in *Raging Bull,* and many of the women in *After Hours.* Furthermore, most of Scorsese's protagonists have objectionable traits.

Here, Scorsese fully indulges his interest in meanness and toughness. In *GoodFellas,* the characters are coarse, aggressive, hardened. They are not reflective, sensitive types. They are not even in the mainstream, for they are people without conscience. They are all appetite. Scorsese comments,

> Basically I was interested in what they *do.* And, you know, they don't think about it a lot. They don't sit around and ponder about [laughs] "Gee, what are we doing here?" The answer is to eat a lot and make a lot of money and do the least amount of work as possible for it. I was trying to make it as practical and primitive as possible. Just straight ahead. Want. Take. Simple. I'm more concerned with showing a lifestyle and using Henry Hill [Ray Liotta] as basically a guide through it [quoted in Smith 1990, 28].

Scorsese illustrates this part of their personality with all the shots of food. *GoodFellas* provides a picture of men who move slowly, who do little work, who dominate others by beating or killing whoever gets in their way. In short, this is a different type of character study because it is about men lacking in depth and fineness of feeling.

Henry, however, is not quite one of them. Consistently, he is not as cold-blooded as his cronies. From his sympathy for the first man he saw shot while at the pizzeria one day to his lack of participation in the brutal slaying of Billy Batts (Frank Vincent) to his shock and concern for Spider, the waiter whom Tommy shoots, Henry is the typical Scorsese outsider. Henry, however, is an outsider with an insider's view. Because Henry is half Irish and only half Sicilian, he can never be a full member of the all–Italian inner circle, a "made man." Nevertheless, Henry is an ideal narrator because he observes with both the longing and the detachment of an outsider's perspective.

GoodFellas is also a Scorsese film in its revisionist viewpoint. It shows the excitement and appeal of mob life, but it also shows gangsters probably much as they really are, as crude, greedy, and sometimes psychotic. There is no code of honor or dignity as there is in Coppola's *Godfather* trilogy. *GoodFellas* brazenly shows us the raw and disgusting brutality of beatings and slayings. Violent scenes are shown in their full horror. They are not tastefully abbreviated nor is the blood and gore minimized in any way. Scenes like the bloody brutality of Jimmy's bashing the head of the man in Tampa; Billy Batts's being kicked, shot, and later bludgeoned to death; and the cold-blooded slaying of Morrie, a friend of Jimmy's and Tommy's for years, all make the Mafia violence visceral. It is no longer "just a movie."

These thugs are not romanticized. They are shown in their full inhumanity.

GoodFellas is based on the book *Wiseguy,* published in 1985 by crime writer Nicholas Pileggi. Pileggi recounts the true life experiences of Henry Hill, who started working for the mob when he was eleven years old, in 1956, until he left the life when he entered the witness protection program in 1980. Scorsese read the text of the book while it was still in galleys. Intrigued by the book's realism and by Henry's narration, he was immediately interested in making a movie of it. He contacted Pileggi and later they collaborated on writing the script, which evolved from several drafts over a five-month period.

GoodFellas shows the appeal of fast-lane life. Along with Henry's voiceover commentary, the visuals of the 1950s Mafia tell the story. From the eyes of an eleven-year-old boy from a poor neighborhood "full of nobodies," it is easy to see why Henry is attracted to this life, for it offers power, money, belonging, excitement, and recognition. We see the attraction as young Henry watches these men pull up in luxury sedans and playfully jab at one another outside the cab stand across the street. In warm amber tones, we see slightly slowed close-ups of the neighborhood men and their finery: a polished shoe, a gold ring, the fender of a shiny Cadillac, images of privilege.

When Henry takes a job at the cab stand, although he is only a young boy, he becomes a respected figure in the neighborhood. He no longer has to wait in line at the bakery. One day other kids carry his mother's groceries home for her. He can barely see over the dashboard, yet he's given the privilege of parking Cadillacs. He has more money than he can spend and is able to outfit himself in an expensive new suit and shoes. He feels as though he is living a fantasy. Most of all, he was a part of something, and being a part of this gangster life, he says, is where he belonged.

GoodFellas is about the strong allures that captivate us and how we allow these fascinations to dictate the decisions we make. It is about how we are tacitly drawn to a way of living, to the type of person we aspire to be, to the values we select that embody a certain way of life. And, like Henry, our actions and decisions are made according to this powerful, private connection we've made. Young Henry finds himself instinctively drawn to life at the cab stand. Giving the decision little thought, he stops going to school, yielding to the strong attraction of the gangster lifestyle. The warm, happy picture of life as one of the 1950s goodfellas is powerfully romantic and appealing.

As the years pass, however, Henry's story grows darker. Romantic attractions such as Henry's can add sparkle and magic to life. They can motivate positively. Unfortunately, the excitement of romance has the potential for both highs and lows. Although not in the way most people would think of the term, *GoodFellas* is also about addiction. It is about being so powerfully drawn to excitement, to "the life," that at some point a line is crossed, and, like being caught in a vortex, one surrenders control. The rush can be seen in the face of Jimmy Conway as he quickly crushes out his cigarette and springs to the bar to hear the machinations for the latest airport heist. It is in Henry's and Tommy's exuberance in hijacking a truck and Tommy's firing his pistol into the air like a boy playing cowboys and Indians. As the story unfolds, however, the specters of the darker side to addiction loom larger: the compulsive behavior, self-centeredness, growing fear and alienation from others, escalating need, paranoia, and a life that spins out of control.

Morrie's obsessiveness leads directly to his death. Jimmy's appetite for wealth becomes so compulsive that he systematically annihilates all connected with the Lufthansa heist. Six million dollars should have been enough to go around, but Jimmy wanted it all. Despite Karen's obvious agony and heartbreak at her husband's infidelity, Henry shows no remorse, no compunction, no regard for her feelings. By the end of the film, Henry is on his own, with no allegiance to Jimmy or Paulie. They also feel no loyalty to him. It is Henry and his new best friend and powerful ally — cocaine. With fear stalking his every move, Henry does lines of coke to help him navigate the minefields of an ordinary day. The drug gives him a false sense of control through the hazy, nerve-jangling consciousness of his life.

The main characters of *GoodFellas* are Henry Hill, Jimmy Conway, Tommy DiVito, Paul Cicero, and Henry's wife, Karen. The movie features a large supporting case as well, including Henry's mother (Elaine Kagan) and father (Beau Starr) and handicapped brother Michael (Keven Corrigan); Karen's mother (Suzanne Shepherd); Henry's girlfriends, Janice (Gina Mastrogiacomo) and Sandy (Debi Mazar); Tommy's mother (Catherine Scorsese); and a cadre of other goodfellas and their wives and Friday night girlfriends as well as many small parts.

Paulie, the head of the local mob, gets a share of the profits from all of the heists of the men who work for him. A heavyset man, he moves slowly "because he didn't have to move fast for anyone." Like all the other goodfellas, Paulie has other eccentricities as well. For example, he doesn't like telephones, so he won't have one in his house. Others, like his brother Tuddy or Henry, take his calls, talk to Paulie, then call back with his response. Paulie also doesn't like having a conversation with more than one person. All concerns must be handled one on one.

Jimmy Conway, "Jimmy the Gent," is a legendary wiseguy, fabulously successful at thievery, a man who "rooted for the bad guys" at movies and "who loved to steal." Jimmy smartly gives a payoff to those whom he robs, thereby smoothly greasing the wheel of his operations while creating

Left to right: Ray Liotta, Robert De Niro, Paul Sorvino, Joe Pesci. *GoodFellas* is primarily a revisionist film. Instead of focusing on the gangsters' mythic qualities, it reveals their coarseness, greed, and craziness. However, it also adheres to a number of conventions: The gangsters dress in fancy suits, frequent nightclubs, make lots of money, and have power and prestige within their community. Like many gangsters, Henry also shows unusual loyalty to a family member, in this case his handicapped brother, Michael. Pictured in this scene are four of the goodfellas dressed in their fine clothing (*GoodFellas*, 1990).

goodwill. School-crossing guards, cops, and truck drivers amicably help Jimmy ply his trade, benefitting themselves from his operations. Stolen goods like sweaters, fur coats, suits, shrimp and lobster, and cigarettes are Jimmy's stock-in-trade. To warn a man whose semi he hijacked, Jimmy takes his driver's license and says, "You might know who we are, but we *know* who you are." Jimmy hands him back his wallet with a fifty-dollar bill to establish complicity. As a young boy, Henry is in awe of Jimmy as he walks through the saloon passing out twenties to everyone from Henry to the bartender, for keeping his ice cold. Although Jimmy is a "gent," he also is aggressive and ruthless. Jimmy doesn't mind "doing hits," murdering people. To him, it is just business. As the story progresses, Jimmy becomes more callously violent.

Jimmy introduces Tommy to Henry when they are boys. Both work for Jimmy doing jobs like selling bootleg cigarettes outside factories. Known for his humor and storytelling, Tommy is one of Henry's closest friends. However, in Tommy, Scorsese shows us the darkest personality of any of the wiseguys, for Tommy is clearly psychotic. His psychosis is most evident in two instances: one is the scene in which Henry tells Tommy that he is funny. Tommy takes the remark personally, assuming that he has been insulted. He reacts as though Henry's comment is an assault to his dignity. Finally, Henry jokes Tommy out of this tense confrontation.

The other scene showing the dangerously crazy side to Tommy is when Tommy shoots Spider (Michael Imperioli), the waiter, first in the foot and later in the heart. Tommy quickly dismisses the act with, "All right, so he got shot in the foot. What is it? Big fucking deal. Don't get me upset. Don't make a big fucking thing out of it. Trying to make me think what the fuck I did here. An accident. Fuck it." When Jimmy and others confront him about the insanity of killing the waiter over a trivial comment, Tommy's minimization of the incident is chillingly astonishing. He casts off even a twinge of second thoughts over the incident with, "[I'm a] Good shot. What do you want from me? You got a problem with what I did Anthony? His whole family were all rats. He would have grown up to be a rat." Tommy's insecurity and hotheadedness later lead directly to his death over his killing a made man, Billy Batts, a move that is not allowed by the Mafia code.

Karen, Henry's wife, is a middle-class Jewish woman from the suburbs. Attractive and strong-willed, she is an ideal match for Henry. Like other Scorsese leading women, Karen is strong, bright, and capable. She contributes to the story as a narrator by giving us yet another outsider's view of the Mafia. Significantly, she recognizes that the life they were leading was aberrant. She sees how a perverse, violent, criminal lifestyle was made to seem sane, routine, justified.

> After awhile it got to be all normal. None of it seemed like crimes. It was more like Henry was enterprizing and he and the guys were making a few bucks hustling while the other guys were sitting on their asses waiting for handouts. Our husbands weren't brain surgeons. They were blue collar guys. The only way they could make extra money, real extra money, was to go out and cut a few corners.

Karen explains that this odd normalcy evolved, in part, because of the insularity of their world. "We were all so very close. I mean there were never any outsiders. Absolutely never. And being together all the time made everything seem all the more normal." All events and activities from visiting each other, playing cards, and taking vacations to anniversaries and christenings were done together. "No outsiders. Ever."

The visuals also show this peculiar way of living when two officers come to search Henry and Karen's house. Karen is calm. As though merely letting in a repairman, she signs the warrant, admits the police officers, offers them coffee, picks up her baby, and continues to watch an old Al Jolsen movie on television. "There was always a little harassment," she comments, "Mostly they were looking for a handout."

Karen admits an attraction to the glitter, glamour, and privilege of the world to which Henry introduces her. She beams as Henry ushers her into the Copa through a side entrance, whirling past people who know Henry to a VIP table set up in the front row especially for them. She also admits to an attraction to the danger. When Henry beats up a man who had treated her shabbily, Henry hands Karen the gun he used to pummel his victim. Karen comments, "There are some women, like my best friends, who would have run if their boyfriend had given them a gun to hide. But I've got to be honest. It turned me on."

Karen's honesty, intelligence, and middle-class background make her an interesting narrator, able to see the absurdities of the life that she has joined. At a hostess party given by Jimmy Conway's wife, Mickey (Julie Garfield), Karen feels as though she has entered a bizarre world. Insightfully, she observes their shabby looks and their melodramatic, downbeat, gossipy preoccupations. "They had bad skin and wore too much makeup. They didn't look very good. They looked beat up. The stuff they wore was thrown together and cheap. Pantsuits and double knits. They talked about how rotten their kids were and hitting them with broom handles and leather belts and the kids still didn't listen."

In collaboration with cinematographer Michael Ballhaus, Scorsese uses the camera expressively to unfold Henry Hill's story, to reveal character, and to allow the viewer to vicariously experience the lifestyle of a wiseguy. *GoodFellas* is a rich film visually. It engages the viewer, so much that one might not notice the film's exceptional length, 146 minutes. Using a wide variety of techniques, Scorsese crafted a sophisticated and technically superior film. Some of Scorsese's signatures are the use of red, the use of slow motion, and the moving camera.

Scorsese uses a red filter during the opening scene, dated June 11, 1970, and later when that scene is repeated chronologically within the story. He also uses this filter when Jimmy, Tommy, and Henry dig up Billy Batts's body six months after they buried him. The reddish glow casts a

Left to right: **Christopher Serrone, Robert De Niro, Joseph D'Onofrio. In this shot, Jimmy Conway introduces young Henry Hill to young Tommy De Vito. With an arm around each boy, Jimmy shows a warm fatherly interest in them while he teaches them how to score (*GoodFellas*, 1990).**

sinister tone to these events, making them look like scenes from hell. Red is also used during the introduction of Henry's friends in one of the nightclub scenes. Like in the bar scenes in *Mean Streets*, the red filter suggests vividness, excitement, danger, and romance.

Just as Scorsese used slow motion to reveal the private preoccupations of Charlie in *Mean Streets* and Jake in *Raging Bull,* he uses this technique in a similar way in *GoodFellas.* For example, during Karen and Henry's wedding reception, the camera highlights Karen's private reverie. In slightly slowed motion, she drifts around the dance floor, as if living a happy dream. The camera is slowed later on when it focuses on Jimmy, deep in thought and worried as he smokes a cigarette at the bar while he contemplates killing Morrie, who has become more trouble than he is worth.

Slow motion is also used to highlight gory circumstances and sinister acts. When collaborators of the Lufthansa heist are found dead tumbling through a garbage truck, hanging on a hook in a meat truck, and gunned down in a pink Cadillac, slow motion underscores the gruesome slayings. When Tommy stabs Billy Batts in the trunk, the dagger plunges in a slightly slowed motion, intensifying the slaughter. Finally, when the Lufthansa heist driver, Stacks Edwards (Samuel L. Jackson), is killed by Tommy, his murder is repeated in slow motion from a high angle, magnifying the violence and making Stacks look like a wounded animal. This scene also reinforces Tommy as a psychopath, for he shoots Stacks five times.

The moving camera scans all the action, whether quickly following behind or methodically observing the participants and their environs. When we first meet Henry's mother, the camera follows her, a busy young mother of five with much to attend to, as she walks through their apartment at a brisk pace. Similarly, the camera follows the winding path of Henry and Karen as Henry goes into the Copa through a special entrance. The camera notes the savory staples of the good life as it glides over fat sausages frying in a pan and other delectables at a backyard barbecue, trays of lunch meats and cheeses at a local club, and a long table of lobster dinners at a nightclub.

An interested viewer, the camera scouts out and observes all the participants in this drama. It browses through the crowd as Henry introduces us to the various goodfellas at a club, Freddy No Nose (Mikey Black), Frankie Carbone (Frank Sivero), and others; it points out all of the men involved in the Lufthansa heist; and, to check out the action, it typically scans the length of the bar to observe the scene. The camera also astutely observes the wiseguys' living quarters in jail and the congested mass of humanity taking care of intimate needs elbow to elbow at the visitors's area in jail.

By contrast, the camera halts with grim attentiveness in the "Tommy, you're a funny guy" scene. The scene is simple and spare. There is no music, and the camera uses simple over-the-shoulder two-shots, focusing first on Tommy, then on Henry's reaction and back again. When Tommy has just finished entertaining his friends with a story, Henry compliments him by saying, "You're a funny guy." Thinking this comment is an affront, Tommy becomes angry. Deadly serious, he confronts Henry. Astonished, Henry tries to explain that his remark was positive, but Tommy persists in challenging Henry. Scorsese notes,

> If he [Henry] doesn't try laughing about it, he's going to be killed; if he tries laughing about it and the guy doesn't think it's funny, he's going to be killed. Either way he's got nothing to lose. You see, things like that, they could turn on a dime, those situations. And it's just really scary [quoted in Smith 1990, 69].

Moments later Tommy breaks a bottle over the head of the bar owner and attacks a waiter who happened to glance at the violent act. The mood of the scene shifts abruptly from playfulness to danger and alerts the audience to a frightening and dangerous part of Tommy's personality. The stark simplicity of the frozen camera setup helps spotlight Tommy's aberrant behavior.

In several scenes Scorsese uses light dramatically and atmospherically to express thematic ideas. Because murder and other criminal activity are associated with the shadowy world of darkness, bringing such activities out into the light of day is incongruous and alarming. When Karen lets police officers search her home, the scene is full of bright daylight. For most people, this event would be a startling request and a shocking invasion of privacy; however, here it is routine, and the sunny daylight provides an ironic contrast. Similarly, when Henry hoses down his trunk to deodorize it from the stench of Billy Batts's body, incongruously, the washing down takes place in the driveway of his home located in a comfortable, modern residential neighborhood in bright light. In another scene, children play at "sword fights" with sticks in gentle daylight. They casually approach a pink Cadillac, which contains the bodies of a murdered man and woman, their faces blood-spattered and expressionless.

One of the most jarring uses of bright light occurs when Henry and Karen talk to the FBI agent, Ed McDonald, who informs them about the witness protection program. Karen and Henry look like frightened nocturnal animals caught in a trap and brought out into startling daylight. Wearing a green silk suit, Henry looks like an aging greaser. His eyes are glassy, his face is puffy, and his movements are jittery. Looking completely dysfunctional and out of his element, he speaks with strain and without conviction. By contrast, the agent, looking crisp and contemporary in his white shirt and power tie, represents reality. Strong and authoritative, he is the type of straight person Karen and Henry have managed to avoid having contact with for years.

The camera also occasionally finds elements of humor in a story of much grim reality. For example, it seems to enjoy the fun of meeting the goodfellas as Henry introduces them. Each man is caricatured affectionately, the camera resting politely at each introduction. Similarly, in good humor, it tracks all the Peters, Pauls, and Maries to whom Paulie introduces Karen at the Hills' wedding. In like manner, it notices all the women at the hostess party given by Jimmy's wife, Mickey, as it wryly records the satire of this scene. Finally, the camera also records the black humor in the scene where the man in Florida is about to be fed to the lions. Showing us what the man sees as he is hung upside down — the lion waiting below — it provides a small moment of grotesque comic relief in an otherwise cruel scene.

Freezeframes are the climax of several scenes during the first part of the film. They serve as snapshots of childhood memories. Scorsese points out, "It's very important where the freezeframes are in that opening sequence. Certain things are embedded in the skull when you're a kid" (quoted in Smith 1990, 30). The various freezes are impressionistic, a way we remember the past, not necessarily anything to do with the actual cause-effect of events or with linear or objective storytelling. Frozen in memory are such instances as Henry's father beating him for not attending school, a postman's being warned not to deliver truancy letters to Henry's home, Henry's running away after setting fire to a fleet of competing cabs, Henry's first meeting with Jimmy Conway, and the warm circle of older wiseguys who embrace young Henry after his day in court.

Scorsese's editing style often juxtaposes light-hearted scenes with serious ones, or vice versa, catching the viewer off guard. This contrasting style of editing captures both the fun and the underlying horror that become a part of young Henry's experience with the Mafia. For example, one scene features young Henry showing off a new suit to his mother. Instead of complimenting him, however, she looks astonished at his appearance and says in disbelief, "You look like a gangster!" The dress-up shot is followed by the pizzeria scene during which Henry first sees a man who has been shot. He tries to help the man, wrapping his wound with aprons; however, Tuddy scoffs at Henry's compassionate response, commenting that he needs to toughen Henry up and saying that Henry wasted eight aprons.

Scorsese also uses contrast as an editing principle in the courtship scenes, alternating between violence and lyricism. Through slow motion and editing, Karen's marriage to Henry seems like a whirlwind, dreamy affair. This sequence begins at the end of the scene during which Henry has just beaten up a man who had been abusive towards Karen. At the end of that scene, Karen comes out of her house in slow motion and Henry gives her a gun to hide. This scene shifts from the close-up of the gun in Karen's hand to a close-up of a glass being wrapped and stepped on punctuated by "Mazel Tov!" as Henry and Karen are married in a Jewish ceremony. This ceremonial act is followed by rapturous slow-motion photography of Karen being introduced to wedding guests who are friends of Henry's and then dancing with Henry in slow motion.

During the fast-paced final fifth of the movie, editing accelerates the action. Scorsese dramatically shows the deterioration of the characters as he knits several scenes together, showing the characters' moral decline and how their lives have spun out of control. The scenes revolve around adultery, murder, and emotional breakdowns. In the first scene, Henry tosses his girlfriend, Janice, on a bed, and moments later he flirts with one of her friends, Sandy. In the next scene, Tommy flippantly shoots a waiter, Spider, in the foot. Then Karen, suspecting her husband's adultery, throws Henry's car keys out the window and warns that he's not going out. The scene ends with a shot of one of their little girls watching her parents' argument. Next, Tommy kills Spider. Afterwards, Karen, accompanied by her children, frantically buzzes Janice's apartment and the rest of the tenants as she rages about the affair Janice is having with Henry. The final scene in this sequence shows Karen pointing a revolver at Henry. In close-up and medium shots, they both look bloated and emotionally strung out. Karen is so desperate that she points a gun at her husband to get his attention. When Henry convinces her to put the gun down, he angrily wrestles her to the floor and then walks out on her. The scene ends with her forlorn wail, "I'm sorry." Scorsese comments on this sequence: "Those five scenes, pushed together, tell you everything about the energy level and the psychic ambience of living a lifestyle like that. At that point, they're all trapped in it; they can't get out. That's what's interesting to me" (quoted in Strauss 1990, 8-H).

The visual style of *GoodFellas* is richly sensuous. Many of the compositions in the early part of the film express the attractiveness of the 1950s era: the luxury and pleasure of their fellowship. One of the first shots of the goodfellas is at the cab stand. The men are in the background of the frame while a luxurious car dominates the foreground. After young Henry's day in court, his older friends gather round him, literally circling him en masse with support and bonhomie. Years later this same sense of fellowship and good cheer is apparent when Tommy tells funny stories to his fellow card players, all of them huddled together, a circle of unity at least for the moment. Unity and brotherhood are also rendered in the scene when Jimmy, Tommy, and Henry drink together at the bar, celebrating the news that Tommy is being made.

The mise-en-scène is not merely visually striking; it is also functional. When Henry gets out of jail and looks for the cocaine he had intended to sell for sixty thousand dollars, he discovers that Karen flushed the drug down the toilet when the agents stormed their house. Henry is sickened and stunned by the news. He cries out achingly that it can't be so, that that was all the money they had, that he was counting on that money. Henry is in desperate trouble, and his one hope has just been vanquished. Karen defends her action, "They would have found it!" Then she joins her husband in grief, sobbing in anguish. The mise-en-scène captures their vulnerability as it pictures them huddled in a corner of their bedroom, collapsed in desperation and misery at their hopeless situation.

Close-ups and camera angles also express fast-lane life as lived by the goodfellas. For instance, a number of close-ups help reveal its intimacy, excitement, and sensual pleasures. When Henry helps Jimmy sell bootleg cigarettes, the camera closes in on them, establishing the intimacy of a shared illicit activity. Similarly, it stops on a close to medium shot of Jimmy, Henry, and another pal as they huddle in obvious excitement at plans for the Air France heist. The camera focuses on Henry's eyes in an extreme close-up as he gazes with wonder at the cab stand across the street. From a high angle, it captures the glamour and sensuousness of Karen and Henry

Robert De Niro (*left*) and Ray Liotta. One of the ironies in *GoodFellas* is the false intimacy of the brotherhood of the mob. As a boy, Henry was initially attracted to their warm camaraderie, and he longed to be one of them. However, what unites the Mafia is the greed of pure capitalism. Like many gangster stories, this one too is a perverse version of the rags-to-riches American dream. Self-interest, which necessitates murdering an old friend, precludes "family" loyalty. In this shot, Henry intuitively knows his long-time pal Jimmy is planning to "whack" him. (*GoodFellas*, 1990).

in a convertible on a starlit night, each wearing elegant clothing and drinking champagne from fine crystal. On the other hand, camera angles soberly capture the grimmer aspects of this lifestyle too. From a bird's-eye-view shot (directly overhead), it fatalistically observes the sad, helpless picture of Tommy lying face down on a rec-room floor in a pool of his own blood.

Music is a very important artistic element in *GoodFellas*. It is richly atmospheric. Its lyrics sometimes comment on the visuals, and it sets the emotional tone of many scenes. It suggests a great deal about each time period of the film from the affectionate nostalgia of the 1950s to the distraught uncertainty of the 1970s. It also expresses the themes of the film.

Just as Scorsese does in *Mean Streets* and *New York, New York,* he sometimes selects songs with lyrics that comment on the visuals which they underscore. The words to "Leader of the Pack" are a funny and appropriate commentary featured during the hostess party scene when we meet the goodfellas' wives. The song's story is told by a middle-class teenage girl whose parents disapprove of her boyfriend, who "came from the wrong side of town." Karen, the narrator of this scene, is, similarly, a woman from a middle-class background who has married someone working-class. Moreover, the song is richly connotative of the 1960s, recalling the rebels of that era, greasers in black leather jackets and their girlfriends with teased-up, hairsprayed bouffant hairdos. The women in this scene are the purveyors of that ethos.

Sometimes music works to soften the violence or aggressiveness of a scene; sometimes it works in counterpoint to the visuals. When Henry gets in trouble with his father because he hasn't been in school in months, the goodfellas help him out so he can keep his cab stand job. They grab Henry's mailman off the street, throw him into the backseat of a car, and rough him up at the pizzeria. This violent act is diminished, however, by Henry's narration and the accompanying music, "Hearts of Stone." The song features men harmonizing a boogy woogy song with a saxophone in rhythm and blues. The friendly, smooth sound tones down the violence while Henry remarks wryly that not only did no more letters from school arrive at his house, his family didn't receive any mail for two weeks. Finally his mother had to go to the post office to complain.

In another scene a restaurant owner asks Paulie to become his partner to help save his business. However, this decision turns out to be a serious mistake. Ordered goods now come into the restaurant sold at 100 percent profit, with the owner paying the bills. While this process is shown visually, with boxes of goods being dollied in and out, the song "Playboy" underscores the scene. The bebop girl-group, fast-paced, sassy lyrics make the sad exploitation of the restaurant owner seem routine, normal, even fun.

Also, when Jimmy greets the men who pulled off the Lufthansa heist, "Frosty the Snowman" plays in the background. The song suggests the happiness of the holiday season and innocence of childhood fun. The song fits. As some of the more dim-witted members of the theft team enter, they proudly show off expensive items they just purchased: a pink Cadillac and a fur coat. Like children, they can't wait to buy themselves gifts with their share of the stolen money. However, Jimmy had warned them not to buy anything because of the danger of calling attention to themselves.

In addition to lyrics commenting on a visual and music sometimes softening a violent scene, one of the primary ways music is used in *GoodFellas* is to suggest the mood and atmosphere of the time periods portrayed in the film and to express the movie's themes.

During the 1950s scenes, the songs are nostalgic. The first tune, "Rags to Riches," sung by Tony Bennett, has an inviting, friendly, safe sound. It underscores young Henry, from his living-room window, longingly watching the guys at the cab stand. This song suggests the romantic attraction of being one of the goodfellas. It also expresses the emotional tone of the romantic yearnings that pull people to a set of values, a lifestyle, a type of person to aspire to.

Similarly, the music of the early 1960s suggests a time of romance and innocence. When Henry comes of age during this period, the first shot is of him waiting to hijack goods from a truck with Tommy at a diner near the airport. In a grey silk suit and knit sweater and with slicked-back hair, he looks polished and confident. Announcing this scene is a 1960s crooner song, "Sometimes I Wonder," smooth, elegant, and romantic.

The late 1960s, a transitional time, is marked by more traditional songs like Jack Jones's "Wives and Lovers" and "Beyond the Sea," as well as more modern tunes like Donovan's "Atlantis." "Wives and Lovers" suggests the smugness of the 1960s, reflecting a naive sense of security and assurance that would be shattered by violent social upheavals, political assassinations and scandals, and the aftermath of cynicism from the Vietnam War. "Beyond the Sea," sounding smooth and elegant, suggests the snug oasis of the goodfellas in jail, enjoying one another's fellowship apart from the seamier environment of the other prisoners. The modern sound of "Atlantis" forebodes the sinister step Tommy and Jimmy take in killing Billy Batts, a made man, an act that will later have grave consequences.

The tumultuous decade of the 1970s is reflected vividly through the music that underscores scenes taking place during that time period. This music is radically different in melody and lyrics than the fifties and sixties counterparts. Whereas the music of the fifties and sixties sounds innocent, romantic, and safe, the music of the seventies sounds threatening, dangerous, and out of control. This music is hard rock, straight out of the drug culture, and reflective of a society ripped apart.

During the scene when Henry's girlfriend, Sandy, is cutting coke, "Gimme Shelter" blares in the background, a wild, hard-rock song with lyrics suggestive of the lure of drugs. That great high is "just a shot away," they promise. Lois, the sullen baby-sitter and drug runner, shows Karen the baby she will be transporting to Pittsburgh. As she does, "Monkey Man" by the Rolling Stones shouts in the background, sounding frenetic, seductive, and insolent.

When Jimmy smokes a cigarette while he thinks about killing Morrie, he is photographed in slightly slowed motion, putting special focus on him as he contemplates this act. "Sunshine of Your Love" plays in the background, sounding aggressive, grinding, and intense, expressive of the violent act he is pondering. Henry comments that he "could see Jimmy was a nervous wreck. His mind was going in eight directions at once."

But perhaps the most vivid use of wild rock and roll occurs during the scenes of May 11, 1980. That day starts with a fast, pounding bass which sets the pace and tone for Henry's day: frantic, wired, nerve-jangling, paranoid, strung out. The first visuals are a close-up of Henry doing lines of coke. By

8:05 Henry is driving down the highway, anxiously looking up at a helicopter which is tracking him. His movements are jerky, nervous. The lyrics, "I want it. I want it. I want it" reverberate, reflecting Henry in his full-blown addiction, all wants and needing to have it all.

Henry nearly gets into an accident and brakes to a dead stop inches from the car in front of him. Loud, speeded-up drums symbolize the adrenalin rushing through Henry's body. The lyrics scream out the promise of intimacy, of happiness, from this new lover, cocaine: "We can make each other happy." The lyrics "I'm a monkey" elbow into the musical score as the day progresses, set to screaming, shrill rock. One of the final shots featuring music on this day is a close-up of Henry snorting coke, his nostrils red and his eyes glassy. Underneath this picture, a hard-driving blues drones, "I'm a rolling stone." A small speeded-up drumbeat suggests the nervous energy with which Henry tries to embark for Rockaway to get Lois's lucky hat before she flies to Pittsburgh.

The song played during the credits is a discordant version of "My Way." In this distorted interpretation of the famous Frank Sinatra song, punk-rocker Sid Viscious's performance is abrasive, stuttering, indecipherable. In contrast to the original's smooth, straightforward proclamation of individuality, this version is nasal, harsh, and nasty. Appropriately, it reflects a warped concept of individual enterprise and the more positive connotation of the self-made man. Here men have "succeeded" through ruthlessness, selfishness, extortion, and killing.

Like other Scorsese films, *GoodFellas* is well cast. Even small roles are played by actors with the looks and mannerisms that make their characters authentic and vividly etched.

Scorsese is especially good at selecting actors who show a distinctive New York City style: the school-crossing guard who buys cigarettes from Jimmy; the policeman who takes a payoff from Jimmy; the plain-clothes officers who arrest young Henry outside the factory; the man at the airport who fakes the hijacking of his truck; the trucker to whom Jimmy says, "You might know who we are, but we *know* who you are"; and Henry's brother, Michael, whom Henry picks up from the hospital.

Many other small roles are also memorable. Scorsese often captures the expression of an emotion, mood, or idea of a scene with sensitivity to detail and precise timing. For example, when Henry sees Sandy, she is annoyed that he won't stay longer with her. This small scene is convincing and striking, however, because Debi Mazar acts the part of being stoned and feeling resentful so well. Her performance is not overacted; and her resentment resonates from pent-up feeling. Scorsese also captures emotion with precise timing when Henry's father vents his anger over Henry's not attending school; when Karen's mother argues with Karen over Henry's staying out all night with his friends; and when Belle (Margo

Winkler) comes to Henry's house, frantic with worry because she knows something has happened to her husband, Morris.

The lead characters—Henry, Jimmy, Tommy, Karen, and Paulie—were all well-acted, each vivid, full, and distinctive. Ray Liotta looks the part of a 1950s leading man in style and spirit. He resembles Ed Burns (the parking lot attendant in the popular detective show *77 Sunset Strip*), a rebel without a cause of the 1950s era, an outsider and an underling, but hip and a part of the action too.

Liotta plays Henry in an understated manner. Henry is not as tough and thick-skinned as his gangster buddies. He has not lost his humanity. We identify with Liotta when he shows Henry's visceral response to some of the brutality he witnesses: Henry is moved to help the man shot in front of the pizzeria; he is shocked at Tommy's shooting Spider and comes to his aid; and he gets sick at digging up a corpse while Jimmy and Tommy crack jokes about it. Liotta acts this side of Henry well.

Liotta's performance is especially powerful when his life is overcome by the insanity of addiction. For example, when Henry is high on coke, Liotta is the picture of someone in the throes of addiction: he looks sweaty and has bloodshot eyes. He is jittery driving his car as he looks up at the helicopter, nearly crashing into the car in front of him. His movements are quick and jerky, his nerves shattered. One of the most compelling scenes revolves around the way Liotta shows Henry's vulnerability as he talks to Ed McDonald, the FBI agent. Henry squirms, his speech is strained, all his fears are exposed.

Robert De Niro gives another completely different performance in this Scorsese film. Jimmy Conway is a thug: tough, hardened, all defenses, private and distant. Jimmy is harder to sympathize with than other characters De Niro has played because, except when his friend Tommy is killed, Jimmy shows no vulnerability. Still, the strength and inviolability De Niro brings to this performance are commanding. The aggressiveness and tough-mindedness, performed in a spare, minimalist acting style, push through in each scene while De Niro keeps other emotions well hidden. One example is when Jimmy talks to Karen about whether Henry has said anything to the police and later offers her some designer dresses. De Niro conceals Jimmy's motivations, making the scene ambiguous and suspenseful.

Joe Pesci's performance as Tommy is a complete contrast to his performance as Joey, Jake La Motta's brother, in *Raging Bull*, a role marked by warmth and humanity. As Tommy, Pesci fleshes out a character who is funny, psychotic, insecure, and cold-blooded. Tommy is the raconteur of the goodfellas. Interestingly, his stories aren't very funny. They're based on thug shop talk, stories about gangsters bullying other gangsters. One would have to be a thug to fully appreciate the humor in these anecdotes.

Pesci is especially forceful in the scenes where he shows Tommy's insecurity, hot-headedness, and psychotic behavior. The "You're a funny guy" scene is serious and frightening one minute and then the tone shifts to welcome relief and humor. This episode foreshadows Tommy's killing Billy Batts and his wounding and later killing Spider. In recognition for his remarkable acting, Pesci won an Academy Award for best supporting actor for his role as Tommy.

Lorraine Bracco gives a memorable performance as Henry's wife, Karen. Bright and attractive, Karen is an interesting character and an important voiceover narrator. Wearing the fashions and hairdos of each era, Karen reflects changing attitudes and styles from the conservative 1950s to the glitzy 1970s. Bracco's acting is powerful: She lives the part of Karen, an intelligent and strong woman who loves Henry. We see her during the happy times—the excitement of their courtship and wedding—and the miserable ones, when she grieves as her husband goes to prison. We also see the determination she shows in standing by Henry, writing letters to the parole board, sneaking in goods to him in jail, and caring for their children alone. Some of the most memorable scenes, which reveal the depth of her love for Henry, are those in which Bracco movingly shows Karen's passionate agony over Henry's affair with Janice Rossi.

Finally, Paul Sorvino brings strength, toughness, and authority to his role as Paul Cicero. Paulie's very presence, his mere walking into one of the opening scenes, for example, makes Tuddy and one of his buddies look at one another sheepishly and stop their playful jabbing. Sorvino shows Paulie's affection for Henry, how loving he is towards "the kid," and how proud he is of Henry as a young man, earning a lot of money in Henry's first big heist, Air France. Private, idiosyncratic, and powerful, Paulie is an original as the Mafia boss.

GoodFellas was a notable commercial success. It was one of Scorsese's highest grossing films. *GoodFellas* is a landmark film for Scorsese in that it combines some of his finest craftsmanship and elements of personal style while also being a very available work of art for a wide audience. *GoodFellas* was the first Scorsese film many had ever seen. It was also well received by critics. Considered a favorite by many, *GoodFellas* was selected by a number of film critics as the movie they believed should receive the Academy Award for best picture of 1990.

CONCLUSION

Scorsese is clearly an auteur. His personal vision is imprinted all over his films. Looking at a single frame of a crowd scene, one could identify it as part of a Scorsese film. Scorsese's artistic signature comes across in his choice of characters and actors; in the stories he chooses to tell and the emotion he invests in telling them; and in the look and bold camera movements of his films.

Perhaps more than any other quality, passion is characteristic of Scorsese's work. His movies are intense. In making his character studies, he is willing to risk being personal, to show the anguish and lonelienss that are a part of his characters' lives. Scorsese shows us their struggles, and we might feel uncomfortable at the personal nature of what he reveals on screen. But life is worth living in a Scorsese movie. Other directors who also have a passionate and intense style lack this vitality and hopefulness: Ingmar Bergman's characters are self-absorbed and tend to be depressed. John Cassavetes's neurotic characters have a similar hopelessness. Elia Kazan's characters are too mired in a system that oppresses. By contrast, Scorsese's charactes are out hustling, making it in a world that still holds out the possibility of fulfillment of hopes and dreams. Unlike other modern characters, his do not live lives of "quiet desperation." His characters are shown from the point of view of the swirling vortex of camera movement punctuated by the beat of contemporary rock music drawing us into their lives.

Scorsese's films are rich visually. His camera, typically, is always moving. His well-framed shots, quick editing, and a participatory camera are all characteristics of his films. What the camera photographs is frequently a richly atmospheric scene meaningfully depicting time and place, not just soft nostalgia or quaintly decorated scenes. Frequently, the camera is lyrical in a Scorsese film.

Scorsese is a New York director in style and spirit. His work reflects many of the characteristics of the Big Apple. His appreciation for individual style and eccentricity, the tough guys who populate his movies, the violence and aggressiveness, the beauty and art, the ethnicity, the humanity, and the humor are all characteristics found in a Scorsese film.

His interest in city types is shared by New York–oriented film makers like Kazan, Cassavetes, Francis Ford Coppola, Spike Lee, and others. Furthermore, Scorsese characteristically dignifies the working class, respecting them, rather than belittling them with stereotypes that middle-class people often have about blue-collar people. In a similar spirit, Scorsese's use of ethnic detail and characterization is truthful, respectful, and appreciative. His characters are, for example, more than conventionally Italian. They are individuals as well, not media cliches.

There is a romanticism in Scorsese's optimistic view of the world, but even more, there is a search for truth, at least in the willingness to probe deeper than the formulas of most movies. Scorsese is consistently a revisionist director. In *Mean Streets,* he goes beyond the cliches about working-class and ethnic neighborhoods to show a plausible coming-of-age story about a young man and his friends in Manhattan's Little Italy. In *Alice,* he looks beyond the predictable woman's story to a woman and her relationships with other women and men and her son while she reconstructs her life after the death of her husband. In his contemporary film noir *Taxi Driver,* Scorsese shows us a sad and frightening picture of modern angst and alienation. In *New York, New York,* instead of telling the usual boy-meets-girl love story, Scorsese attempts the uncharted territory of real intimacy in a love relationship. In *Raging Bull,* he looks beyond the cliches of the typical boxer-hero story to explore the paradox that the same fury which helped bring Jake La Motta success in the ring destroys his life. In *GoodFellas,* he captures the excitement of a gangster's lifestyle, but he also communicates its shocking criminality as well.

Just as Frank Capra and John Ford were directors of their times, the 1930s and 1940s, so has Scorsese been a chronicler of his time, the 1970s, 1980s, and 1990s. Ford and Capra reflected their era by making movies that mirrored a simpler, more idealistic time, and Scorsese is an artist of alienation and anxiety. His search for psychological accuracy, his consistent use of antiheroes, and his unsentimental, yet humanistic approach are all characteristic and expressive artistic elements reflective of contemporary society.

Scorsese brings together the diverse elements of character, story, camera, music, and action in a new and unique way that draws the audience into the film. His creative individuality and startling vision will ensure that Scorsese's works will last. They will be studied not only for their own artistic sake, but also for what they say about America during a tumultuous era of social upheaval and change.

FILMOGRAPHY

As Director

1963
What's a Nice Girl Like You Doing in a Place Like This?
Producer: New York University Department of Television, Motion Picture and
   Radio Presentations, Summer Motion Picture Workshop
Screenplay: Martin Scorsese
Still photography (black and white): Frank Truglio
Editor: Robert Hunsicker
Music: Richard H. Coll
Cast: Zeph Michaelis (Harry), Mimi Stark (wife), Sarah Braveman (analyst),
   Fred Sica (friend), Robert Uricola (singer)
9 minutes

1964
It's Not Just You, Murray!
Producer: New York University Department of Television, Motion Picture and
   Radio Presentations
Screenplay: Martin Scorsese, Mardik Martin
Cinematography (black and white): Richard H. Coll
Editor: Eli F. Bleich
Music: Richard H. Coll
Production designers: Lancelot Braithwaite, Victor Magnotta
Cast: Ira Rubin (Murray), Andrea Martin (wife), San De Fazio (Joe), Robert
   Uricola (singer), Catherine Scorsese (mother), Victor Magnotta, Richard
   Sweeton, Mardik Martin, John Bivona, Bernard Weisberger
15 minutes

1967
The Big Shave
Producer: Martin Scorsese
Screenplay: Martin Scorsese
Cinematography (color): Ares Demertzis
Editor: Martin Scorsese
Art director: Ken Gaulin
Special effects: Eli Bleich

Cast: Peter Bernuth (young man)
6 minutes

1969
Who's That Knocking at My Door?
(First version, 1965, *Bring on the Dancing Girls*; second version, 1967, *I Call First*; also released in 1970 under title *J.R.*)
Producers: Joseph Weill, Betzi Manoogian, Haig Manoogian
Screenplay: Martin Scorsese
Cinematography (black and white): Michael Wadleigh, Richard H. Coll
Editor: Thelma Schoonmaker
Art director: Victor Magnotta
Cast: Harvey Keitel (J.R.), Zina Bethune (girl), Lennard Kuras (Joey), Michael Scala (Sally GaGa), Anne Colette (young girl in dream), Harry Northup (Harry, the rapist), Robert Uricola (young man at party with gun), Bill Minkin (Iggy/radio announcer), Wendy Russell (GaGa's girlfriend), Phil Carlson (guide on the mountain), Susan Wood (Susan), Marissa Joffrey (Rosie), Catherine Scorsese (J.R.'s mother), Tsuai Yu-Lan, Saskia Holleman, Anne Marieka (dream girls), Victor Magnotta, Paul de Bionde (boys in street fight), Martin Scorsese (gangster)
90 minutes

1970
Street Scenes 1970
Producer: New York Cinetracts Collective
Production supervisor and post-production director: Martin Scorsese
Cinematography (black and white/color): Don Lenzer, Harry Bolles, Danny Schneider, Peter Rea, Bob Pitts, Bill Etra, Tiger Graham, Fred Hadley, Ed Summer, Nat Trapp
Editors: Peter Rea, Maggie Koven, Angela Kirby, Larry Tisdall, Gerry Pallor, Thelma Schoonmaker
Cast: William Kunstler, Dave Dellinger, Alan W. Carter, David Z. Robinson, Harvey Keitel, Verna Bloom, Jay Cocks, Martin Scorsese
75 minutes

1972
Boxcar Bertha
Production company: American International Pictures
Producer: Roger Corman
Screenplay: Joyce H. Corrington and John William Corrington, based on *Sister of the Road* by Bertha Thompson as told to Ben L. Reitman
Cinematography (color): John Stephens
Music: Gib Guilbeau and Thad Maxwell
Visual consultant: David Nichols
Cast: Barbara Hershey (Bertha), David Carradine (Billy Shelley), Barry Primus (Rake Brown), Bernie Casey (Von Morton), John Carradine (H. Buckram Sartoris), David R. Osterhout and Victor Argo (the McIvers), Grahame Pratt

(Emeric Pressburger), "Chicken" Holleman (Michael Powell), Marianne Dole (Mrs. Mailer), Harry Northup (Harvey Hall), Doyle Hall (dice player), Joe Reynolds (Joe), Martin Scorsese and Gayne Rescher (clients in brothel)
88 minutes

1973
Mean Streets
Production company: Warner Brothers
Producer: Jonathan T. Taplin
Executive producer: E. Lee Perry
Screenplay: Martin Scorsese, Mardik Martin
Cinematography (color): Kent Wakeford
Editor: Sid Levin
Visual consultant: David Nichols
Cast: Harvey Keitel (Charlie), Robert De Niro (Johnny Boy), David Proval (Tony), Amy Robinson (Teresa), Richard Romanus (Michael), Cesare Danova (Giovanni), George Memmoli (Joey Catucci), Victor Argo (Mario), Lenny Scaletta (Jimmy), Murray Moston (Oscar), David Carradine (drunk), Robert Carradine (assassin), Jeannie Bell (Diane), Lois Walden (Jewish girl at bar), D'Mitch Davis (black cop), Dino Seragusa (old man), Julie Andelman (girl at party), Peter Fain (George), Harry Northup (soldier), Robert Wilder (Benton), Jaime Alba (first young boy), Ken Konstantin (second young boy), Nicki "Ack" Aquilino (man on docks), Catherine Scorsese (woman on landing), Ken Sinclair (Sammy), B. Mitchell Reed (disc jockey), Martin Scorsese (Shorty, Michael's hired killer), Barbara Weintraub (Heather Weintraub), Ron Satloff (Carl), Anna Uricola (neighbor at window)
110 minutes

1974
Alice Doesn't Live Here Anymore
Production company: Warner Brothers
Producers: David Susskind, Audrey Maas
Associate producer: Sandra Weintraub
Screenplay: Robert Getchell
Cinematography (color): Kent Wakeford
Editor: Marcia Lucas
Music: Richard La Salle
Production designer: Toby Rafelson
Cast: Ellen Burstyn (Alice Hyatt), Kris Kristofferson (David), Alfred Lutter (Tommy), Diane Ladd (Flo), Billy Green Bush (Donald), Vic Tayback (Mel), Jodie Foster (Audrey), Harvey Keitel (Ben), Lelia Goldoni (Bea), Lane Bradbury (Rita), Valerie Curtin (Vera), Harry Northup (bartender), Murray Moston (Jacobs), Mia Bendixsen (Alice at age eight), Ola Moore (old woman), Dean Casper (Chicken), Henry M. Kendrick (shop assistant), Martin Brinton (Lenny), Mardik Martin (customer in club), Martin Scorsese and Larry Cohen (patrons at the diner)
112 minutes

Italianamerican
Production company: National Communications Foundation
Producers: Saul Rubin, Elaine Attias
Treatment: Martin Scorsese, Mardik Martin, Larry Cohen
Cinematography (color): Alex Hirschfield
Editor: Bertram Lovitt
Cast: Charles Scorsese, Catherine Scorsese, Martin Scorsese
45 minutes

1975
Taxi Driver
Production company: Columbia Pictures
Producers: Michael Phillips, Julia Phillips
Screenplay: Paul Schrader
Cinematography (color): Michael Chapman
Editors: Marcia Lucas, Tom Rolf, Melvin Shapiro
Music: Bernard Herrmann
Visual consultant: David Nichols
Cast: Robert De Niro (Travis Bickle), Jodie Foster (Iris), Cybill Shepherd
   (Betsy), Harvey Keitel (Sport/Matthew), Steven Prince (Andy, the gun sales-
   man), Albert Brooks (Tom), Peter Boyle (Wizard), Leonard Harris (Charles
   Palantine), Diahnne Abbott (woman at concession stand), Frank Adu (angry
   black man), Richard Higgs (Secret Service agent), Gino Ardito (policeman
   at rally), Garth Avery (Iris's companion), Copper Cunningham (prostitute in
   cab), Harry Fischler (cab dispatcher), Harry Cohn (cabbie in Bellmore),
   Brenda Dickson (woman on soap opera), Nat Grant (stick-up man), Robert
   Martoff (mafioso), Beau Kayser (man on soap opera), Victor Magnotta
   (Secret Service photographer), Norman Matlock (Charlie T.), Murray
   Moston (caretaker at Iris's apartment), Harry Northup (doughboy), Bill Minkin (Tom's assistant), Gene Palma (street drummer), Peter Savage (the john),
   Robert Shields (Palantine aide), Robin Utt (campaign worker), Joe Spinell
   (personnel officer), Maria Turner (angry prostitute on street), Carey Poe
   (campaign worker), Ralph Singleton (television interviewer), Martin Scorsese (man watching silhouette)
113 minutes

1977
New York, New York
Production company: United Artists
Producers: Irwin Winkler, Robert Chartoff
Screenplay: Earl Mac Rauch, Mardik Martin
Cinematography (color): Laszlo Kovacs
Editors: Irving Lerner, Marcia Lucas
Music and songs; John Kander, Fred Ebb
Production designer: Boris Leven
Cast: Robert De Niro (Jimmy Doyle), Liza Minnelli (Francine Evans), Lionel
   Stander (Tony Harwell), Barry Primus (Paul Wilson), Mary Kay Place (Bernice),

Georgie Auld (Frankie Harte), George Memmoli (Nicky), Dick Miller (Palm Club owner), Murray Moston (Horace Morris), Lenny Gaines (Artie Kirks), Clarence Clemons (Cecil Powell), Kathy McGinnis (Ellen Flannery), Norman Palmer (desk clerk), Adam David Winkler (Jimmy Doyle, Jr.), Dimitri Logothetis (desk clerk), Frank Silvera (Eddie de Muzio), Diahnne Abbott (Harlem Club singer), Margo Winkler (argumentative woman), Steven Prince (record producer), Don Calfa (Gilbert), Bernie Ruby (justice of the peace), Selma Archerd (wife of justice of the peace), Bill Baldwin (announcer in Moonlight Terrace), Mary Lindsay (hatcheck girl in Meadows), Jon Cutler (musician in Frankie Harte's band), Nicky Blair (cab driver), Casey Kasem, (DJ), Jay Salerno (bus driver), William Tole (Tommy Dorsey), Sydney Guilaroff (hairdresser), Peter Savage (Horace Morris's assistant), Gene Castle (dancing sailor), Louie Guss (Fowler), Shera Danese (Doyle's girl in Major Chord), Bill McMillan (DJ), David Nichols (Arnold Trench), Harry Northup (Alabama)

Original release version, 136 minutes; re-release version, 163 minutes

1978
The Last Waltz
Production Company: United Artists
Producer: Robbie Robertson
Cinematography (color): Michael Chapman, Laszlo Kovacs, Vilmos Zsigmond, David Myers, Bobby Byrne, Michael Watkins, Hiro Narita
Editors: Yeu-Bun Yee, Jan Roblee
Production designer: Boris Leven
Cast: The Band (Robbie Robertson, Rick Danko, Levon Helm, Garth Hudson, Richard Manuel), Paul Butterfield, Eric Clapton, Neil Diamond, Bob Dylan, Emmylou Harris, Ronnie Hawkins, Dr. John, Joni Mitchell, Van Morrison, The Staples, Ringo Starr, Muddy Waters, Ron Wood, Neil Young, Martin Scorsese, Michael McClure, Lawrence Ferlinghetti
117 minutes

American Boy: A Profile of Steven Prince
Production company: New Empire Films/Scorsese Films
Producers: Bertram Lovitt
Treatment: Mardik Martin, Julia Cameron
Cinematography (color): Michael Chapman
Editors: Amy Jones, Bertram Lovitt
Cast: Steven Prince, Martin Scorsese, George Memmoli, Mardik Martin, Julia Cameron, Kathy McGinnis
55 minutes

1980
Raging Bull
Production company: United Artists
Producers: Irwin Winkler, Robert Chartoff in association with Peter Savage

Screenplay: Paul Schrader, Mardik Martin, from the book *Raging Bull* by Jake La Motta with Joseph Carter and Peter Savage
Cinematography (black and white/color): Michael Chapman
Editor: Thelma Schoonmaker
Production designer: Gene Rudolf
Cast: Robert De Niro (Jake La Motta), Cathy Moriarty (Vickie La Motta), Joe Pesci (Joey La Motta), Frank Vincent (Salvy), Nicholas Colasanto (Tommy Como), Theresa Saldana (Lenore), Mario Gallo (Mario), Frank Adonis (Patsy), Joseph Bono (Guido), Frank Topham (Toppy), Lori Anne Flax (Irma), Charles Scorsese (Charlie, man with Como), Don Dunphy (himself), Bill Hanrahan (Eddie Eagan), Rita Bennett (Emma, Miss 48's), James V. Christy (Dr. Pinto), Bernie Allen (comedian), Michael Badalucco (soda fountain clerk), Thomas Beansy Lobasso (Beansy), Paul Forrest (Monsignor), Peter Petrella (Johnny), Sal Serafino Thomassetti (Webster Hall bouncer), Geraldine Smith (Janet), Mardik Martin (Copa waiter), Maryjane Lauria (first girl), Linda Artuso (second girl), Peter Savage (Jackie Curtie), Daniel P. Conte (Detroit promoter), Joe Malanga (bodyguard), Sabine Turco, Jr., Steve Orlando, Silvio Garcia, Jr. (bouncers at Copa), John Arceri (maître d'), Joseph A. Morale (first man at table), James Dimodica (second man at table), Robert Uricola (man outside cab), Andrea Orlando (woman in cab), Allan Malamud (reporter at Jake's house), D. J. Blair (State Attorney Bronson), Laura James (Mrs. Bronson), Richard McMurray (J.R.), Mary Albee (underage ID girl), Liza Katz (woman with ID girl), Candy Moore (Linda), Martin Scorsese (Barbizon stagehand), Johnny Barnes ("Sugar" Ray Robinson), Floyd Anderson (Jimmy Reeves), Eddie Mustafa Muhammad (Billy Fox), Louis Raftis (Marcel Cerdan), Johnny Turner (Laurent Dauthuille)
129 minutes

1982
The King of Comedy
Production company: Twentieth Century-Fox
Producer: Arnon Milchan
Screenplay: Paul Zimmerman
Cinematography (color): Fred Schuler
Editor: Thelma Schoonmaker
Production designer: Boris Leven
Cast: Robert De Niro (Rupert Pupkin), Jerry Lewis (Jerry Langford), Diahnne Abbott (Rita), Sandra Bernhard (Masha), Ed Herlihy (himself), Lou Brown (bandleader), Loretta Tupper, Peter Potulski, Vinnie Gonzales (stage door fans), Whitey Ryan (stage door guard), Doc Lawess (chauffeur), Marta Heflin (young girl), Catherine Scorsese (Rupert's mom), Cathy Scorsese (Dolores), Chuck Low (man in Chinese restaurant), Margo Winkler (receptionist), Shelley Hack (Cathy Long), Mick Jones, Joe Strummer, Paul Simonon, Kosmo Vinyl, Ellen Foley, Pearl Harbor, Gabu Salter, Jerry Baxter-Worman, Don Letts (street scum), Fred de Cordova (Bert Thomas), Edgar J. Scherick (Wilson Crockett), Kim Chan (Jonno), Dr. Joyce Brothers, Victor Borge, Tony Randall (themselves), Jay Julien (Langford's lawyer),

Harry Ufland (Langford's agent), Martin Scorsese (television director), Charles Scorsese (first man at bar), Mardik Martin (second man at bar)
108 minutes

1985
After Hours
Production company: Double Play/The Geffen Company
Producers: Amy Robinson, Griffin Dunne, Robert Colesberry
Screenplay: Joseph Minion
Cinematography (color): Michael Ballhaus
Editor: Thelma Schoonmaker
Music: Howard Shore
Production designer: Jeffrey Townsend
Cast: Griffin Dunne (Paul Hackett), Rosanna Arquette (Marcy), Verna Bloom (June), Thomas Chong (Pepe), Linda Fiorentino (Kiki), Terri Garr (Julie), John Heard (Tom, the bartender), Cheech Marin (Neil), Catherine O'Hara (Gail), Dick Miller (waiter), Will Patton (Horst), Robert Plunket (Mark), Bronson Pinchot (Lloyd), Rocco Sisto (coffee-shop cashier), Larry Block (taxi driver), Victor Argo (diner cashier), Murray Moston (subway attendant), John P. Codiglia (transit cop), Clarke Evans (first neighbor), Victor Bumbalo (second neighbor), Bill Elvermann (third neighbor), Joel Jason (first biker), Clarence Felder (bouncer), Henry Baker (Jett), Margo Winkler (woman with gun), Robin Johnson (punk girl), Stephen J. Lim (Club Berlin bartender), Frank Aquilino, Maree Catalano, Paula Raflo, Rockets Redglare (angry mob members), Martin Scorsese (man with spotlight)
97 minutes

Mirror, Mirror
(episode in "Amazing Stories" TV series)
Production company: Amblin
Producer: David E. Vogel
Screenplay: Joseph Minion, from a story by Steven Spielberg
Cinematography (color): Robert Stevens
Editor: Joe Ann Fogle
Music: Michael Kamen
Production designer: Rick Carter
Cast: Sam Waterston (Jordan), Helen Shaver (Karen), Dick Cavett (himself), Tim Robbins (Jordan's phantom), Dana Gladstone (producer), Valerie Grear (host), Michael C. Gwynne (jail attendant), Peter Iacangelo (limo driver), Jonathan Luria (cameraman), Harry Northup (security guard), Glenn Scarpelli (Jeffrey Gelb), Jack Thibeau (tough guy)
24 minutes

1986
The Color of Money
Production company: Touchstone
Producers: Irving Axelrad, Barbara De Fina

Screenplay: Richard Price, based on the novel by Walter Tevis
Cinematography (color): Michael Ballhaus
Editor: Thelma Schoonmaker
Music: Robbie Robertson
Production designer: Boris Leven
Cast: Paul Newman ("Fast" Eddie Felson), Tom Cruise (Vincent Lauria), Mary
   Elizabeth Mastrantonio (Carmen), Helen Shaver (Jazelle), John Turtorro
   (Julian), Bill Cobbs (Orvis), Keith McCready (Grady Seasons), Robert Agins
   (Earl at Chalkies), Alvin Anastasia (Kennedy), Elizabeth Bracco (Diane at
   bar), Joe Guastaferro (Chuck the bartender), Grady Matthews (Dud), Steve
   Mizerak (Duke, Eddie's first opponent), Jerry Piller (Tom), Forest Whitaker
   (Amos), Bruce A. Young, (Moselle), Vito D'Ambrosio (Lou in Child World),
   Randall Arney (first Child World customer), Lisa Dodson (second Child
   World customer), Ernest Perry, Jr. (eye doctor), Iggy Pop (skinny player on
   road), Richard Price (guy who calls Dud), Alex Ross (bartender who bets),
   Charles Scorsese (first high roller), Fred Squillo (second high roller)
119 minutes

Armani Commercial (I)
Production company: Emporio Armani
Producer: Barbara De Fina
Treatment: Martin Scorsese
Cinematography (black and white): Nestor Almendros
Cast: Christophe Bouquin, Christina Marsilach
30 seconds

1987
Bad
Production company: Optimum Productions
Producers: Quincy Jones, Barbara De Fina
Screenplay: Richard Price
Cinematography (black and white/color): Michael Chapman
Editor: Thelma Schoonmaker
Choreography: Michael Jackson, Gregg Burge, Jeffrey Daniel
Cast: Michael Jackson (Daryl), Adam Nathan (Tip), Pedro Sanchez (Nelson),
   Webley Sniper (Mini Max), Greg Holtz, Jr. (Cowboy), Jaime Perry (Ski),
   Paul Calderon (dealer), Alberto Alejandrino (Hispanic man), Horace Daily
   (street bum), Marvin Foster (crack customer), Roberta Flack (Daryl's
   mother)
16 minutes

1988
Somewhere Down the Crazy River
Production company: Limelight
Producers: Amanda Pirie, Tim Clawson
Treatment: Martin Scorsese
Cinematography (color): Mark Plummer

Production designer: Marina Levikova
Cast: Robbie Robertson, Sammy BoDean, Maria McKee
4½ minutes

The Last Temptation of Christ
Production company: Universal Pictures
Producer: Barbara De Fina
Screenplay: Paul Schrader, based on the novel by Nikos Kazantzakis
Cinematography (color): Michael Ballhaus
Editor: Thelma Schoonmaker
Music: Peter Gabriel
Production designer: John Beard
Cast: Willem Dafoe (Jesus), Harvey Keitel (Judas), Paul Greco (Zealot), Steven
   Shill (Centurion), Verna Bloom (Mary, Mother of Jesus), Barbara Hershey
   (Mary Magdalene), Roberts Blossom (Aged Master), Barry Miller (Jero-
   boam), Gary Basaraba (Andrew Apostle), Irvin Kershner (Zebedee), Victor
   Argo (Peter Apostle), Michael Been (John Apostle), Paul Herman (Philip
   Apostle), John Lurie (James Apostle), Leo Burmeister (Nathaniel Apostle),
   André Gregory (John the Baptist), Peggy Gormley (Martha, sister of Laza-
   rus), Randy Danson (Mary, sister of Lazarus), Thomas Arana (Lazarus), Alan
   Rosenberg (Thomas Apostle), Del Russel (moneychanger), Nehemiah Per-
   soff (Rabbi), Donald Hodson (Sadducee), Harry Dean Stanton (Saul/Paul),
   Peter Berling (beggar), David Bowie (Pontius Pilate), Juliette Caton (girl
   angel)
163 minutes

Armani Commercial (2)
Production company: Emporio Armani
Producer: Barbara De Fina
Treatment: Martin Scorsese
Cinematography (color): Michael Ballhaus
Cast: Jens Peter, Elisabetha Ranella
20 seconds

1989
New York Stories: Life Lessons
Episode in three-part film; other parts—*Oedipus Wrecks,* directed by Woody
   Allen, and *Life without Zoe,* directed by Francis Coppola.
Production company: Touchstone
Producers: Barbara De Fina, Robert Greenhut
Screenplay: Richard Price
Cinematography (color): Nestor Almendros
Editor: Thelma Schoonmaker
Production designer: Kristi Zea
Cast: Nick Nolte (Lionel Dobie), Rosanna Arquette (Paulette), Patrick O'Neal
   (Philip Fowler), Jesse Borrego (Reuben Toro), Steve Buscemi (Gregory
   Stark), Peter Gabriel, Richard Price, Michael Powell
44 minutes

1990
GoodFellas
Production company: Warner Brothers
Producer: Irwin Winkler
Executive producer: Barbara De Fina
Screenplay: Nicholas Pileggi, Martin Scorsese, based on the book *Wiseguy* by
   Pileggi
Cinematography (color): Michael Ballhaus
Editor: Thelma Schoonmaker
Production designer: Kristi Zea
Cast: Robert De Niro (James Conway), Ray Liotta (Henry Hill), Joe Pesci
   (Tommy DeVito), Lorraine Bracco (Karen Hill), Paul Sorvino (Paul Cicero),
   Frank Sivero (Frankie Carbone), Tony Darrow (Sonny Bunz), Mike Starr
   (Frenchy), Frank Vincent (Billy Batts), Chuck Low (Morris Kessler), Frank
   DiLeo (Tuddy Cicero), Henny Youngman (himself), Gina Mastrogiacomo
   (Janice Rossi), Catherine Scorsese (Tommy's mother), Charles Scorsese
   (Vinnie), Suzanne Shepherd (Karen's mother), Debi Mazar (Sandy), Margo
   Winkler (Belle Kessler), Welker White (Lois Byrd), Jerry Vale (himself),
   Julie Garfield (Mickey Conway), Christopher Serrone (young Henry),
   Elaine Kagan (Henry's mother), Beau Starr (Henry's father), Kevin Cor-
   rigan (Michael Hill), Michael Imperioli (Spider), Robbie Vinton, (Bobby
   Vinton), John Williams (Johnny Roastbeef), Daniel P. Conte, Tony Conforti,
   Frank Pellegrino, Ronald Maccone, and Tony Sirico (Cicero's 50's crew),
   Joseph D'Onofrio (young Tommy), Steve Forleo (City Detective #1),
   Richard Dioguardi (City Detective #2), Frank Adonis (Anthony Stabile),
   John Manca (Nickey Eyes), Joseph Bono (Mikey Franzese), Katherine
   Wallach (Diane), Mark Evan Jacobs (Bruce), Angela Pietropinto (Cicero's
   wife), Marianne Leone (Tuddy's wife), Marie Michaels (Mrs. Carbone), Lo
   Nardo (Frenchy's wife), Melissa Prophet, Illeana Douglas, and Susan Varon
   (women at cosmetics party), Elizabeth Whitcraft (Tommy's girlfriend at the
   Copa), Clem Caserta (Joe Buddha), Samuel L. Jackson (Stacks Edwards),
   Fran McGee (Johnny Roastbeef's wife), Paul Herman (dealer), Edward
   McDonald (himself), Edward Hayes (defense attorney), Daniela Barbosa
   (young Henry's sister #1), Gina Mattia (young Henry's sister #2), Joel Calen-
   drillo (young Henry's older brother), Anthony Valentin (young Michael), Edward D. Murphy (liquor cop #1), Michael Citriniti (liquor cop #2), Peter
   Hock (mailman), Erasmus C. Alfano (barbeque wiseguy), John DiBenedetto
   (bleeding man), Manny Alfaro (gambling doorman), Thomas Lowry (hijacked
   driver), Margaret Smith (school guard), Richard Mullally (cop #1), Frank
   Albanese (mob lawyer), Paul McIssac (judge 1956), Bob Golub (truck driver
   at diner), Louis Eppolito (Fat Andy), Tony Lip (Frankie the Wop), Mikey
   Black (Freddy No Nose), Peter Cicale (Pete the Killer), Anthony Powers
   (Jimmy Two Times), Vinny Pastore (man with coatrack), Anthony Alessan-
   dro and Victor Colicchio (Henry's 60's crew), Mike Contessa and Philip
   Suriano (Cicero's 60's crew), Paul Mougey (terrorized waiter), Norman
   Barbera (bouncer), Anthony Polemeni (Copa Captain), James Quattrochi
   (Henry greeter #1), Lawrence Sacco (Henry greeter #2), Dino Laudicina

(Henry greeter #3), Thomas E. Camuti (Mr. Tony hood #1), Andrew Scudiero (Mr. Tony hood #2), Irving Welzer (Copa announcer), Jesse Kirtzman (Beach Club waiter), Russell Halley (Bruce's brother #1), Spencer Bradley (Bruce's brother #2), Bob Altman (Karen's dad), Joanna Bennett (Marie #1), Gayle Lewis (Marie #2), Gaetano Lisi (Paul #3), Luke Walter (truck driver), Ed Deacy (Detective Deacy), Larry Silvestri (Detective Silvestri), Johnny Cha Cha Ciarcia (Batts's crew #1), Vito Picone (Vito), Janis Corsair (Vito's girlfriend), Frank Aquilino (Batts's crew #2), Lisa DaPolito (Lisa), Michael Calandrino (godfather at table), Vito Antuofermo (prizefighter), Vito Balsamo, Peter Fain, Vinnie Gallo, Gaetano LoGiudice, and Garry Blackwood (Henry's 70's crew), Nicole Burdette (Carbone's girlfriend), Stella Kietel (Henry's older child [Judy]), Dominque DeVito (Henry's baby [Ruth]), Michaelangelo Graziano (bar patron), Paul Gallo (Janice's girlfriend #1), Nadine Kay (Janice's girlfriend #2), Tony Ellis (bridal shop owner), Peter Onorati (Florida bookie), Jamie DeRoy (bookie's sister), Joel Blake (Judge 1971), H. Clay Dear (security guard with lobsters), Thomas Hewson (drug buyer), Gene Canfield (prison guard in booth), Margaux Guerard (Judy Hill at 10 years), Violet Gaynor (Ruth Hill at 8 years), Tobin Bell (parole officer), Berlinda Tolbert (Stacks's girlfriend), Nancy Ellen Cassaro (Joe Buddha's wife), Adam Wandt (kid), Joseph P. Gioco (garbage man), Isiah Whitlock, Jr. (doctor), Alyson Jones (Judy Hill at 13 years), Ruby Gaynor (Ruth Hill at 11 years), Richard "Bo" Dietl (arresting narc)
146 minutes

As Editor

1970
Woodstock
Production company: Warner Brothers
Director: Michael Wadleigh
Supervising editor: Martin Scorsese
184 minutes

1971
Medicine Ball Caravan
(also released as *We Have Come for Your Daughters*)
Production company: Warner Brothers
Director: François Reichenbach
Supervising editor: Martin Scorsese
88 minutes

1972
Unholy Rollers
Production company: AIP
Director: Vernon Zimmerman
Supervising editor: Martin Scorsese
88 minutes

Elvis on Tour
Production company: MGM
Director: Pierre Adidge, Robert Abel
Montage supervisor: Martin Scorsese
93 minutes

As Actor

1969
Who's That Knocking at My Door?
as gangster

1972
Boxcar Bertha
as client in brothel

1973
Mean Streets
as Shorty, Michael's hired killer

1974
Alice Doesn't Live Here Anymore
as patron at diner

1976
Taxi Driver
as man watching silhouette

1976
Cannonball
Directed by Paul Bartel
as mafioso

1980
Raging Bull
as Barbizon stagehand

1981
Il Pap'occhio (In the Eye of the Pope)
Directed by Renzo Arbore
as television director

1982
The King of Comedy
as television director

Pavlova: A Woman for All Time
Directed by Emil Lotianou
as Gatti-Cassaza, director of the Metropolitan Opera House

1985
After Hours
as man with spotlight

1986
Round Midnight
Directed by Bertrand Tavernier
as Goodley, the manager of Birdland

WORKS CITED

Bobrow, Andrew. "The Filming of Mean Streets." *Filmmakers Newsletter* 7, no. 3 (January 1974): 28–31.

Cateura, Linda Brandi. *Growing Up Italian*. New York: William Morrow & Company, 1987.

Ciment, Michel, and Michael Henry. "Entretien avec Martin Scorsese." *Positif*, no. 170 (June 1975): 8–23.

Crist, Judith. "A Star Outshining in Its Galaxy." *New York*, 27 January 1975, 64.

Delson, James. "Mean Streets." *Take One* 3, no. 12 (July/August 1972): 28–29.

Denby, David. "*Mean Streets:* The Sweetness of Hell." *Sight and Sound* 4, no. 1 (Winter 1973–74): 48–50.

Ferretti, Fred. "The Delicate Art of Creating a Brutal Film Hero." *New York Times*, 23 November 1980, 1, 28.

Fischler, Steven, and Joel Sucher. (Producers and Directors). 1990. "American Masters Martin Scorsese Directs" [television documentary]. New York: Pacific Street Film Projects, Inc. in association with Thirteen/WNET.

Flatley, Guy. "At the Movies." *New York Times*, 24 June 1977, C-8.

————. "He Has Often Walked Mean Streets." *New York Times*, 16 December 1973, 17–28.

————. "Martin Scorsese's Gamble." *New York Times Magazine*, 8 February 1976, 34–43.

Gambino, Richard. "Despair, Italian Style." *Village Voice*, 23 May 1974, 105, 107–8.

Giannetti, Louis. *Masters of the American Cinema*. Englewood Cliffs, N.J.: Prentice-Hall, 1981.

Hodenfield, Chris. "*New York, New York:* Martin Scorsese's Back-Lot Sonata." *Rolling Stone*, 16 June 1977, 36–44.

Howard, Steve. "The Making of *Alice Doesn't Live Here Anymore*." *Filmmakers Newsletter*, 8, no. 5 (March 1975): 21–26.

Jacobs, Diane. *Hollywood Renaissance.* South Brunswick, N.J., and New York: A. S. Barnes, 1977, 122–48.

James, Caryn. "Fascination with Faith Fuels Work by Scorsese." *New York Times,* 8 August 1988, C11, 14.

Kael, Pauline. "The Current Cinema: Woman on the Road." *New Yorker,* 13 January 1975, 74–78.

————. "The Current Cinema: Underground Man." *New Yorker,* 9 February 1976, 82–85.

Kroll, Jack. "Hackie in Hell." *Newsweek,* 1 March 1976, 82–83.

Landau, Jon. "Films: *Mean Streets.*" *Rolling Stone,* 8 November 1973, 80.

Lindsey, Robert. "The Director of *Taxi Driver* Shifts Gear." *New York Times.* 8 August 1976, 1, 11.

Macklin, Anthony. "It's a Personal Thing for Me." *Film Heritage* 10, no. 3 (Spring 1975): 13–28, 36.

Oumano, Ellen. *Film Forum Thirty-Five Top Filmmakers Discuss Their Craft.* New York: St. Martin's Press, 1985.

Pond, Steve. "Movies: Newman, Cruise and Mastrantonio." *Rolling Stone,* 20 November 1986, 30–32.

Rosen, Marjorie. "New Hollywood: Martin Scorsese Interview." *Film Comment* 11, no. 2 (March–April 1975): 42–46.

Smith, Gavin. "Martin Scorsese Interviewed by Gavin Smith." *Film Comment* 26, no. 5 (September–October 1990): 27–30, 69.

Sterritt, David. Review of *New York, New York. Christian Science Monitor,* 15 July 1977, 22.

Strauss, Bob. "Scorsese: An Artistic Cornucopia of Contradictions." *The Plain Dealer.* 23 September 1990, 8H.

Thompson, David, and Ian Christie. *Scorsese on Scorsese.* London: Faber and Faber, 1989.

INDEX

Abbott, Diahnne 93, 129
After Hours 90, 95, 102, 103–112, 113, 138, 139
Alice Doesn't Live Here Anymore 15, 17–32, 83–84, 88, 95, 102, 104, 138, 139, 158
Allen, Woody 95, 133
Amazing Stories 112
Arquette, Rosanna 103–112, 129, 133–135
Artie (*New York, New York*) 65
Astaire, Fred 60
Auld, George 62, 66

Baby (*Dirty Dancing*) 110
Ballhaus, Michael 104, 144
Barnes, Johnny 76
Batts, Billy (*GoodFellas*) 139–155
Bea (*Alice Doesn't Live Here Anymore*) 18–32, 88
Behar, Henri 18
Ben (*Alice Doesn't Live Here Anymore*) 18–32, 139
Bennett, Tony 137, 151
Bergman, Ingmar 157
Berlin Club (*After Hours*) 111
Bernhard, Sandra 87–102
Bertolucci, Bernardo 13
Betsy (*Taxi Driver*) 36–48
Bickle, Travis (*Taxi Driver*) 33–48, 85, 88, 131
Black, Mikey 146
Bleak House 78
Bliss, Michael x, 24
Boxcar Bertha 125, 129

Boyle, Peter 43
Bracco, Lorraine 138–155
Bridges, Kiki (*After Hours*) 105–112
Bronson, Charles 41
Brooks, Albert 36, 46
Burns, Ed 154
Burstyn, Ellen 17–32
Bush, Billy Green 17–32

Canby, Vincent 113
Cannes Film Festival 48, 112
Capra, Frank 158
Carbone, Frankie (*GoodFellas*) 146
Carmen (*The Color of Money*) 114–123
Carradine, David 125, 129
Cassavetes, John x, 112, 157, 158
Cateura, Linda Brandi 5
Chapman, Michael 34, 43
Charles, Ray 97
Charlie (*Mean Streets*) 1–15, 88, 131, 145
Chips 9, 11
Christ, Judith 27
Ciardi, John 5
Cicero, Paul (*GoodFellas*) 138–155
Cicero, Tuddy (*GoodFellas*) 138
Citizen Kane 25, 44
Cocks, Jay 125
Collins, Judy 108
The Color of Money 95, 112, 113–123
Colosanto, Nicholas 70–85
Como, Tommy (*Raging Bull*) 70–85

Conway, Jimmy (*GoodFellas*) 85, 138–155
Conway, Mickey (*GoodFellas*) 144
Copacabana 144
Coppola, Francis Ford 133, 139, 158
Corman, Roger 125
Crawford, Joan 20
Cruise, Tom 114–123
Curtain, Valerie 32

Dafoe, Willem 126–135
Dali, Salvadore 130
Danova, Cesare 1
Dante 42
David (*Alice Doesn't Live Here Anymore*) 18–32
Day, Doris 20
Debonaire Social Club (*Raging Bull*) 79
Decca Records 51
De Cordova, Fred 100
Denby, David 6, 10, 13
De Niro 1–15, 33–48, 50–67, 69–85, 87–102, 129 138–155
De Palma, Brian x
De Vito, Tommy (*GoodFellas*) 145–155
Diane (*Mean Streets*) 10
Dickens, Charles 77, 78
Di Leo, Frank 138
Dirty Dancing 110
Disney Studios 113
Dobie, Lionel (*New York Stories*) 133–135
Donald (*Alice Doesn't Live Here Anymore*) 17–32
Donald (*New York, New York*) 63
D'Onofrio, Joseph 145
Donovan 152
Dorcey, Tommy 58–60
Doughboy (*Taxi Driver*) 43, 47
Doyle, Jimmy (*New York, New York*) 49–67, 85, 88, 131

Duke (*The Color of Money*) 123
Dunne, Griffin 103–112

Eastwood, Clint 41
Easy Andy (*Taxi Driver*) 47
Ebert, Roger 101
Edwards, Stacks (*GoodFellas*) 146
Eliot, T.S. 33, 42, 77
Evans, Francine (*New York, New York*) 49–67, 88

Faye, Alice 25–26
Felson, Fast Eddie (*The Color of Money*) 113–123
Fiorentino, Linda 105–112
Fitzgerald, F. Scott 77
Flatley, Guy 6
Flo (*Alice Doesn't Live Here Anymore*) 18–32, 88
Ford, John 25, 158
Forty-Second Street 63
Foster, Jody 36–48, 129
Francis, Saint (*Mean Streets*) 1
Freddy No Nose (*GoodFellas*) 146

Gaines, Lenny 65
Gambino, Richard 4
"The Gambler" 133–135
Garfield, Julie 144
Garland, Judy 63
Garr, Terri 106–112
Garrity, Inspector (*King of Comedy*) 96, 100
Getchell, Robert 31
Giovanni, Uncle (*Mean Streets*) 1–15
The Godfather 10, 139
Goldoni, Lelia 19–32
GoodFellas 85, 134, 137–155
Grant, Nat 39

Great Expectations 78
Growing Up Italian 5
Gulliver's Travels 89

Hack, Shelley 100–102
Hackett, Paul (*After Hours*) 103–112
Happy Endings (*New York, New York*) 51, 67
Harlem Club (*New York, New York*) 51–67
Harris, Leonard 36–48
Harte, Frankie (*New York, New York*) 58, 63
Harwell, Tony (*New York, New York*) 63
Hermann, Bernard 44
Hershey, Barbara 125, 129
Hill, Henry (*GoodFellas*) 137–155
Hill, Karen (*GoodFellas*) 138–155
Hill, Michael (*GoodFellas*) 153
Hitchcock, Alfred 25, 44, 110, 111
Horst (*After Hours*) 106
Hurt, John 109–112
The Hustler 112
Hyatt, Alice (*Alice Doesn't Live Here Anymore*) 17–32

Imperioli, Michael 143
The Inferno 42
Interiors 95
Iris (*Taxi Driver*) 36–48
Italianamerican 32
It's Not Just You, Murray! x

Jackson, Samuel L. 146
Jacobs (*Alice Doesn't Live Here Anymore*) 24
Jazelle (*The Color of Money*) 113
Jimmy (*Mean Streets*) 7, 14–15

John, Elton 28–29
John the Baptist (*The Last Temptation of Christ*) 130–131
Johnny Boy (*Mean Streets*) 1–15, 48, 85
Jolsen, Al 144
Jones, Jack 152
Jonno (*King of Comedy*) 92
Judas (*The Last Temptation of Christ*) 131–132
Julie (*After Hours*) 106–112
Julien, Jay 103
June (*After Hours*) 107–108

Kael, Pauline 38
Kagan, Elaine 141
Kazan, Elia 77, 112, 157–158
Kazantzakis, Nikos 125
Keitel, Harvey 1–15, 31, 46, 129
King of Comedy 87–102, 103, 104, 112, 138
Kirks, Artie (*New York, New York*) 55, 65
Kovac, Laszlo 60
Kristofferson, Kris 18–32
Kroll, Jack 38
Krupa, Gene 45

Ladd, Diane 32
La Motta, Jake (*Raging Bull*) 69–85, 88, 131, 139, 145, 157–158
La Motta, Joey (*Raging Bull*) 70–85, 88, 154
La Motta, Lenore (*Raging Bull*) 79
La Motta, Vickie (*Raging Bull*) 70–85
Landau, Jon 15
Langford, Jerry (*King of Comedy*) 87–102
The Last Supper (*The Last Temptation of Christ*) 130

The Last Temptation of Christ
    (Kazantzakis) 125
The Last Temptation of Christ
    (Scorsese) 102, 103, 125–131
Lee, Spike 158
Life (magazine) 60
"Life Lessons" 133–135
Linda (*After Hours*) 106–112
Liotta, Ray 137–155
Lois (*GoodFellas*) 152
Long, Cathy (*King of Comedy*)
    89–102
"The Love Song of J. Alfred
    Prufrock" 33
Lucas, Marcia 30
Lutter, Alfred 17–32

McBride, Jim x
McCabe, Clarence (*King of Com-
    edy*) 93, 99
McCready, Keith 123
McDonald, Ed (*GoodFellas*) 147
Macklin, Anthony 4
Mafia 6, 46, 70, 82, 137–155
Manoogian, Haig x
Marcy (*After Hours*) 103–112
Marnie 111
Martin, Mardik 7, 14, 65, 84, 129
*Martin Scorsese and Michael
    Cimino* x
Marvalettes 11
Mary Magdalene (*The Last Tempta-
    tion of Christ*) 130
Mascagni, Pietro 79
Masha (*King of Comedy*) 87–102
Mastrantonio, Mary Elizabeth 114–
    123
Mastrogiacomo, Gina 141
Mazar, Debi 141, 153
Mean Streets 1–15, 21, 25, 27, 31,
    32, 49, 88, 104, 105, 131, 138,
    139, 145, 150, 158
Memmoli, George 14, 129
Michael (*Mean Streets*) 1–15, 139

Mildred Pierce 20
Minion, Joe 103
Minnelli, Liza 50–67, 96
Mr. Smith Goes to Washington 92
Mizerak, Steve 123
Monkees 108, 110
Moriarty, Cathy 70–85
Moorie (*GoodFellas*) 139, 152
Moston, Murray 129
Mott the Hoople 26

Nashville 28
National Endowment for the
    Humanities 32
New York, New York 48–67, 77,
    88, 104, 131, 150, 158
New York Stories 133–135
Newman, Paul 112
Nolte, Nick 133–135
Northrup, Harry 43, 47, 129

O'Hara Catherine 106
On the Waterfront 83

Palantine, Senator (*Taxi Driver*)
    36–37, 46
Paramount 126
Paulette (*New York Stories*) 133–
    135
Pepy (*After Hours*) 110
Pesci, Joe 70–85, 129, 142–155
Pileggi, Nicholas 140
Pond, Steve 121
Powell, Michael 129
Powers, Cecil (*New York, New
    York*) 63
Price, Richard 118
Primus, Barry 55, 129
Prince, Steven 129
Procol Harum 134

Proval, David 1–15
Psycho 44
Pupkin, Rupert (*King of Comedy*) 85, 87–102

Rafelson, Toby 30
Raging Bull 69–85, 88, 104, 131, 138, 139, 145, 154, 158
Rambo 116
Randall, Tony 93–102
Rauch, Earl Mac 65
Reeves, Jimmy (*Raging Bull*) 76
Researcher's Guide to Martin Scorsese x
Rita (*King of Comedy*) 87–102
Robinson, Amy 1–15
Robinson, Sugar Ray 76
Rocky 71
Rogers, Ginger 60
Rolling Stones 8, 152
Romanus, Richard 1–15
Ronettes 10, 110
Rooney, Mickey 63
Rossi, Janice (*GoodFellas*) 141–155
Round Midnight 112
Russell, Leon 28

Saldana, Theresa 79
Salvy (*Raging Bull*) 74
Sandy (*GoodFellas*) 148
Scaletta, Lenny 7, 129
Schoonmaker, Thelma 85
Schuler, Fred 95
Schrader, Paul 33, 84, 125
Scorsese, Catherine ix, 129
Scorsese, Charles ix, 129
Segal, George 103
Send Me No Flowers 20
Serrone, Christopher 145
Sessions, Grady (*The Color of Money*) 123

77 Sunset Strip 154
Shadows x
Shallit, Gene 57
Shaver, Helen 113
Shearer, Norma 20
Sheckie (*The Color of Money*) 120
Shepherd, Cybill 36–48
Shepherd, Suzanne 141
Shylock 12
Sinatra, Frank 97
Siskel, Gene 101, 109
Sivero, Frank 146
Smith, Peggy (*Happy Endings* in *New York, New York*) 63
Sorvino, Paul 138–155
Spider (*GoodFellas*) 139, 143
Spielberg, Steven 112
Sport (*Taxi Driver*) 46
Stander, Lionel 66
Starlight Terrace 58–59
Starr, Beau 141
Storm of Strangers 32
Strasberg, Lee 14
Suslova, Apollinaria 133
Swift, Jonathan 89

Tavernier, Bertrand 112
Taxi Driver 32, 33–48, 49, 85, 88, 104, 125, 131, 138, 158
Tayback, Vic 22
Theresa (*Mean Streets*) 1–15
Thomas, Bert (*King of Comedy*) 92, 100
Tom 36, 46
Tom (*After Hours*) 109–112
Tommy (*Alice Doesn't Live Here Anymore*) 17–32
Tony (*Mean Streets*) 1–15
Tropic of Cancer 104

Up Club 55

Vera (*Alice Doesn't Live Here Any-more*) 19, 30
Vincent (*The Color of Money*) 114–123
Vincent, Frank 74, 129, 139
Viscious, Sid 153

Wadleigh, Michael x
Warner Bros. 15
"The Wasteland" 33, 42, 77
Wayne, John 25
Weintraub, Sandy 30–31
Weiss, Marion x
Welles, Orson 44

West Side Story 7
What's a Nice Girl Like You Doing in a Place Like This? x
Who's That Knocking at My Door? 14, 125
Williams, William Carlos 7
Wilson, Paul (*New York, New York*) 55, 65, 66
Winkler, Margo 129, 153
Wise, Robert 114
Wiseguy 140
Wizard (*Taxi Driver*) 43–48
The Women 20
Woodstock x